COMPUTER LITERACY FOR IC3™

UNIT 1: COMPUTING FUNDAMENTALS

COMPUTER LITERACY FOR IC3™

UNIT 1: COMPUTING FUNDAMENTALS

John Preston

Sally Preston

Robert L. Ferrett

IC3® INTERNET AND COMPUTING CORE CERTIFICATION
GLOBAL STANDARD 4

PEARSON

Boston Columbus Indianapolis New York San Francisco Upper Saddle River
Amsterdam Cape Town Dubai London Madrid Milan Munich Paris Montreal Toronto
Delhi Mexico City Sao Paulo Sydney Hong Kong Seoul Singapore Taipei Tokyo

Library of Congress Cataloging-in-Publication Data

Preston, John M.

Computer literacy for IC3 / John Preston, Robert L. Ferrett, Sally Preston.

p. cm.

Includes index.

ISBN-13: 978-0-13-302859-1

ISBN-10: 0-13-302859-3

1. Electronic data processing personnel—Certification—Study guides. 2. Computer literacy—Examinations—Study guides. 3. Computers—Examinations—Study guides. 4. Internet—Examinations—Study guides. I. Ferrett, Robert. II. Preston, Sally. III. Title. IV. Title: Computer literacy for IC3.

QA76.3.P743 2009

004—dc22

2009004932

Editor in Chief: Michael Payne	**Marketing Manager:** Nathan Anderson
Acquisitions Editor: Samantha McAfee	**Marketing Coordinator:** Susan Osterlitz
Product Development Manager: Laura Burgess	**Marketing Assistant:** Darshika Vyas
Editorial Project Manager: Keri Rand	**Sr. Managing Editor:** Camille Trentacoste
Development Editor: Toni Ackley	**Sr. Production Project Manager/ Procurement Lead:** Natacha Moore
Editorial Assistant: Laura Karahalis	**Senior Art Director:** Jonathan Boylan
VP, Director of Digital Strategy: Paul Gentile	**Composition:** GEX Publishing Services
Director of Digital Development: Taylor Ragan	**Full-Service Project Management:** GEX Publishing Services
Digital Editor: Eric Hakanson	**Cover Printer:** LSC Communications
Production Media Project Manager: John Cassar	**Printer/Binder:** LSC Communications/Kendallville
Director of Marketing: Maggie Moylan Leen	

Credits and acknowledgments borrowed from other sources and reproduced, with permission, in this textbook appear on appropriate page within text.

Microsoft and/or its respective suppliers make no representations about the suitability of the information contained in the documents and related graphics published as part of the services for any purpose. All such documents and related graphics are provided "as is" without warranty of any kind. Microsoft and/or its respective suppliers hereby disclaim all warranties and conditions with regard to this information, including all warranties and conditions of merchantability, whether express, implied or statutory, fitness for a particular purpose, title and non-infringement. In no event shall Microsoft and/or its respective suppliers be liable for any special, indirect or consequential damages or any damages whatsoever resulting from loss of use, data or profits, whether in an action of contract, negligence or other tortious action, arising out of or in connection with the use or performance of information available from the services.

The documents and related graphics contained herein could include technical inaccuracies or typographical errors. Changes are periodically added to the information herein. Microsoft and/or its respective suppliers may make improvements and/or changes in the product(s) and/or the program(s) described herein at any time.

Microsoft® and Windows® are registered trademarks of the Microsoft Corporation in the U.S.A. and other countries. This book is not sponsored or endorsed by or affiliated with the Microsoft Corporation.

Pearson Education Ltd., London	Pearson Education North Asia Ltd., Hong Kong
Pearson Education Singapore, Pte. Ltd	Pearson Education de Mexico, S.A. de C.V.
Pearson Education, Canada, Inc.	Pearson Education Malaysia, Pte. Ltd.
Pearson Education–Japan	Pearson Education, Upper Saddle River, New Jersey
Pearson Education Australia PTY, Limited	

PEARSON

ISBN-13: 978-0-13-302859-1
ISBN-10: 0-13-302859-3

Dedication

We have been working as a collaborative team since 1996. Our many years of friendship have been the glue holding this project together. We would like to dedicate this book to that unique camaraderie.

Acknowledgments

Our thanks go to Samantha McAfee for asking us to write this book. We appreciate the careful tech edits from Sean Portnoy, Linda Pogue, and Julie Boyles, who paid attention to all the little details and offered helpful suggestions for improvement. We also appreciate the contributions of Keri Rand of Pearson Education and Toni Zuccarini Ackley.

Additionally, we would like to thank the following people for their valuable contributions to this book:

Shelley Allen	Elizabeth Lockley
Michelle August	Thomas McKenzie
Linda Bird	Lawrence Metzelaar
Lynn Bowen	Keith Mulbery
Julie Boyles	Phyllis Pace
Peter Casey	Ralph Phillips
Linda Collins	Janet Pickard
Lew Cousineau	Jennifer Pickle
Doug Cross	Anita P. Ricker
Annette Duvall	Steven Rubin
Denise Farley	Rafaat Saade
Marianne Fox	Cheryl L. Slavik
Anthony Garner	Jan Snyder
Laurie Grosik	Barbara Taylor
Carson Haury	Pam Toliver
Christine Held	Philip Vavalides
Bill Holmes	June West
Cheryl Jordan	

About the Authors

John Preston is an Associate Professor at Eastern Michigan University in the College of Technology in the Technology Management program. He has been teaching, writing, and designing computer courses since the advent of PCs, and has authored and co-authored more than 60 books on computer applications and the relationship between technology and society. He teaches courses in global technologies, managing information systems, project management, and quantitative reasoning. He served as program coordinator of the Energy Management program and has trained commercial energy auditors for all of the major utilities in Michigan. Prior to his tenure at EMU, he was a partner in an energy management consulting firm.

Sally Preston teaches computing in a variety of settings, which provides her with ample opportunity to observe how people learn, what works best, and what challenges are present when learning a new software program. This diverse experience provides a complementary set of skills and knowledge that is blended into her writing. Sally has been writing computer textbooks for over 10 years and, in addition to the IC^3 books, has authored books for the *GO! Series,* the *Learn Series,* and the *Essentials Series.* Sally has an MBA from Eastern Michigan University. When she is away from her computer, she is often found planting flowers in her garden.

Robert L. Ferrett recently retired as Director of the Center for Instructional Computing at Eastern Michigan University, where he provided computer training and support to faculty. He has authored or co-authored more than 80 books on Access, PowerPoint, Excel, Publisher, WordPerfect, Windows Vista, and Word. He has been designing, developing, and delivering computer workshops for nearly two decades. Bob has written for the *GO! Series,* and was a series editor for the *Learn 97, Learn 2000,* and *Learn XP* books. He has a BA in Psychology, an MS in Geography, and an MS in Interdisciplinary Technology from Eastern Michigan University. His doctoral studies are in Instructional Technology at Wayne State University. As a sidelight, Bob teaches a four-week Computers and Genealogy class, and has written genealogy and local history books.

IC³ Series **Contents**

Unit 1: Computing Fundamentals

Unit 2: Using Productivity Software

Unit 3: Living Online

Contents

chapter **four**   Identifying Software and Hardware
Interaction and Types of Software   **119**

chapter **five**   Identifying Operating System Functions   **151**

Why We Wrote This Book

"I know how to use a computer"

We've probably all heard this statement at some point from our students and employees and wondered exactly what it meant—or, at least, what it meant to them. To those of us in the business of teaching computer skills, it's not just a matter of semantics. There is, in fact, a great deal of confusion out there about what constitutes computer literacy.

Even the best and most prepared students have significant gaps in their knowledge at the basic level. Some know how to surf the Internet, but have only a vague idea of how it works. Others, returning to school as adults, might know a few isolated applications but lack the concepts to learn software more thoroughly. All would benefit from a foundation course that teaches computers in the real world context that students must master in order to succeed—in college and in their careers.

That is why we made the decision to partner with Certiport to develop a text that prepares students for the IC^3 certification. The philosophy behind IC^3 certification helps define the concepts all students must know in order to be considered computer literate. Even if they never take the certification tests, this "common baseline" approach will give your students the confidence to say, "I know how to use a computer" and know exactly what that means.

Why IC^3?

Not just applications
- Unlike other certifications, IC^3 offers a well-rounded approach to computer literacy that covers basic computer concepts, applications, and the Internet.

Software is not vendor specific
- Although we wrote the operating systems chapter using Microsoft Windows 7 and the applications section using Microsoft Office 2010 because they are the most current version of the industry-standard software, students will learn about other operating systems such as Linux and Mac OS and other applications suites like Google Docs.

Flexibility
- Because of the division of topics into three major areas—Computing Fundamentals, Key Applications, and Living Online—students can choose to focus on areas where they need more work. Faculty have the freedom to be creative while working within IC^3's defined framework.

Why Computer Literacy for IC³?

Comprehensive coverage of objectives

- Each of the IC³ objectives is covered comprehensively and a map of the coverage of IC³ objectives is included at the beginning of each chapter so you can be assured that your students are learning everything necessary to meet the standard.

Extensive end-of-project material

- Several levels of reinforcement exercises to choose from at the end of each chapter.

Skills-based, hands-on instruction

- Students grasp the material quickly and easily with clearly numbered, bold, step-by-step instructions within these hands-on tutorials.

Typeface Conventions Used in This Book

Computer Literacy for IC^3 uses the following typeface conventions to make it easier for you to understand the material.

Monospace type appears frequently and looks like this. It is used to indicate text that you are instructed to key in.

Italic text indicates text that appears onscreen as (1) warnings, confirmation, or general information; (2) the name of a file to be used in a lesson or exercise; and (3) text from a menu or dialog box that is referenced within a sentence, when that sentence might appear awkward if it were not set off.

Student Resources

Companion Website (www.pearsonhighered.com/ic3). This companion website provides students with additional information and exercises to reinforce their learning. Features include: additional end-of-project reinforcement material; online Study Guide; easy access to *all* chapter data files; and much, much more!

Accessing Student Data Files. The data files that students need to work through the chapters can be downloaded from the companion website (www.pearsonhighered.com/ic3). Data files are provided for each chapter. The filenames correspond to the filenames called for in this book. After you open the file, you will save it with the same name followed by your name to identify the file as yours.

Instructor's Resources

The Instructor's Resource Center contains all necessary files to prepare for class, teach the class, and assess your students' performance. It is flexible so you can collect the materials that are most relevant to your interests, edit them to create powerful class lectures, copy them to your own computer's hard drive, and/or upload them to an online course management system. The Instructor's Resource Center includes the following:

- The Instructor's Manual in Word and PDF formats—includes solutions to all questions and exercises from the book and companion website
- Customizable PowerPoint slide presentations for each chapter
- Data and Solution Files
- Complete Test Bank
- TestGen Software

TestGen is a test generator that lets you view and easily edit test bank questions, transfer them to tests, and print in a variety of formats suitable to your teaching situation. The program also offers many options for organizing and displaying test banks and tests. A built-in random number and text generator makes it ideal for creating multiple versions of tests that involve calculations and provides more possible test items than test bank questions. Powerful search and sort functions let you easily locate questions and arrange them in the order you prefer.

CourseSmart

CourseSmart is an exciting choice for students looking to have a more digital experience. As an alternative to purchasing the print textbook, students can purchase an electronic version of the same content and save up to 50% off the suggested list price of the print text. For more information, or to purchase access to the CourseSmart eTextbook, visit www.coursesmart.com.

Companion Website @ www.pearsonhighered.com/ic3

This text is accompanied by a companion website at www.pearsonhighered.com/ic3. Features of this site include an interactive study guide, downloadable supplements, additional practice projects, and web resources links.

COMPUTER LITERACY FOR IC³™

Visual Walk-Through

In addition to being newly written to the 2012 GS4 Certiport Guidelines for IC³ Certification and featuring a vibrant new design, the series utilizes the following pedagogical features, making it the IC³ series that provides a relevant approach to computer literacy for today's students:

The new and improved **Learning Outcome** mapping allows students to navigate chapter content more efficiently and effectively, while identifying where IC³ learning objectives are being covered throughout the chapter.

Chapter at a Glance

Lesson	Learning Outcomes	Page Numbers	Related IC3 Objectives
1	Identify different computer types based on relative size and capacity	4	2.2.1
1	Identify different computer types based on the computer's user	5	2.2.1
1	Identify different computer types based on where the computer is used	5	2.2.1
1	Identify different computer types based on intended use	6	2.2.1
1	Identify different computer types based on operating system	8	2.2.1
1	Identify other types of computers such as appliances and media players	10	2.2.1
2	Identify the role of the central processing unit	12	2.1.1
2	Identify factors that affect the processing speed of the CPU including measurements in hertz and gigahertz	12	2.1.1
2	Identify the functions of volatile random access memory (RAM) and non-volatile read-only memory (ROM)	13	2.1.1
2	Identify the features and benefits of different types of secondary storage including magnetic hard disks and solid state drives (SSD)	13	2.1.1
2	Identify units of measure of bits and bytes combined with prefixes including *mega-, giga-, tera-,* and *peta-*	13	2.1.2
2	Identify the purpose of input and output devices	15	2.1.1
3	Identify the numeric system used by computers	15	2.3.2
3	Identify how computer memory is measured	15	2.1.2
3	Identify how memory relates to different types of items stored on a computer	16	2.1.2
3	Identify the general flow of data through a computer	17	2.3.2
3	Determine the capacity of a computer hard drive	18	2.1.2
3	Identify how to boot a computer	20	1.1.2
3	Identify how to start a computer application	20	2.1.2
3	Identify how to create a document	21	3.3.5
3	Identify how to save a file	22	2.1.2
3	Identify how to close a file	22	2.1.2
3	Identify how to exit an application	22	2.1.2
3	Identify how to turn off a computer	23	1.1.2
4	Identify the role of each type of system in an organization	23	2.2.0
4	Identify the importance of sharing hardware, software, and data	25	2.2.0
4	Identify the purpose of distributed databases	26	3.3.2
4	Identify the purpose of distributed processing	26	1.1.3
4	Determine if a folder is set up for sharing	26	1.2.2

Why Would I Do This?

Many computer programs use the same methods for accomplishing common tasks. In this chapter, you practice the procedures that are common to several programs. *Application software* is the term used for computer programs that accomplish a specific set of tasks. They are also referred to as applications or *programs*. *Windows-based applications* are computer programs that are written to work on a computer using a Microsoft Windows operating system. *Microsoft Office* is a suite of applications that performs tasks commonly used in an office environment, such as writing documents, managing finances, and presenting information.

Whether you are using a Microsoft Office application or another Windows-based program, you will use the same basic procedures to start and exit each application and to interact with the various programs. Before you can use a software application effectively, you need to know how to work with the program's on-screen elements. Microsoft Office applications use a *graphical user interface*, commonly referred to as *GUI* (pronounced "gooey"), which includes windows, dialog boxes, command buttons, and menus. A mouse and keyboard are the most common input devices used to interact with the on-screen elements. In this chapter, you practice using the Microsoft Office 2010 user interface.

Why Would I Do This? effectively explains why each task and procedure is important so that students will be able to apply them in real life scenarios.

GREEN ENERGY EXPRESS™
One Plaza Drive, Detroit, MI 48231-1001
www.greenenergyexpress.net

August 23, 2010

Rob and Marla Franklin
6236 Daleview Drive
Ypsilanti, MI 48197

Dear Mr. and Mrs. Franklin:

Congratulations! You are the recipients of a donation on your behalf to the *Green Energy Express™* program. Your benefactors, Jake and Sara Prescott, have purchased a month's supply of green energy for your home.

The *Green Energy Express™* program helps fund research and develops new sources of electrical energy. The following two projects will produce the electrical energy for your home in the coming month:

- **Wind** – Our newest wind generator is named Express One. It generates one megawatt of electrical power from the wind while producing no exhaust gases.
- **Biomass** – We are partnering with the largest dairy herd owners in the state to capture the methane gas that is produced by natural processes in the animal waste and burning it to generate electricity.

Because new technologies cost more to get up and running, the electricity costs a bit more but the benefits to our state and country are worth it. Your bill for the following month will not change but an additional $.02 will be added to Jake and Sara Prescott's bill for each kilowatt-hour of electricity you use. The amount you are already paying, plus the small increase funded by your benefactors, will pay for a month's green energy that does not add to air pollution or send your dollars overseas.

At the end of the month, you will have the opportunity to continue to participate in the *Green Energy Express™* program. You have three options; you can do nothing and your bill will not be affected, you can sign up for the *Green Energy Express™* and assume the additional cost yourself, or you can be the benefactor of someone else.

We hope that this experience of using electricity for a month in the most environmentally friendly way possible will be a satisfying experience. We want to invite you to get on the Green Express by continuing the program yourself or by being a benefactor to a friend.

Sincerely,

Student Name
Director, *Green Energy Express™*

Make sure your students see the big picture with the **Visual Summary**, a graphical presentation of the concepts and features in each chapter that also includes the final results of the completed project.

Visual Summary

In this chapter, you will open several applications and identify elements that are common to all applications. You will then open a file and use common features in Microsoft Office Word 2010 to edit a letter to a customer about green energy technology, as shown in Figure 1.1.

⑤ **In the lower-right corner of the Open dialog box, click the Open button to open the selected file. On the Protected View bar, click Enable Editing.** You can also double-click a file name to open it. The protected view allows the user to preview a document before he or she edits or saves it to limit exposure to files that might contain hidden codes that are intended to harm the computer.

⑥ **On the File tab, click Save As.** In the displayed Save As dialog box, you can give the file a new name and save it to a location on your computer, USB drive, or network drive.

⑦ **In the Save As dialog box, in the File name box, type** U2Ch01EnergyStudentName **replacing the words** *StudentName* **with your own name.** Each time you save a file used in this textbook, you will add your name to the end of the file name so that your work can be easily identified.

⑧ **In the left panel of the Save As dialog box, click Computer, and then double-click the drive location where you want to save your files—such as a USB drive or removable disk.**

⑨ **Click the New Folder button, type** Chapter01 **and then press** ⏎Enter**. Compare your screen with Figure 1.8.** The folder name and path display in the Address bar, with the new file name in the File name box. The new folder is empty. It is helpful to organize your files into folders so that you can locate all of the completed files when it is time to submit your work.

Provide students with **Step-by-Step Tutorials**, a feature that encourages students to learn as they follow instructions in a clear numbered format.

 Extend Your Knowledge

SAVING AND OPENING FILES

When you save a file, it is important to first select the folder where you want it to be saved. If you open a file and click the save button, it will be saved to the folder and drive in which it was previously stored.

A saved file can be opened from within the computer's file management program or from the desktop. If you save a file to the desktop, you can double-click the file name icon on the desktop to open the file. When you double-click on a file name, it launches the program that it was created with, and then displays the file. If you save your files to the Documents folder, you can open the files by selecting Documents from the Start menu, which will display a dialog box with the Documents folder selected. Locate the file you want to open and double-click the file name. The key to good file management is to use folders and to be sure you identify the location where the file is saved before you click the Save button.

Show your students alternative ways to complete a process, give them special hints about using the software, and provide them with extra tips and shortcuts with the **Extend Your Knowledge** feature.

 How Do You Feel About It?

APPLIANCES AND MICROPROCESSORS IN YOUR LIFE

Today's cars have up to 50 appliance computers, such as the processor that controls the antilock brakes. What are some of the other appliance (special purpose) computers in an automobile? What are examples of appliance computers in household devices? (Hint: Look for a digital readout.) How does the inclusion of computers in cars and household appliances affect your sense that you can fix things yourself (or at least have a friend or relative who can) and your pride in being able to do so? How does this affect your decision to repair or replace a car or an appliance?

Encourage students to think critically about environmental and ethical issues related to technology by incorporating these discussion topics in class with the **How Do You Feel About It?** feature

Capture teachable moments with **Good Design**, a Unit 2 feature that introduces design tips in the most applicable section of the material. This feature is assessed in the **Fix It** end-of-chapter exercises.

 Good Design

BLOCK-STYLE LETTER

There are a few generally accepted styles for a professional letter or memo. The most common is the block style, which aligns all of the text at the left margin. In a letter, the spacing between the inside address and the salutation is one blank line, created by pressing ⏎Enter two times at the end of a line of text. The inside address is single-spaced and includes the name and address of the person to whom you are writing, as demonstrated in the previous steps and shown in Figure 1.12. The salutation should be personalized using the name or names of the person to whom the letter is being sent.

Help students anticipate or solve common problems quickly and effectively with **If You Have Problems**, a feature that provides short troubleshooting notes.

 If You Have Problems

IS THE TASKBAR HIDDEN?

If the taskbar is hidden, you may not see the Word button name on the taskbar. If the taskbar is hidden, move your pointer to the bottom of the screen. The taskbar will pop up. If you want to display or hide the taskbar, right-click in an open area of the taskbar, and then select Properties from the shortcut menu. On the Taskbar tab, select the *Auto-hide the taskbar* check box to turn the Auto-hide feature on or off. The taskbar will be displayed through the end of this chapter and will then be hidden for the rest of the book to give you the maximum work area on the screen.

 Fix It

One way to appreciate the value of good design is to fix a file that is not designed well. In this exercise, you open a file that has several errors and design flaws and fix it according to good design elements, using the skills that you practiced in the lessons.

Navigate to the folder with the student files, open **U2Ch01FixIt**, and save it as U2Ch01FixItStudentName

Examine the letter and make the changes that are necessary to correct errors and comply with the good design principles that were introduced in this chapter. Here is a list of corrections needed and the design principles introduced in this chapter, along with some tips on how to fix the letter.

- Recolor the recycle symbol in the letterhead to dark green (*Olive Green, Accent color 3 Dark*).
- The Recycle Center name was recently changed to *Green City Recycling™*. Replace all references to Recycle Center to the new name, including the trademark symbol.
- Replace *Date* with the current date and space per the stated design principles for a letter.
- This letter is being sent to Joseph Paellas, at 367 Huntington Drive, Toledo, OH 43604. Enter the inside address in the proper location.
- Enter the proper spacing between the date line, inside address, salutation, and the body of the letter.
- Correct all spelling and grammar errors.
- Move the last sentence in the letter so that it is the third sentence in the first paragraph.

Encourage hands-on design practice with **Fix It**. This feature asks students to improve a file containing several errors and design flaws by having them use the skills and good design elements that they practiced in their lessons.

Prepare students to use the skills from each lesson outside the classroom with the extensive **end-of-chapter exercises**. These exercises include: **Checking Concepts and Terms**, **Skill Drill**, **Explore and Share**, **In Your Life**, **Related Skills**, and **Discover**.

Skill Drill

The Skill Drill exercise repeats the lessons in the chapter but with different data. The instructions are less detailed, and your speed and familiarity should increase with practice. There is a figure at the end against which you can check your results. The purpose of this exercise is to build your confidence and speed in using the skills introduced in this chapter and to set them in your memory for later recall. mbers. You are welcome to refer back to the lessons ry.

In Your Life

Information workers add value to data by organizing, selecting, displaying, communicating, interpreting, and using data to communicate information and support decisions. In Your Life exercises simulate a situation where you are given data, and your job is to add value to it using the skills you practiced in this chapter. Success in these exercises indicates that you have a valuable skill to offer an employer.

Explore and Share

The questions in this section are based on the topics in the Explore and Share section of the chapter.

1. Examine a letter that you have received recently from a company. Identify the parts of the letter and the formatting that has been used to help convey the information. Demonstrate your knowledge of the topics in this chapter in your answer. Describe any errors that you find in the letter.

2. Describe an example from your experience where you have had difficulty printing a document.

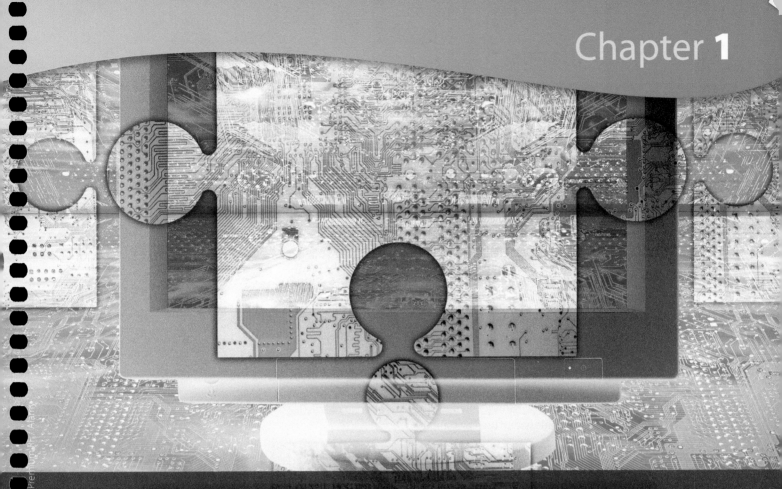

Chapter 1

Identifying Types of Computers

Why Would I Do This?

Computers are in our homes, cars, and workplaces. In this book, you learn how they influence our lives and how to use them effectively. Computers come in many sizes and types. When we talk about them, we use a variety of terms, many of which overlap. You might take part in a conversation and hear people talk about a microcomputer, a desktop computer, a personal computer, and a Mac, even though they are all talking about the same kind of computer. Before you can learn more about computers, it is necessary to develop a common vocabulary. A good place to start is to learn the terms commonly used to categorize computers.

A computer is defined by a few basic functions. Once you know what the functions are, you can identify how parts of a new computer may work, even if you have not seen that particular type of computer before.

The performance of a computer often depends upon the speed of its processor, the amount of memory it has, and the speed of its connections to other computers. You need to know how these factors are measured in order to compare them and to estimate how long certain tasks will take.

If you understand the way data flows through a computer during start-up, operation, and shutdown, you will have a better idea of what effect a malfunction would have at each stage. This may help you to take appropriate actions to fix problems or recover data files.

If you want to use computers effectively, you need to understand how they interact with each other and share resources. This knowledge will help you save money by reducing duplication of resources and by specifying the right computer equipment for the computer's role in the organization.

Chapter at a Glance

Lesson	Learning Outcomes	Page Numbers	Related IC3 Objectives
1	Identify different computer types based on relative size and capacity	4	2.2.1
1	Identify different computer types based on the computer's user	5	2.2.1
1	Identify different computer types based on where the computer is used	5	2.2.1
1	Identify different computer types based on intended use	6	1.1.3., 2.2.1
1	Identify different computer types based on operating system	8	1.1.3., 2.2.1
1	Identify other types of computers such as appliances and media players	10	1.1.3., 2.2.1
2	Identify the role of the central processing unit	12	2.1.1
2	Identify factors that affect the processing speed of the CPU including measurements in hertz and gigahertz	12	2.1.1
2	Identify the functions of volatile random access memory (RAM) and non-volatile read-only memory (ROM)	13	2.1.1
2	Identify the features and benefits of different types of secondary storage including magnetic hard disks and solid state drives (SSD)	13	2.1.1
2	Identify units of measure of bits and bytes combined with prefixes including *mega-*, *giga-*, *tera-*, and *peta-*	13	2.1.2
2	Identify the purpose of input and output devices	15	2.1.1
3	Identify the numeric system used by computers	15	2.3.2
3	Identify how computer memory is measured	15	2.1.2
3	Identify how memory relates to different types of items stored on a computer	16	2.1.2
3	Identify the general flow of data through a computer	17	2.3.2
3	Determine the capacity of a computer hard drive	18	2.1.2
3	Identify how to boot a computer	20	1.1.2
3	Identify how to start a computer application	20	2.1.2
3	Identify how to create a document	21	3.3.5
3	Identify how to save a file	22	2.1.2
3	Identify how to close a file	22	2.1.2
3	Identify how to exit an application	22	2.1.2
3	Identify how to turn off a computer	23	1.1.2
4	Identify the role of each type of system in an organization	23	2.2.0
4	Identify the importance of sharing hardware, software, and data	25	2.2.0
4	Identify the purpose of distributed databases	26	3.3.2
4	Identify the purpose of distributed processing	26	1.1.3
4	Determine if a folder is set up for sharing	26	1.2.2

Visual Summary

In this chapter, you will become familiar with the components of computers, how computers are categorized, the role their relationships play in an organization, and basic concepts of memory measurement and flow of information.

FIGURE 1.1
Flow of information between types of computers.

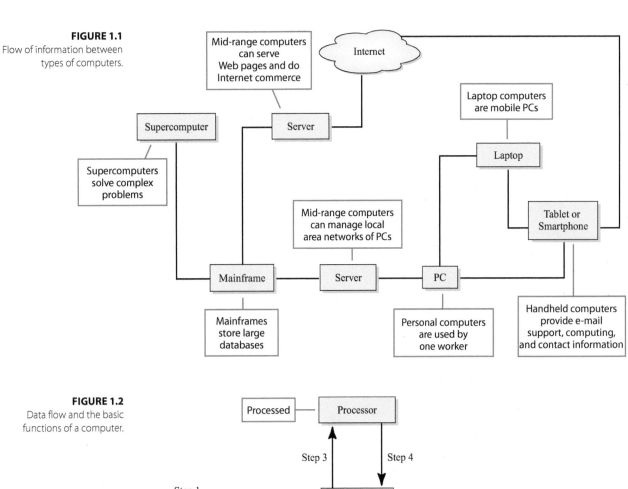

FIGURE 1.2
Data flow and the basic functions of a computer.

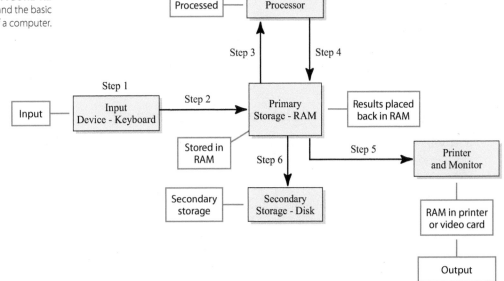

List of Student Files

In most cases you will create files by capturing screens. You will add your name to the file names and save them on your computer or portable memory device. Table 1.1 lists the files you start with and the names you give them when you save the files.

Lesson 1 ▶ Identifying Categories of Computers

Computers vary in their relative size, capacity, software, and intended use. They can be categorized in several different ways, and the terms used to do so often overlap. In this lesson, you learn about several common computer categories.

Categories Based on Size and Use

Computers are commonly categorized by their physical size. This often represents their computing capacity as well as who uses them, where they are used, and their intended use.

Categories Based on Relative Size and Capacity

The following list categorizes computers based on relative size and capacity from the smallest and least capable to the largest and most capable. The division between some of these categories is not well defined.

- Smartphone
- Handheld/ultra portable/pocket computer
- Tablet computer
- Laptop/notebook/portable computer/netbook
- Personal/desktop computer
- Server
- Mainframe computer
- Supercomputer

These categories refer to the computer's relative size or capability. However, the capability and size of computers changes rapidly. Today's personal computer has more computing power than a supercomputer from 40 years ago; therefore, it is important to remember that these categories are relative to each other.

Categories Based on the Computer's User

Another way to categorize computers is by who uses them. Computers may be separated into two broad categories:

Personal/Desktop Computers *Personal computers*, also referred to as *microcomputers*, are typically operated by one person who can customize the functions to match personal preferences. Personal computers, notebook computers, and pocket computers may all be personalized to meet individual needs.

Business Computers An organization often needs more powerful and expensive computers that are shared by many people. These computers require standardization—rather than personalization—as well as specially trained administrators and maintenance technicians. Supercomputers and mainframe computers fit in this category.

Categories Based on Where the Computer Is Used

Another way to categorize computers is by where they are typically used. The following categories apply to smaller computers.

Desktop Computers A *desktop computer* sits on, next to, or under an individual user's desk. It is too large to carry around and usually comes in several pieces that are connected with wires. A desktop computer has a keyboard, mouse, speakers, display, and system unit, as shown in Figure 1.3. Even though some companies, such as Apple, combine their computer's display, speakers, and case into a single unit, the system is still too large to carry conveniently and is intended to sit on a desk. A desktop computer is usually a personal computer.

FIGURE 1.3
Desktop computers sit on or near the user's desk.

Dino Ablakovic / istockphoto.com

Laptop Computers *Laptop computers*—also called portable or notebook computers—are portable, fit on your lap or in a briefcase, and have batteries that are used when a power outlet is not accessible. The screen is a flat-panel display, and the mouse is often replaced by a *touch pad*, *track ball*, or very small *pointing stick* embedded in the keyboard. The screen and case are connected by a hinge, and the unit closes to protect the screen and keyboard during transport. Some units have a screen that pivots from its regular position and becomes a tablet that recognizes handwriting. Netbook computers are small laptop computers that are primarily used for Internet access. A laptop computer is shown in Figure 1.4.

FIGURE 1.4
Portable computers are often called laptop or notebook computers.

bravobravo / Shutterstock.com

Smartphones *Smartphones* are cellular telephones that have a virtual keypad on a touch screen or a small keypad that slides out, as shown in Figure 1.5, and can be used almost anywhere. Smartphones have an operating system and can run mobile versions of software applications such as word processing and spreadsheets that are adapted to the small screen. They can be used to store and play recorded music and videos and to display digital pictures or video. When in range of a cell tower, they can also be used for text messaging, instant messaging, uploading and downloading files, surfing the Web, and reading and sending e-mail. Most smartphones have built-in cameras that can record still pictures and video.

Oleksiy Mark / shutterstock.com

Categories Based on Intended Use

Another way to categorize computers is by how the computer is typically used.

Smartphones Smartphones are cell phones that also have computer functions. They are small enough to fit in a pocket and are highly portable. Smartphones are used primarily as a phone, but they are often used as an appliance for connecting to the Internet to send text and images and to check e-mail and social media postings.

Tablet Computers A *tablet computer*, shown in Figure 1.6, is usually about the size of a sheet of notebook paper. It has a touch screen and can connect to the Internet through a cell phone service or through a wireless connection. Order forms may be displayed and filled out using a special inkless pen as if they were paper forms. The handwriting and boxes checked on a form are automatically converted into text and ***data***—a collection of unprocessed facts and figures. Tablet computers can be used without a keyboard, with input and navigation performed using a mouse or a fingertip. However, many tablet computers can display a keyboard and can function as a laptop computer.

FIGURE 1.6

Yunus Arakon / istockphoto.com

Workstation The term *workstation* originally referred to a desktop computer that had more capability than most other desktop computers for specific tasks, such as animating movies or managing computer-aided designs of complex machines. Although this meaning is still used, general-purpose personal computers have become increasingly powerful; therefore, the distinction between workstations and personal computers is less clear. The term *workstation* is now often used when referring to any personal computer (PC) at an organization that is connected to the company's network. However, there are still specialized, high-power workstations designed for specific tasks in areas such as graphics, medicine, games, and engineering.

Servers

Servers are powerful, fast computers that run special software to serve specific purposes for many users at once. Servers might not have their own monitors or keyboards, as shown in Figure 1.7.

FIGURE 1.7

Network servers may not have keyboards or monitors connected to them.

Crusitu Robert / istockphoto.com

Network Server Computers in an organization may be connected to form a network that is coordinated by specialized software running on a personal computer or workstation.

Web Server A *Web server* is a computer that runs specialized software to support Web pages. It may be a personal computer, workstation, or mainframe, depending on the capacity needed to meet the demand.

File Server An organization's records are critical to its existence. Billing, sales, accounting, and customer information databases are often kept on computers that are more powerful than a typical workstation or network server. These computers vary in capability, depending on the size of the organization and the size of the data files they manage. They are also known by their function of managing database files and are called *file servers*.

Users often communicate directly with file servers via a *dumb terminal* or a *point-of-sale (POS) terminal*. Dumb terminals have no storage and are useless if disconnected from the file server. When you check out at a supermarket, order food at a major fast-food chain, or buy clothing at a department store, the transaction is handled by a POS terminal, as shown in Figure 1.8. A POS terminal may be a dumb terminal or it can be an appliance that is dedicated to handling sales.

FIGURE 1.8
POS terminals must be connected to a computer to function.

istockphoto.com

Mainframe computer *Mainframe computers* are large computer systems used by organizations to process large amounts of information. Typical uses for mainframe computers include processing insurance claims, evaluating census data, tracking credit card purchases, payroll processing, and customer billing. Mainframe computers are highly reliable, usually very secure, and have ongoing backup and redundancy built in. Prices range from $100,000 up to millions of dollars.

Supercomputer *Supercomputers* are characterized by their ability to evaluate complex interactions quickly. One use of supercomputers is *modeling* using *finite element analysis*. For example, supercomputers are used to design airplanes. A design drawing of an airplane is divided into very small pieces (finite elements). Formulas are provided to determine how each part of the plane reacts to airflow and stress, as well as how movement or stress on each part affects the parts next to it. The interaction of these elements is evaluated thousands of times each second to simulate how the plane will perform. Designers can simulate many different maneuvers with this type of model to evaluate and modify a new design before the plane is ever built.

Supercomputers can evaluate millions of these complex interaction formulas each second to simulate the behavior of an airplane in a reasonable amount of time, whereas a mainframe may take weeks to evaluate the same information. Rapid evaluation also enables designers to test the formulas and assumptions they use to gain better understanding of how elements affect each other. Supercomputers are found at national research laboratories, large research universities, government facilities, and military research facilities. They are typically the most expensive computers and prices usually exceed a million dollars.

Categories Based on Operating System and Manufacturer

Another way to categorize computers is by their manufacturer or basic programming. The fundamental programming that controls the way computers interact with their various parts and with users is called the *operating system*. The largest computers that run entire companies often use proprietary operating systems that are supplied by the manufacturer of the computer. IBM and SUN are two manufacturers of large computers that also provide their own operating systems. Many medium-size computers use operating systems, such as *UNIX*, that are independent of a manufacturer. Personal computers typically use one of three operating systems, which are often used to categorize personal computers. The operating system directly affects the user's computing experience, and each has its devoted users. A fourth type of operating system is used for mobile devices such as tablets and smartphones.

Mac Operating System

Personal computers from Apple Corporation use the Mac operating system, which is named after one of its most popular lines, the Macintosh. A personal computer from Apple Corporation that runs the Mac operating system, like the one shown in Figure 1.9, is often called a *Mac*. A Macintosh personal computer can also run software that enables it to run application software written for other operating systems. A devoted user might refer to him- or herself as a Mac person or a Mac user.

FIGURE 1.9

Apple Corporation makes the Macintosh computer.

Jill Fromer / istockphoto.com

Windows Operating System

When the IBM Corporation decided to enter the personal computer business in the late 1970s, the operating system it used on its organization computers was too large to work on the limited resources of a personal computer. It did not write a new operating system for personal computers, but contracted the work to Microsoft Corporation with the agreement that Microsoft could sell the operating system to other manufacturers. As a result of operating system developments following this agreement, *Windows* is the operating system now used on a large majority of personal computers from a wide variety of manufacturers, as shown in Figure 1.10.

FIGURE 1.10

Computers running Windows are often called PCs.

Users of the Windows operating system are in the majority; therefore, they assume that a personal computer uses Windows unless otherwise stated. A Mac user, on the other hand, will often distinguish between a Mac and a Windows machine by calling the latter a PC. Unfortunately, this usage is confusing because computers that use Mac and Windows operating systems are both personal computers.

Linux

As personal computers gained capacity, they became capable of running mainframe operating systems. A few personal computers were adapted to run UNIX, but it did not become popular due to competing claims of ownership and lack of uniformity between different versions. Linus Torvalds adapted the UNIX operating system to work on a variety of computers—including personal computers—and renamed it *Linux*. The programming code for Linux is not owned by a particular company and is available free of charge. It runs on organization and personal computers.

Natural User Interface

Early operating systems processed instructions that were entered from a keyboard. The next generation of operating systems utilized input from a pointing device like a mouse in addition to keystrokes. Mobile devices like smartphones and tablets with touch screens use a variety of inputs including voice commands and dragging fingers across the screen. These inputs are more intuitive for the user, and an operating system that can interpret these types of inputs is called a *natural user interface (NUI)*. Examples of NUI operating systems are Apple's iOS and the Android operating system, which is based on Linux.

Other Types of Computing Devices

Early computing devices were dedicated to solving particular problems such as calculating tables of expected distances for artillery or breaking enemy codes. Changing the setup of one of these computers to solve a different problem often took days of moving wires or resetting switches. Computers began to take their modern form when it became possible to change their programming electronically. Tasks performed by computers could change by simply loading a new program. Dedicated devices still exist in numerous forms, however, because they are faster and cheaper. Some devices use parts of a computer but do not have all the characteristics of a computer. Others are hybrid devices that have characteristics of a computer combined with another function.

Appliances

A computer that is dedicated to one function is called an *appliance*. Examples of appliances are computer game boxes, Web browsers that work with a television, calculators, and bar code scanners, such as the one shown in Figure 1.11.

FIGURE 1.11
Appliances are dedicated to one task.

Konstantin Voznikevich / istockphoto.com

Media Players

In recent years, media players of all kinds have become enormously popular. Portable media players such as the Apple iPod, the SanDisk Sansa Clip+, and the Microsoft Zune enable you to listen to music or videos that you have downloaded from the Web or copied to your personal computer from other media. These devices are available in different models that provide varying amounts of memory and perform various tasks. For example, some of the devices are only intended to play music, whereas others play music, display pictures, play videos, and store data files.

Another type of media player that has become popular is the e-book reader. ***E-books*** are electronic books that can be read on computers or on special reading devices (see Figure 1.12). These devices have been around for a decade, but until very recently the quality of the readers was not high enough to attract many customers. The most popular e-book readers are the Amazon Kindle and the Barnes and Noble Nook. The basic versions of these e-readers use a type of black-and-white display called ***electronic paper***. Instead of emitting light like a computer monitor, electronic paper reflects light from the surroundings. It is much easier to read in bright light outdoors, but it is usually restricted to black-and-white text. Tablets like the iPad also can be used to read books, and Amazon and Barnes and Noble have produced color e-readers that have tablet features. E-book readers can display books, magazines, and newspapers that can be downloaded using cell phone or wireless connections.

FIGURE 1.12

An e-book reader enables you to use wireless connectivity to download books, magazines, and newspapers.

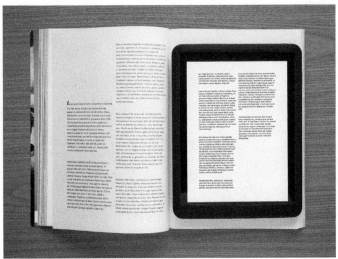

Yunus Arakon / istockphoto.com

Computer Game Systems

Game systems are dedicated devices that use an operating system designed just for gaming. The game controllers (see Chapter 2) that are used to play the games are designed to be used with a computer or with a television set. The games designed for computers require special software that is installed on the computer, whereas the games designed for use with television sets have the software in the controller or in a separate device attached to the television.

Microprocessors

Many devices contain a microprocessing unit with a limited amount of memory that is dedicated to a single task. Examples of this type of device are calculators, some digital clocks and radios, and the engine ignition controller in your automobile.

Identifying Basic Components of a Computer

A computer has four major functions: input, processing, storage, and output. A computer can be any size or located almost anyplace. It is a device that can sit on a desk or be implanted in a pacemaker next to your heart. It can fill a room or fit through the eye of a needle.

Central Processing Unit

At the heart of the computer is the **central processing unit (CPU)**, a term that, when used in reference to personal computers and workstations, is synonymous with **microprocessor**. It is made up of millions of microscopic parts connected together to form **integrated circuits (ICs)**, as shown in Figure 1.13. It is sealed in a thin, rigid container with dozens of connector pins. Some of the companies that manufacture integrated circuits for computers—also referred to as **microchips** or simply **chips**—are Intel, AMD, and IBM.

FIGURE 1.13
A CPU contains an integrated circuit with millions of components.

Oleksiy Mark / istockphoto.com

Role of the CPU

A computer manipulates data according to a set of instructions, resulting in the creation of **information**—data that is organized in a useful and meaningful manner. This data manipulation is known as **processing**. Instructions for early computers were provided by changing gears or wires, which limited their flexibility. Later-model computers were designed for a variety of tasks, and sets of instructions could be stored and used as required.

A procedure that a computer can follow to accomplish a task is called an **algorithm**. Translating algorithms into code that a computer can use is called **programming**, and computers that can change programs are **programmable**. People who write programs are called **programmers**.

How the Speed of the CPU Is Measured

The speed of a CPU depends primarily on its word size and clock speed. Many of the more powerful computers—such as dual-core or quad-core computers—now use multiple processors that can also increase the speed of a computer if the software is designed to separate tasks for individual processing.

Word Size The **word size** is the amount of data processed in one operation. A processor works with binary numbers that consist of zeros and ones. Each digit of the number is called a **bit (b)**. The unit of data that a processor can work with is called a **word**. Early processors worked with 8 bits at a time, which means that they had an 8-bit word length. This size word is also called a **byte (B)**, which is a common measurement unit for data. An 8-bit binary number can only represent decimal numbers from 0 to 255, which limited the number of colors the screens could display, the alphabets and languages a computer could interpret, as well as the accuracy of scientific numbers.

One of the biggest differences between early personal computers and mainframe computers was the word size. Early personal computers used 8-bit words whereas mainframes used 32-bit words. Most personal computers now have processors that use 32-bit words, and 64-bit processors are becoming more common. These processors have the potential to perform some tasks faster, but the software must be written to take advantage of that potential, which currently limits the effectiveness of 64-bit processors to special applications.

Clock Speed   Another measure of the speed of a processor is its *clock speed*. The *clock* in a computer does not keep track of time; it is a circuit on a computer chip that emits pulses. The processor performs an action with each pulse of the clock. Clock pulses are measured in *hertz*, with one pulse per second equaling one hertz. Processors work at very high speeds, and even the first personal computers operated at about five *megahertz*—about 5 million pulses per second. Current processors work with clock speeds that are measured in *gigahertz* or billions of pulses per second. Some processors make more efficient use of each action, so the clock speed is not the only measurement of processor speed. However, one can generalize for most purposes and assume that with similar types of CPUs, the faster the clock speed, the more actions the processor will perform each second.

Memory and Storage

A computer must have the capability of storing data and instructions while it is processing data. This type of storage is known as *primary storage* or *memory*. Computers must also be able to store the results of the processed data for later retrieval. This type of storage is referred to as *secondary storage*.

Memory

A computer has two distinct types of memory:

Read-Only Memory (ROM)   The type of memory that contains the instructions used by the computer when it starts up and communicates with its internal components is called *read-only memory (ROM)*. It is programmed at the factory and is *non-volatile*—it does not need constant power to function.

Random Access Memory (RAM)   The memory that is used to store programs and data while the computer is working is called *random access memory (RAM)*. The processor retrieves data from memory, processes it, and returns it to memory. RAM is designed to keep up with the processor, and the time it takes to read or write data to RAM is measured in *nanoseconds*—billionths of a second. RAM capacity is rated in *megabytes*, *gigabytes*, *terabytes*, or *petabytes*. A byte of memory can store enough data to identify one character of text; a megabyte of RAM can store over a million characters of text, a gigabyte over a billion characters of text, a terabyte over a trillion characters of text, and a petabyte over a quadrillion characters of text. RAM consists of computer chips that are mounted on small plastic boards inside the computer case. Present technology uses RAM that is *volatile*—it must have constant power to function, otherwise the data is lost.

The RAM typically used in personal computers is called *synchronous dynamic random access memory (SDRAM)*, most often a specific type called *double-data-rate 2 (DDR2)* SDRAM. When shopping for a computer, these are the terms you will most often see in the computer description. DDR2 is a recent development of faster memory that uses less power and can store more data.

Secondary Storage

Secondary storage includes any device on which information can be stored for later retrieval and that does not require constant power. The three main types of secondary storage devices are classified according to the technology used to store the data.

Magnetic Media   Coatings of magnetic material on a disk can record and store data by magnetizing small spots on the disk in one direction or the other. Examples are a computer's main hard drive, external hard drives used for supplemental storage or for backup, and removable disks. It is common practice to use the term *disk* for magnetic media.

Optical Media   Data may be recorded in the form of small pits in a reflective surface on a disc. To read the data, a disc drive shines a beam of light on the surface and a sensor picks up variations in the reflection. The flickering reflection is converted into a stream of data. The discs, shown in Figure 1.14, are called **compact discs (CDs)** or **digital video—or versatile—discs (DVDs)**. There are several distinctive types of CDs and DVDs, which will be examined in detail in the next chapter. It is common practice to use the term *disc* for optical media.

FIGURE 1.14
Optical media.

Grigory Bibikov / istockphoto.com

Flash Memory   Unlike magnetic or optical media, **flash memory** has no moving parts. It is similar to RAM but slower, and it does not require constant power to store data. Flash memory—shown in Figure 1.15—can be plugged into USB ports on computers or into card slots in digital cameras. It can be removed easily and is often used to transfer data between personal computers or between digital cameras and personal computers. As the price of flash memory decreases, it is becoming competitive with magnetic disks for use as the computer's memory storage. A unit with a large amount of flash memory that is intended to replace the hard drive is called a **solid state drive (SSD)**. A standard hard drive and an SSD are shown in Figure 1.16.

FIGURE 1.15
Flash memory.

Nadezda Ledyaeva / istockphoto.com. Rafa Irusta / istockphotos. Tom Brown / istockphoto.com

FIGURE 1.16
A hard drive with moving parts (left) and a solid state drive with flash memory (right).

Ludovit Repko / istockphoto.com

Input and Output Devices

Input refers to the action of transferring instructions or data into the computer. Data is a collection of unprocessed facts and figures such as names and addresses or items purchased. A keyboard and mouse are examples of input devices, as are bar code readers and magnetic card swipes used at grocery stores. The results of the processing—known as *output*—must be reported in some manner to the user. The monitor and printer are examples of output devices, as is the dashboard warning light that indicates it's time to service your car. In some computers, such as handheld computers and smartphones that use a touch screen, the screen is both an input and an output device.

Lesson 3

Measuring Memory and Identifying Flow of Information

Memory is a vital part of the computer, and its capacity is often an important factor that determines how fast the computer performs. You need to know how memory is measured to determine if you have enough. If you know how data flows through the computer during typical processes, you can understand the importance of each part of the process and understand how limitations in processor speed, memory, storage, input, or output can affect overall performance.

Memory Measurement

We are familiar with the decimal numbering system, which uses 10 digits from zero to nine. Early computer designers found that mechanical or electrical devices like switches could represent digits using a simple numbering system with only two digits, 0 and 1, known as the *binary* numbering system. Electrical devices were eventually replaced by electronic switches called *transistors*, but the simple binary numbering system is still in use. For a comparison of decimal and binary numbers, see Table 1.2.

TABLE 1.2 **COMPARISON OF DECIMAL AND BINARY NUMBERS**

DECIMAL	EQUIVALENT BINARY
0	0
1	1
2	10
3	11
4	100
5	101
6	110
7	111
8	1000
9	1001
10	1010

Text and Numbers

In order for computers to communicate with each other, a standard code was developed. The ***American Standard Code for Information Interchange (ASCII)*** is a standard that began by assigning a binary number to each capital and lowercase letter in the alphabet and to the 10 decimal digits, as well as to other commonly used function keys such as Enter and Backspace.

The early ASCII code used seven binary numbers and was limited to only 128 different characters. The code was later expanded to 8-digit binary numbers to provide an additional 128 binary numbers to represent additional computer functions and keys, for a total of 256. A newer code, ***Unicode***, has been developed that uses up to 32-digit binary numbers and includes codes for characters in many languages besides English.

Each digit in a binary number is called a *bit*. An 8-digit binary number, such as one used by the ASCII code, is called a *byte*. Data transmission rates are often measured in bits per second, and data storage is usually measured in bytes. Large amounts of data are common, so standard prefixes are used to denote multiples of the basic units. Memory is typically measured in megabytes (MB), which are approximately 1 million bytes, or gigabytes (GB), which are approximately 1 billion bytes. See Table 1.3 for a list of International System of Units (SI) prefixes and the multipliers they represent.

TABLE 1.3

SI MULTIPLIER	SIZE
Kilo-	1,000
Mega-	1,000,000
Giga-	1,000,000,000
Tera-	1,000,000,000,000
Peta-	1,000,000,000,000,000

Extend Your Knowledge

MULTIPLES OF BINARY NUMBERS

Computers use binary numbers, and most measurements of their capacity and speed use bits or bytes. Larger measurement units are based on multiples of 2, the base for binary numbers. There are 8 bits in a byte because 8 is a convenient multiple of 2; for example, $2 \times 2 \times 2 = 8$. Another convenient multiple of 2 is 1,024 because it is close to 1,000. The International System of Units (SI) provides standard prefixes such as *kilo-* to indicate 1,000. It is common to refer to 1,024 bytes as a *kilobyte* even though it is slightly larger than 1,000 bytes. Similarly, another multiple of 2—1,048,576—is close to 1 million. Therefore, we often use a megabyte—where mega is the SI prefix for 1 million—to refer to 1,048,576 bytes. For the purposes of estimating the capacity of disks or the speed of a connection, it is usually acceptable to approximate kilobytes and megabytes as 1,000 and 1 million bytes, respectively.

Pictures

Computers communicate with us visually, either on paper or on a computer screen. To convert binary numbers into letters on the screen or on paper, computers display patterns of individual dots. If the dots are close enough and small enough, they look like continuous lines. If you take a close look at your computer screen, you will see that the screen is made up of many small elements that can turn on (bright) or off (dark). These picture elements are called ***pixels***. If the available space on the screen is divided into smaller, more numerous pixels, finer details can be displayed. For example, if a monitor is set to display images that are 800 pixels wide by 600 pixels high, it may not display small fonts as well as would a monitor set to 1,024 by 768.

Sound

Using computers to communicate and manipulate sound is a challenge because sound waves are not static like a page of text or a picture. Everything about music or speech, such as the volume and pitch, varies with time. Before the use of digital computers, music was converted with a microphone into electrical signals that varied in a way that was analogous to the way the volume and pitch varied. This type of signal is called an *analog* signal because it behaves in a way that is analogous—similar to the thing it represents. These signals were transmitted, received, amplified, and sent to a speaker that converted the electrical signals back into sound waves.

A computer takes the analog signal from the microphone and samples the signal thousands of times each second. Each time it samples the signal, it assigns numbers to the volume and pitch, converting the analog signal into a series of binary numbers. The specialized integrated circuit that converts analog signals to a series of digital numbers is called an *A to D converter* or *analog to digital converter*. A computer is so fast at this task that it can sample music thousands of times each second, compare the volume and pitch of each individual sample with the ones that come before and after it, and fix problems if the values of the numbers vary too much from the ones that come before and after. This is why you can play a music CD that has many small scratches on it without hearing any static. It is also how telephone conversations can be transmitted thousands of miles and sound like the people are next door to each other.

The digital signal, which consists of a series of numbers, can be changed back into an analog electrical signal by a *D to A converter* or *digital to analog converter*. The analog electrical signal moves the cone of the speaker, producing the sound waves we hear. Whenever a digital computer works with something that varies continuously with time, it uses this process of converting from analog to digital and back.

Computers are good at manipulating numbers and communicating with sound and images. They have not yet been developed to the point where they are good at communicating with us through our senses of touch, smell, and taste.

Flow of Information

If you understand the interaction between storage devices and a processor and how information flows between input and output devices, you will be able to follow common processes such as starting the computer, using application programs, and shutting down the computer.

Data Flow and the Basic Functions of a Computer

The functions of a computer and their relationship to each other may be understood by following the flow of data as it moves through a computer. Data goes in, it gets processed according to a set of instructions, and information comes out. Events occur in a particular order that uses both primary and secondary storage.

The following sequence, also shown in Figure 1.17, is typical of how data flows through a computer:

Step 1	Input	The user types words, numbers, or commands on the keyboard or uses the mouse to point to a part of the screen and click.
Step 2	Primary Storage	The data, program, and commands are stored in RAM.
Step 3	Processing	The processor takes data from RAM and processes it according to a program and the commands provided by the user.
Step 4	Primary Storage	The results of the processing are stored in another location in RAM.
Step 5	Output	The processed data is transferred from the memory to the printer's RAM or the video controller for display on the monitor.
Step 6	Secondary Storage	The processed data is written to the hard disk, flash drive, or optical disc.

FIGURE 1.17

Data flows through storage at several steps in the process.

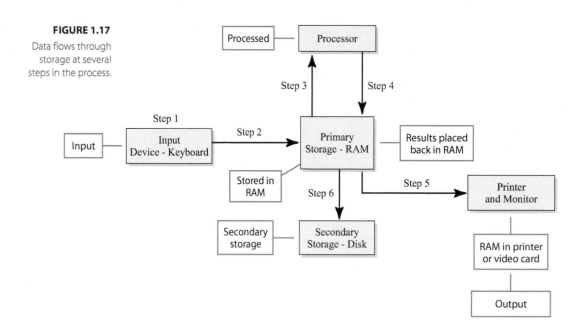

Determine the Storage Capacity of the Hard Disk

The hard disk stores large quantities of data. Its capacity is usually measured in gigabytes (billions of bytes) or even terabytes (trillions of bytes). You can find out how much capacity your hard disk has and how much has already been filled with data. In this exercise, you find the capacity of the hard disk on your computer. This example uses the Windows 7 operating system. You will learn more about operating systems in later chapters.

To find the capacity of your computer's hard disk

① **Turn on your computer and wait until it displays its normal screen, which includes a Start button ⊕.** You may have to log in if you are using a computer in a lab.

② **In the lower-left corner of the computer screen, locate and click the Start button ⊕ one time.** The Start menu displays. The list of programs on the left of the displayed Start menu varies depending on recent use and default settings.

③ **Use the mouse to move the pointer to the right side of the Start menu, and then locate and click Computer.** The Computer window opens. In future instructions, when you are instructed to *point at* an object or location on the screen, use the mouse to move the pointer.

④ **On the left side of the window, under Computer, point to Local Disk (C:) and click the left mouse button.** The local hard disk is selected.

⑤ **In the Command bar, click the Organize button, and then from the displayed menu, click Properties.** The Local Disk (C:) Properties dialog box opens, as shown in Figure 1.18. The amount of used and free space is identified. The number of bytes of storage is measured in bytes and GB (gigabytes).

FIGURE 1.18

The Properties dialog box displays the amount of used and free space on your hard drive.

⑥ **Click the Start button ⊕, click All Programs, click the Accessories folder, and then in the list of programs, click Snipping Tool.**

⑦ **In the Snipping Tool dialog box, click the New Snip button arrow ✂, and then click Window Snip. Point anywhere in the Properties dialog box, and then click one time.**

⑧ **Near the top of the Snipping Tool dialog box, click the Save Snip button 🖫. In the Save As dialog box, navigate to the folder where you store your files. In the *File name* box, type** U1Ch01CapacityStudentName **substituting your name as indicated, and then click Save.**

❓ If You Have Problems

SCREEN CAPTURE

The Snipping Tool is not included in all versions of Windows or in other operating systems. If the Snipping Tool is not available, use the PrintScreen (PrtScrn) button on the keyboard to capture an image of the screen, and then paste it into a blank word processing document. If you have a Macintosh computer, use Help to determine how to find the capacity of the hard drive. Press and hold Command+Control+Shift, and then press 3 to capture the screen, which can be pasted into a blank document.

(9) **In the Local Disk (C:) Properties window, point to the Close button** ![X] **in the upper-right corner, and then click the left mouse button. Alternatively, at the bottom of the dialog box, click the Cancel button.** The Local Disk (C:) Properties dialog box closes.

(10) **In the upper-right corner of the Computer window, point to the Close button** ![X] **and click the left mouse button.** The Computer window closes.

(11) **Submit your snip as directed by your instructor.**

Flow of Information When Creating a Document

Another way to understand how information flows through a computer is to follow a common process from beginning to end.

- **Starting the computer** When you turn on the power from a switch or button on the system unit, a program is automatically moved from ROM to the processor. This program checks to make sure that critical components are connected and functioning. When it confirms that the hardware is working, it copies the operating system from the hard disk into RAM. The operating system takes over and displays the familiar desktop on the screen. This process is called ***booting*** the computer. See Figure 1.19.

FIGURE 1.19

A program from ROM boots the computer when power is turned on.

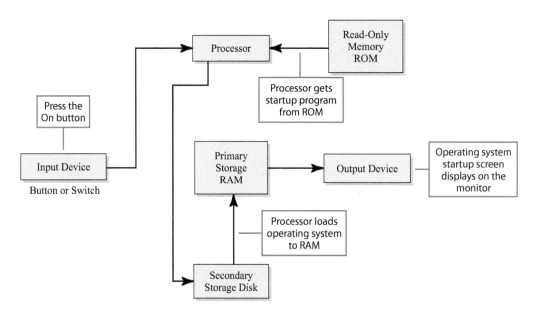

- **Starting an application** The operating system displays a list of programs that have previously been installed on the hard drive. The user selects one, using an input device such as a mouse. The operating system loads the application program into RAM and opens a window on the screen. The application program controls events within the window, but it uses the operating system to interpret and carry out its requests for functions such as file management and printing. See Figure 1.20.

FIGURE 1.20

The application program
is copied from storage
into RAM.

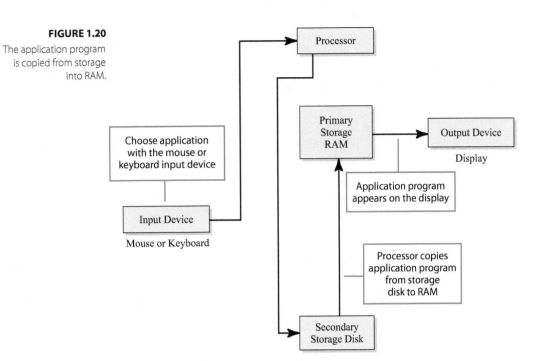

- **Opening a file** The user may choose to open an existing document by using an input device to click on buttons or menu items to select a file. The data that makes up the file is copied from storage—such as the hard disk or flash drive—to RAM memory. The operating system provides specific instructions to manage this process.

- **Editing a file** The user provides input, using a keyboard or mouse to indicate the change—such as inserting new text or correcting an error. The processor loads the affected portion of the data from RAM, processes the request, and places the results in RAM. It may erase the previous data or add to it using additional RAM, depending on the desired changes. The user sees the effect of the change on the screen. The processor also records the date and time when the change was made. See Figure 1.21.

FIGURE 1.21

Files are copied from
RAM to secondary
storage. Temporary
versions are also
stored periodically.

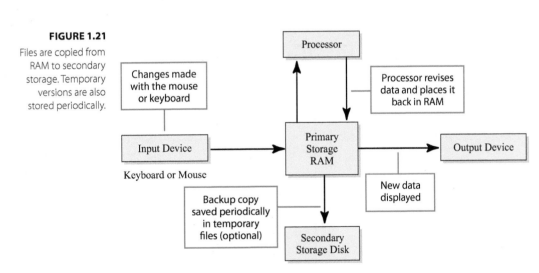

- **Printing a file** The user provides input by clicking on a Print button or selecting the Print option from a menu. The processor sends a copy of the file to the RAM in the printer. The printer has its own memory and processor that are dedicated to the function of printing. The processor in the printer checks the input from sensors that check for the presence of paper and ink. It manages the process of producing patterns of ink or toner on the paper that represent the data in the file.

- **Saving a file** The user provides input by clicking on a Save button or selecting the Save option from a menu. The processor transfers a copy of the file from RAM and writes it in storage. It replaces the existing data with the data from RAM, and the old version of the file is lost. If the user wants to preserve the old version, the Save As option is used instead of Save, and the file is saved either with a different name or in another location. The processor also records the date and time the file was saved to secondary storage. The operating system may periodically save temporary versions of the file automatically to limit the loss of new data in the event of a power loss or other serious problem. See Figure 1.22.

FIGURE 1.22

The processor transfers a copy of the file from RAM and writes it to a storage device.

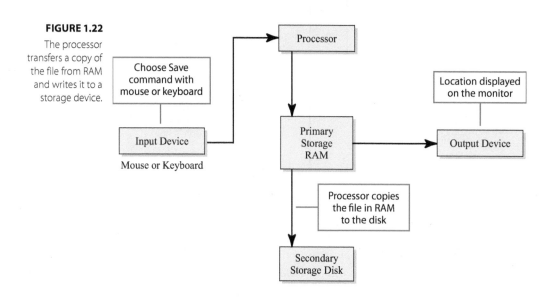

- **Closing a file** The user provides input to close the file by clicking a button or making a menu selection. The processor checks to see if the file has been edited since the last time it was saved. If so, a warning message is displayed on the screen, giving the user the opportunity to save the changes. The file is erased from RAM and temporary backup files are erased from storage. See Figure 1.23.

FIGURE 1.23

Closing a file removes it from RAM and the temporary files are deleted from secondary storage.

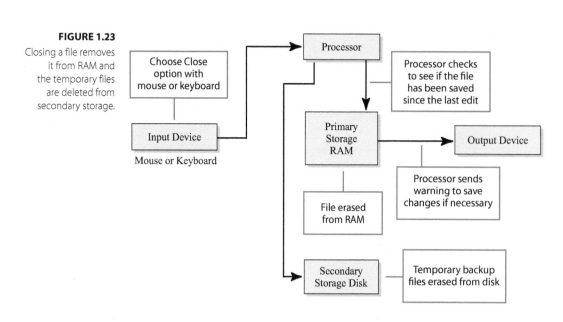

- **Closing an application** The user provides input by clicking on a button or selecting the Close option from a menu. If any documents are open, the program checks to see if all changes have been saved and prompts the user to save changes before closing. The application program is removed from RAM.

- **Turning off the computer** Unlike the operation of a light switch, turning off a computer is not the opposite of turning it on. The user provides input by clicking on a button or selecting the option from a menu. The operating system instructs the processor to check for unsaved files or files in use by someone else who may be connected to your computer by a network. Once the operating system program has completed its checklist, the computer shuts down without using the switch. If the operating system has a problem and stops functioning, the user may shut down the computer by depressing the power button and holding it for several seconds. The next time the computer is started, the operating system will use the temporary backup files to help recover most lost work. See Figure 1.24.

FIGURE 1.24
The operating system checks for applications or files that have not been closed and then shuts down power to most of the computer.

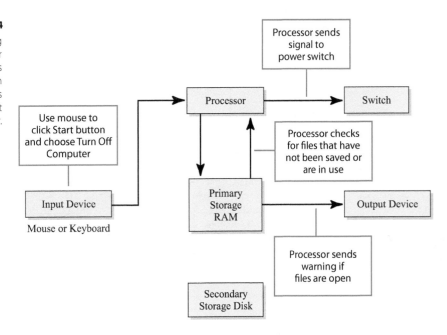

Identifying Relationships Between Computers

Lesson 4

Computers are available in a variety of sizes and capabilities, but they are most effective when they work together. When computers are connected in an organization, each system can be configured to fill a role and share resources.

Role of Each Type of System

Each type of computer system described earlier in this chapter can play an important role in an organization.

Supercomputers

Supercomputers are elite computer systems that may be used to simulate weather systems, design aircrafts, or simulate human intelligence. They are expensive because they use the most advanced technology and equipment available. They are usually found in government and university research centers or at design facilities of large corporations. The first network was created to enable scientists around the country to use supercomputers without having to travel to the computer location.

Mainframe Computers

Most mainframe computers are used to store and share files. These files could contain the financial records of a bank, the customer billing information of a utility company, or the sales history of a retail chain. A file that consists of organized data is called a ***database***. Many mainframe computers are used to manage databases. Mainframes are also capable of functioning as Web servers. They can use Web pages to interact with customers, fill orders, and update inventory files. Figure 1.25 shows how different types of computers relate to each other.

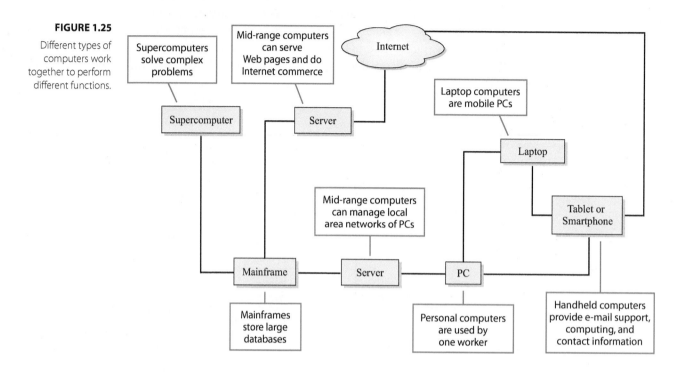

FIGURE 1.25

Different types of computers work together to perform different functions.

Mid-Range Servers

Mid-range servers may serve the same functions as a mainframe computer for smaller companies. They are also commonly used to manage communication between computers on a network within a building, as well as to manage e-mail traffic between computers on the network or with the Internet.

Personal Computers, Desktop Computers, and Workstations

Most people in an organization who work with information have a personal computer at their desk. It is usually connected to other personal computers and the mainframe through a computer that manages the network of connections. A worker may prepare an annual report by downloading the relevant data from the mainframe, which functions as a file server. The worker may use application software to analyze the data and prepare a written report or a slide presentation. The worker can send the report to other workers in the company over the network through the network server or the report could be sent to headquarters through the Internet.

Notebook and Tablet Computers

Notebook or tablet computers are useful for organization members who spend more time traveling than they do at a desk. The portability of notebook and tablet computers enables them to make productive use of time on airplanes or in hotel rooms. They can connect to the organization mainframe through the Internet to exchange files—such as sales results—and update their notebook or tablet computer with current prices and availability data.

Smartphones

Members of an organization must complete tasks by expected deadlines, attend meetings, and keep track of customer and supplier contact information. Many workers carry a smartphone with which they can check e-mail, browse the Internet and social media sites, take pictures, and review documents.

Appliances

Appliances perform a single function. When express delivery service drivers drop off packages, you may see them make a note on a tablet. This is a computing appliance that contains information about the packages loaded into that driver's truck, which was downloaded from the company's mainframe. Throughout the day, the driver notes the time of each delivery; at the end of the day, the appliance is connected to the mainframe, where its files are updated. Some companies now have satellite connections for real-time updates. The mainframe may use its Web server capability to report the status of the delivery to the sender, who can then check on it over the Internet. Many appliances are embedded in other devices—such as an automobile, which has dozens of appliances that monitor and control functions like fuel supply, braking, headlight dimming, and suspension stiffness.

Microprocessors

Some devices have microprocessors that can perform limited functions without the ability to be reprogrammed and have very limited memory or storage. You find these devices in hotel room doors that check the validity of pass codes and point-of-sale terminals in retail stores. Many of these devices can communicate with a server, where the data they gather is processed.

 How Do You Feel About It?

APPLIANCES AND MICROPROCESSORS IN YOUR LIFE

Today's cars have up to 50 appliance computers, such as the processor that controls the antilock brakes. What are some of the other appliance (special purpose) computers in an automobile? What are examples of appliance computers in household devices? (Hint: Look for a digital readout.) How does the inclusion of computers in cars and household appliances affect your sense that you can fix things yourself (or at least have a friend or relative who can) and your pride in being able to do so? How does this affect your decision to repair or replace a car or an appliance?

Resource Sharing

Computers on a network can share data, hardware, software, and Internet connections to reduce costs and improve efficiency. For example, dozens of computers in a building can share a common color laser printer.

Sharing Data

Data files move rapidly between computers over network connections. Mainframe computers store vast amounts of data and share it with other computers by network connections or over the Internet. This ability of computers to share data has caused revolutionary changes in modern society.

Distributed Databases

It is also possible to store a large database on several computers, resulting in a ***distributed database***. A database of customer accounts could be separated into sections, each of which would be stored on a different computer. A coordinating computer would keep track of the location of the files, and users would be unaware that the data was stored in several places.

The Internet can also be used to manage a distributed database. Digital recordings of music and videos may be stored on thousands of different personal computers and shared over high-speed connections. The location of files can be coordinated by a central computer or the individual computers can communicate file locations to each other via ***peer-to-peer network*** communication.

Sharing Software

Some types of software may be stored on a server. When a desktop computer needs to use the software, the necessary portion of the software is copied to the desktop computer, which later erases it once the task has been completed. An advantage to this system is that the software is installed on only one computer and is easily updated with new revisions. The disadvantage is that if the server is not functioning, all the workers who depend upon its software cannot perform their tasks.

Distributed Processing

Some large computing problems can be solved by breaking them into smaller parts that can be solved individually on several different computers and then reassembled into an integrated solution. This process is called ***distributed processing***. For example, a company may own hundreds of powerful workstations, connected by a network, that are idle at night or on weekends. Instead of buying a supercomputer, the company can use its mainframe to assign parts of a large problem to these workstations when they would normally be idle, and then integrate the results during work hours.

Extend Your Knowledge

DISTRIBUTED PROCESSING OVER THE INTERNET

Computers that are continuously connected to the Internet may be used for distributed processing. One creative example is the World Community Grid, which is a group that analyzes the DNA of parasites, bacteria, or viruses to determine what types of drugs might work against them by simulating their interaction with the drug. The DNA molecule is so complex and there are so many drugs that it would take years for one computer to check all the possibilities.

The solution used by World Community Grid is to distribute the simulation to personal computers. Volunteers leave their personal computers on at night and on weekends or during breaks and are connected to the Internet. The World Community Grid downloads some of the data onto their PCs for analysis and then they upload the results when their portion of the task is done. World Community Network coordinates almost 2 million personal computers around the world to process more data than is possible with the most powerful supercomputer.

Sharing Hardware and an Internet Connection

Devices that are not used regularly or that are expensive or take up space may be shared to reduce cost and increase available space in the individual's work area. Most computers on a network share printers and many share extra storage space. Connections to the Internet are usually provided as a service for which a group pays a fee. The connection may be shared among computers on a network.

To look for shared printers

① **Turn on your computer, log in if necessary, and wait until it displays its normal screen, which includes a Start button. Point to the Start button** 🕲 **and click one time with the left mouse button.** The Start button menu displays.

② **On the right side of the Start menu, locate and click Control Panel.** The Control Panel window opens.

③ **At the upper-right of the Control Panel, click the *View by:* option, and then click *Small icons*. In the list of icons, click *Devices and Printers*.** A list of devices displays. Your list will differ from the example.

④ **If there is a printer connected to your computer, right-click its image or name. On the shortcut menu, click Printer Properties.** The properties dialog box displays.

⑤ **In the Printer Properties dialog box, click the Sharing tab.** The sharing option is displayed, as shown in Figure 1.26.

FIGURE 1.26
The Content pane reveals important information about available devices.

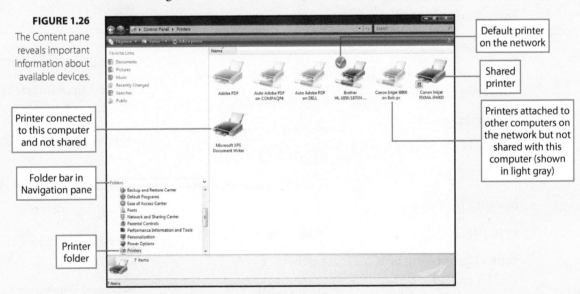

⑥ **Use the skills you practiced previously to start the Snipping Tool program and do a full-screen snip of the Control Panel window. Save a copy of this image to the folder where you store your files. Name the file** U1Ch01PrinterStudentName **substituting your name as indicated.**

⑦ **In the upper-right corner of the Properties dialog box, point to the Close button** ⬛ **, and then click the left mouse button. Repeat this procedure to close the Control Panel window.** The Properties dialog box and Control Panel window close.

⑧ **Submit your snip as directed by your instructor.**

Summary

You learned how to categorize computers based on their capacity and use. You also learned to identify the basic components of a computer and how to measure the speed and capacity of a computer. You learned how to describe the flow of information through the basic parts of a computer when it performs common tasks and to identify the relationships between different types of computers in an organization.

You can extend your learning by reviewing concepts and terms and by practicing variations of skills presented in the lessons.

Key Terms

algorithm *(p. 12)*

American Standard Code for Information Interchange (ASCII) *(p. 16)*

analog *(p. 17)*

analog to digital (A to D) converter *(p. 17)*

appliance *(p. 10)*

binary *(p. 15)*

bit (b) *(p. 12)*

booting *(p. 20)*

byte (B) *(p. 12)*

central processing unit (CPU) *(p. 12)*

chip *(p. 12)*

clock *(p. 13)*

clock speed *(p. 13)*

compact disc (CD) *(p. 14)*

data *(p. 6)*

database *(p. 23)*

desktop computer *(p. 5)*

digital to analog (D to A) converter *(p. 17)*

digital video (or versatile) disc (DVD) *(p. 14)*

distributed database *(p. 26)*

distributed processing *(p. 26)*

double-data-rate 2 (DDR2) *(p. 13)*

dumb terminal *(p. 8)*

e-book *(p. 11)*

electronic paper *(p. 11)*

file server *(p. 8)*

finite element analysis *(p. 8)*

flash memory *(p. 14)*

gigabyte *(p. 13)*

gigahertz *(p. 13)*

hertz *(p. 13)*

information *(p. 12)*

input *(p. 15)*

integrated circuit (IC) *(p. 12)*

laptop computer *(p. 5)*

Linux *(p. 10)*

mainframe computer *(p. 8)*

megabyte *(p. 13)*

megahertz *(p. 13)*

memory *(p. 13)*

microchip *(p. 12)*

microcomputer *(p. 5)*

microprocessor *(p. 12)*

modeling *(p. 8)*

nanoseconds *(p. 13)*

natural user interface (NUI) *(p. 10)*

non-volatile memory *(p. 13)*

operating system *(p. 8)*

output *(p. 15)*

peer-to-peer network *(p. 26)*

personal computer *(p. 5)*

petabyte *(p. 13)*

pixel *(p. 16)*

pointing stick *(p. 5)*

point-of-sale (POS) terminal *(p. 8)*

primary storage *(p. 13)*

processing *(p. 12)*

programmable *(p. 12)*

programmer *(p. 12)*

programming *(p. 12)*

random access memory (RAM) *(p. 13)*

read-only memory (ROM) *(p. 13)*

secondary storage *(p. 13)*

server *(p. 7)*

smartphone *(p. 6)*

solid state drive (SSD) *(p. 14)*

supercomputer *(p. 8)*

synchronous dynamic random access memory (SDRAM) *(p. 13)*

tablet computer *(p. 6)*

terabyte *(p. 13)*

touch pad *(p. 5)*

track ball *(p. 5)*

transistor *(p. 15)*

Unicode *(p. 16)*

UNIX *(p. 8)*

volatile memory *(p. 13)*

Web server *(p. 7)*

word *(p. 12)*

word size *(p. 12)*

workstation *(p. 7)*

Checking Concepts and Terms

MULTIPLE CHOICE

Circle the letter of the correct answer for each of the following.

1. Which of the following groups of characteristics best describes a desktop computer? [L1]

   a. Portable, single user

   b. One user, too large to carry around, several components

   c. Multiple users, special room

   d. Fits in a pocket, has a touch screen

2. Which of the following is the main difference between primary storage (memory) and secondary storage? [L2]

   a. Secondary storage has more capacity than memory but is usually slower, cheaper, and retains data when the computer is turned off.

   b. Primary storage (memory) is measured in petabytes, whereas secondary storage is measured in megabytes or kilobytes.

   c. Memory uses optical methods, whereas secondary storage uses magnetic methods to record and retrieve data.

   d. Secondary storage is nonremovable and located inside the computer, whereas primary storage (memory) may be easily removed and transferred to another computer.

3. Which of the following lists of SI prefixes is in order from smallest to largest? [L3]

   a. *Peta-, giga-, kilo-, mega-, tera-*

   b. *Tera-, giga-, peta-, kilo-, mega-*

   c. *Kilo-, mega-, tera-, giga-, peta-*

   d. *Kilo-, mega-, giga-, tera-, peta-*

4. Which of the following is used to store the initial programming that is used to start the computer when it is first turned on? [L2]

   a. RAM

   b. Hard disk

   c. ROM

   d. CD

5. Supercomputers are best for which of the following problems? [L1]

   a. Serving Web pages

   b. Coordinating computers on a network

   c. Designing and simulating complex systems

   d. Managing dozens of point-of-sale terminals in a supermarket

6. Which of the following is true of read-only memory (ROM)? [L2]

   a. It is non-volatile.

   b. It temporarily stores programs and files while you are working on them.

   c. Its contents are lost when the power is turned off.

   d. It is used as removable storage.

7. RAM stands for which of the following? [L2]

   a. Random access memory

   b. Randomly adjustable memory

   c. Readily available memory

   d. Reliable arranged memory

8. What is the relationship between a byte and a bit? [L2]

   a. A byte may be 8, 16, or 32 bits.

   b. A byte is 2 bits long, either of which may be a 0 or a 1.

   c. A bit is 8 bytes.

   d. A byte is a unit of data 8 bits long.

9. Booting a computer refers to what stage of the flow of information in a computer? [L3]

   a. Startup of the computer

   b. Starting an application program

   c. Opening a file within an application program

   d. Erasing unwanted files

10. Which of the following is *not* a reason to share resources on a network? [L4]

   a. To buy fewer printers

   b. To allow each worker to function independently

   c. To pay for one Internet connection for a group of computers

   d. To transfer files and data easily between computers

MATCHING

Match each term in the second column with its correct definition in the first column by writing the letter of the term on the blank line in front of the correct definition.

_____ 1. A pointing device commonly used on a laptop computer

_____ 2. A popular operating system on a mainframe computer; a version called Linux is used on some personal computers

_____ 3. Using formulas to simulate the behavior of real systems

_____ 4. Arrays of transistors and other electronic devices

_____ 5. A set of instructions that a computer can follow to accomplish a task

_____ 6. Approximately 1 billion bytes

_____ 7. A numbering system that uses only zeros and ones

_____ 8 Converts music to a file a computer can read

_____ 9. A picture element that displays as a dot on a computer monitor

_____ 10. Dividing a task into component parts that can be processed on multiple computers

A. Algorithm

B. Analog to digital

C. Binary

D. Distributed processing

E. Gigabyte

F. Integrated circuit

G. Modeling

H. Pixel

I. Touch pad

J. UNIX

Skill Drill

Skill Drill exercises reinforce chapter skills. Each skill reinforced is the same, or nearly the same, as a skill presented in the chapter. Detailed instructions are provided in a step-by-step format. Each exercise is independent of the others, so you can do the exercises in any order.

1. Finding Storage Capacity of a Folder in Your Hard Drive

Space on your hard disk is divided into smaller sections called *folders*. You can find out how many files are in a folder and how much space is used by the files. The size of folders becomes important when you are planning to write music or picture files to CDs or DVDs.

To find the capacity used by the files in a single folder, follow these steps:

1. Turn on your computer and wait until it displays its normal screen, which includes a Start button. Point to the **Start** button. Click one time with the left mouse button.

2. Point to the right side of the **Start** menu, and then locate and click **Computer** to open the Computer window.

3. In the **Navigation Pane**, if necessary, move the pointer to the left of the **Libraries** folder to display the arrow. Click **Libraries arrow** to display a list of folder types—Documents, Music, Pictures, and Videos.

4. Under **Libraries**, click the **Music** folder arrow.

5. Under **Music**, locate the **Public Music** folder. With the *right* mouse button, click the **Public Music** folder, and then from the displayed menu, click **Properties**.

6. At the top of the dialog box, click the **General** tab if necessary.

7. Read the information about this folder. Note the number of files and other folders it contains.

8. Click the **Start** button, click **All Programs**, click the **Accessories** folder, and then in the list of programs, click **Snipping Tool**.

9. In the **Snipping Tool** dialog box, click the **New Snip** button arrow, and then click **Window Snip**. Point anywhere in the **Public Music Properties** dialog box and click one time.

10. Near the top of the **Snipping Tool** dialog box, click the **Save Snip** button. In the **Save As** dialog box, navigate to the folder where you store your files. In the **File name** box, type U1Ch01MusicStudentName substituting your name as indicated, and then click **Save**.

11. In the upper-right corner of each window, click the **Close** button.

12. Submit your snip as directed by your instructor.

2. Finding Information About an Individual File on Your Hard Drive

Individual files—whether they are songs, videos, pictures, or word processing documents—also have properties.

To find the capacity used by a single file on the hard drive, follow these steps:

1. Turn on your computer and wait until it displays its normal screen, which includes a Start button. Point to the **Start** button. Click one time with the left mouse button.

2. Point to the right side of the **Start** menu, and then locate and click **Computer** to open the Computer window.

3. In the **Navigation Pane**, if necessary, click the **Libraries** arrow to display a list of folder types.

4. Under **Libraries**, click the **Pictures** arrow, and then click the **Public Pictures** arrow.

5. Under **Public Pictures**, click the **Sample Pictures** folder.

6. Select a picture file from the folder, and then right-click the file. From the displayed shortcut menu, click **Properties**. Read the information about this file.

7. Click the **Start** button, click **All Programs**, click the **Accessories** folder, and then in the list of programs, click **Snipping Tool**.

8. In the **Snipping Tool** dialog box, click the **New Snip** button arrow and then click **Window Snip**. Point anywhere in the **Properties** dialog box—it will include the name of the file you selected—and click one time.

9. Near the top of the **Snipping Tool** dialog box, click the **Save Snip** button. In the **Save As** dialog box, navigate to the folder where you store your files. In the **File name** box, type U1Ch01FileStudentName substituting your name as indicated, and then click **Save**.

10. In the upper-right corner of each window, click the **Close** button.

11. Submit your snip as directed by your instructor.

3. Finding Shared Storage

Disk drives or individual folders may be shared with other computers over the network. You can determine whether a folder or drive is shared.

To determine if a folder or disk is shared with others over a network, follow these steps:

1. Turn on your computer and wait until it displays its normal screen, which includes a Start button. Point to the **Start** button. Click one time with the left mouse button.

2. On the right side of the **Start** menu, locate and click **Computer** to open the Computer window.

3. In the **Navigation Pane**, if necessary, click the **Libraries** arrow to display a list of folder types.

4. Under **Libraries**, click the **Documents** arrow, and then click the **My Documents** folder.

5. Navigate to a specific file or folder of your choice. With the *right* mouse button, click the file or folder, from the displayed menu click **Share with**, and then click **Specific people** to display the File Sharing dialog box.

6. Click the **Start** button, click **All Programs**, click the **Accessories** folder, and then in the list of programs, click **Snipping Tool**.

7. In the **Snipping Tool** dialog box, click the **New Snip** button arrow, and then click **Full-screen Snip**. Point anywhere in the **File Sharing** dialog box and click one time.

8. Near the top of the **Snipping Tool** dialog box, click the **Save Snip** button. In the **Save As** dialog box, navigate to the folder where you store your files. In the **File name** box, type U1Ch01ShareStudentName substituting your name as indicated, and then click **Save**.

9. In the upper-right corner of each open dialog box or window, click the **Close** button.

10. Submit your snip as directed by your instructor.

Explore and Share

Explore and Share questions are intended for discussion in class or online. Look for information that is related to the learning outcomes for this chapter as directed. Submit your answers as directed by your instructor.

1. Look in a magazine or newspaper and determine the capacity of the hard disk and RAM that is available on new computers. How does this compare to the hard disk and RAM capacity of the computer you use? How old is your computer, and how much has the hard disk and RAM capacity available on new computers changed? [L2]

2. List the devices you use that probably have microprocessors in them and categorize them as computers, media players, or appliances. Compare your list and how you categorized the items on it with other class members. Discuss your reasons for placing each device in the category you chose. [L1]

3. E-books have been around for many years and are now becoming popular. There are many books available as e-books, including many textbooks. Newspapers, magazines, and blogs also are available through built-in wireless connectivity in e-book readers. What are some of the reasons why people hesitate to use e-books and e-book readers? Do you think these problems will be resolved in the near future? How? What will it take, if anything, for e-books to replace the majority of paper books? [L1]

In Your Life

In Your Life questions are intended for discussion in class or online where you can share your personal experience. Restrict your answers to the topics described in each exercise. Submit your answers as directed by your instructor.

1. Computer hardware is on most desks and in most back rooms of today's workplace. If the building where you work is more than 25 years old, it is likely that the building's designers never had this use in mind. Consequently, the air-conditioning system may be overloaded by the heat from computers, and the wiring that provides power and LAN connections may be in people's way. Is this a problem in your school or place of employment? If so, what has been done to accommodate computers in these older buildings? If this is not a problem in the facility in which you work or go to school, identify how the building's furniture and wiring accommodate computers used by individual workers. [L4]

2. Many computers use wireless communications between the central processing unit and peripherals like a keyboard, mouse, or printer. If you have used a wireless mouse or keyboard, describe the benefits and drawbacks of using a wireless peripheral device compared to one that is connected by a wire.

3. A person can perform the same functions as a computer. What parts of a human function as input, storage, memory, processing, and output? What functions can you perform better than a computer? [L2]

4. If you have used a natural user interface (NUI) on a device like a phone or tablet, compare how basic tasks like scrolling, changing zoom, selecting items, typing text, and file editing are done and describe whether you prefer an NUI or a standard computer interface. [L2]

5. Recall the first time you used Windows to start an application, save a file, close an application, and shut down the computer. Which procedures were easy to figure out and which ones were hard? Reflect on your thinking at the time, and describe why some of these were easy and why some were difficult for you. [L4]

Related Skills

Related Skills exercises expand on—or are somewhat related to—skills presented in the lessons. The exercises provide a brief narrative introduction, followed by instructions in a numbered-step format that are not as detailed as those in the Skill Drill section.

1. Determining the Processor, Clock Speed, and RAM

The computer's operating system has a variety of administrative tools that you can use to determine the capacity of its components.

To determine the brand of processor in your computer as well as the clock speed, hard disk storage, video memory, and RAM capacity, follow these steps:

1. Turn on your computer and wait until it displays its normal screen, which includes a Start button. Point to the **Start** button. Click one time with the left mouse button.

2. Point to the **Control Panel** menu item and click the left mouse button.

3. In the **Control Panel** dialog box, at the upper-right corner, click in the **Search Control Panel** box, type processor speed and then press **Enter**. A list of options appears at the left.

4. Under **System**, click **Check processor speed**. A description of your computer's processor, clock speed, and RAM displays.

5. Open the **Snipping Tool** and select **Window snip**. Click the dialog box. Click the **Save Snip** button. In the **Save As** dialog box, navigate to the folder where you store your files. In the **File name** box, type U1Ch01CPUStudentName substituting your name as indicated, and then click **Save**.

6. In the upper-right corner of each open dialog box or window, click the **Close** button.

7. Submit your snip as directed by your instructor.

2. Applying What You Have Learned to an Advertisement for a Computer

You will learn more about computer hardware and how to make an informed purchase in a later chapter, but you know enough now to pick out key facts from an advertisement for new personal computers and compare them based on type of processor, clock speed, and RAM.

To compare computers for sale that have different processors, clock speeds, and RAM capacity, follow these steps:

1. Find an advertisement for new computers in a newspaper or magazine, or on the Internet, where more than one model is listed.

2. Write down the model, type of processor, clock speed, RAM, and price for at least two computers from the same manufacturer.

3. Repeat Steps 1 and 2 with an advertisement for computers made by a different manufacturer.

4. Answer this question: If the clock speed and RAM are about the same for computers from two different manufacturers, is the difference in price less than $150?

5. If you find that the prices for computers with similar clock speeds and RAM are different by more than $150, look at the ads again and write down or type the features found in the more expensive computer that you think account for the difference. Submit the document as directed.

3. Applying What You Have Learned to Using E-Books in a Library

Many college libraries have subscriptions to electronic books that can be accessed online or through computers in the library.

To check your library for e-books, follow these steps:

1. Go to the website for your school's library or a local community library.

2. Search the interface for references to electronic books or to items that can be read entirely online.

3. Choose a book or article that is available entirely online from the library and open it.

4. Use the skill you practiced earlier to open the Snipping Tool and capture a screen that shows the title of the book and some of its text.

5. Save the screen capture, name it U1Ch01ArticleStudentName and submit the file as directed.

Discover

Discover exercises give you general directions for exploring and discovering more advanced skills and information. Each exercise is independent of the others, so you may complete the exercises in any order.

1. Finding Out What Processes Are Running in the Background

When you first boot your computer, it may appear that no applications are running. However, there will be several (or many) programs running in the background. Many of these will be operating system processes, while others have been added as software is installed. This is particularly true of antivirus programs. Hold down Ctrl and Alt, then press Delete one time. In the displayed menu, click **Start Task Manager**. In the displayed **Windows Task Manager** dialog box, click the **Processes** tab. Watch the **CPU** column to see which processes are currently active—the active processes will change from 00 to 01 or 02 intermittently. Write down the names of the active processes, and then count and write down or type the number of processes running in the background. (Hint: The number of processes running can also be found on the screen.) When you are finished, **Close** the Windows Task Manager dialog box. Submit the document as directed.

2. Learning About Sharing Folders

Click the **Start** button, and then on the **Start** menu, click **Help and Support**. In the **Search** box, type Sharing and click **Enter**. Click **File sharing essentials**. Read the available article on sharing *any* folder on your PC, and then make a list of the steps required to share folders that are not in the Public folder. Submit the document as directed.

3. Finding the Hard Disk Capacity Using Apple OS or Linux

The instructions in this chapter for determining the hard disk capacity assume that you have Windows 7 as your operating system. If you have access to a computer with a different operating system, such as Apple or Linux, use the help features provided with the operating system and write step-by-step instructions like the ones in Lesson 3 to find the capacity of the hard disk. Submit the document as directed.

4. Using the Help and Support Center to Learn About Network Devices

If your computer is part of a network, you will probably have devices available to you, such as printers, scanners, and shared folders on other computers. Click the **Start** button and then on the right side of the Start menu, click **Help and Support**. In the **Search Help** box, type network devices click **Enter**, and then click **View computers and devices on a network**. Follow the directions to view your network devices. Identify and record what network devices are attached to your computer. Submit the document as directed. You will learn more about networks in later chapters.

5. Rebooting a Smartphone

Smartphones have operating systems. On occasion, they can lock up and must be restarted. Read the owner's manual for your smartphone and find out how to reboot the operating system if it freezes. Record the steps necessary to reboot the device, and then submit the document as directed.

Chapter 2

Identifying Computer Components and Their Functions

Why Would I Do This?

Desktop computers are systems of connected components that perform the basic functions of input, storage/memory, processing, and output. If you understand which of the basic functions each component performs, you will be able to recognize and categorize new hardware when you see it or read about it.

Some storage devices are internal (inside the system unit), but most are external and designed for direct interaction with the user. You need to know how each kind of device is used to select the right type of media and to move files between computers.

External devices were originally all connected to each other using special wires or cables. Wireless connections, however, are becoming much more common. When you add a new piece of hardware to a computer system, you need to know how to connect it and how to install it on the system so that it can communicate with other parts of the system.

Chapter at a Glance

Lesson	Learning Outcomes	Page Number	Related IC3 Objectives
1	Identify how different types of computer monitors work	40	2.1.1
1	Identify how different types of computer mice work	41	2.1.1
1	Identify possible problems encountered using computer mice	42	2.1.1
1	Identify mouse alternatives for notebook computers including touchpad and stylus	44	2.1.1
1	Identify the basic functions of a computer keyboard	44	2.1.1
1	Identify the different types of optical discs	46	2.1.2
1	Identify the role of flash memory and solid state drives (SSD)	48	2.1.2
1	Identify the role of external hard drives	49	2.1.2
1	Identify the major printer categories	49	2.1.1
1	Identify the uses of computer speakers	50	2.1.1
1	Identify the uses of computer microphones	50	2.1.1
2	Identify how a game controller works	51	2.1.1
2	Identify the types of still digital cameras	52	2.1.1
2	Identify how a digital video camera works	52	2.1.1
2	Identify the types of computer scanners	53	2.1.1
2	Identify the use of optical character recognition software	54	2.1.1
2	Identify the uses of a graphics tablet	54	2.1.1
2	Identify how a bar code reader works	54	2.1.1
2	Identify the uses of a touch screen	55	2.1.1
2	Identify the uses of sensors and probes	55	2.1.1
2	Identify the different ways remote controls work	55	2.3.1
2	Identify the uses of security input devices	56	2.1.1
2	Identify the uses of adaptive computer devices	56	2.1.1
3	Identify the different types of computer projectors	56	2.1.1
3	Identify the difference between a pen plotter and an electrostatic plotter	57	2.1.1
3	Identify the uses of voice synthesizers	58	2.1.1
3	Identify the uses of robots	58	2.1.1
4	Identify the different types of USB connections	59	4.2.2
4	Identify the uses of a USB hub	61	4.2.2
4	Identify the differences between WiFi and Bluetooth wireless	61	4.2.2
4	Identify the uses of FireWire connections	62	4.2.2
4	Identify the use of a SCSI bus	62	4.2.2
4	Examine connected devices using Device Manager	62	4.3.0
4	Identify special considerations when connecting peripherals	63	4.2.0
4	Identify the use of device drivers	64	4.3.3
4	Update a device driver	64	4.3.3
4	Identify how to install a device driver from a disc	65	4.3.3
4	Identify the use of plug-and-play	65	4.3.0

Visual Summary

In this chapter, you will become familiar with the parts of a desktop computer system, how the parts are connected, and how you install new hardware.

Figure 2.1 shows a photo of a typical desktop computer system.

FIGURE 2.1
A typical desktop computer system.

gabyjalbert / istockphoto.com

List of Student Files

In most cases you will create files by capturing screens. You will add your name to the file names and save them on your computer or portable memory device. Table 2.1 lists the files you start with and the names you give them when you save the files.

TABLE 2.1

ASSIGNMENT:	STUDENT SOURCE FILE:	SAVE AS:
Lessons 1–4	none	U1Ch02ControlStudentName U1Ch02SystemStudentName U1Ch02DriverStudentName
Skill Drill	none	U1Ch02KeyboardStudentName U1Ch02MouseStudentName U1Ch02DVDStudentName U1Ch02MonitorStudentName
Explore and Share	none	U1Ch02BluetoothStudentName U1Ch02SpeechStudentName U1Ch02NarratorStudentName U1Ch02ProbeStudentName
In Your Life	none	none
Related Skills	none	U1Ch02PointerStudentName U1Ch02TrailStudentName U1Ch02DisplayStudentName
Discover	none	none

The desktop computer system consists of a *system unit* that contains the central processing unit. Devices that are visible to the user on the outside of the system unit are input and output components. Some of the components, such as the keyboard and mouse and the built-in storage devices, are intended to remain with one computer. Other components, such as external hard disk drives and other portable storage devices, can be moved from computer to computer. Some devices, such as printers, can be connected to multiple computers.

Monitors

The screen used to display output to the user is called a *monitor*. Older monitors use a glass picture tube called a *cathode ray tube (CRT)*, similar to picture tubes used in older televisions. CRTs use a large glass tube in which an electron beam starts at the small end and strikes the phosphors at the wide end. CRT monitors tend to be large and heavy due to the long, glass picture tube.

The development of portable computers depended on using a different display technology from older computers, called *liquid crystal display (LCD)*. LCD panels have replaced CRT displays in nearly all newer computers. An LCD may use a fluorescent light behind a flat panel. The fluorescent light is called a *backlight*. The panel has small elements that change from transparent to opaque depending on the electric charge applied to them. Filters are used to produce different colors. The computer controls the electric charges applied to the elements to make picture elements, or *pixels*. The number of pixels per inch displayed on the screen determines the *resolution*, or level of detail that can be viewed. Displaying more pixels per inch results in higher resolution.

Monitors are attached to the main processor unit using a *video graphics adapter (VGA)* plug or a *digital video interface (DVI)* plug. Adapters are available that convert VGA and DVI plugs to fit the other form. See Figure 2.2. Many newer LCD panels use light emitting diodes (LED) to replace the fluorescent backlight. These monitors may be called LED but they still use LCD to display the pixels.

FIGURE 2.2
VGA plug (left) and
DVI plug (right).

Anthony Seebaran / istockphoto.com

The Mouse

Most systems use a device that controls a pointer on the screen. The pointer can move up and down, left and right, or in any combination of these directions, and so must the device used to control it. There are several variations of these devices, and they all convert a motion or touch by the user into a motion of a pointer on the screen. The most common of these devices is the ***mouse***.

Mathematicians, scientists, and engineers use a coordinate method of two numbers to locate positions on a flat surface. One number indicates the left-to-right position (the X direction) and the other number indicates the up-and-down position (the Y direction). Some mice hold a rubber ball that rolls on the desk or a mouse pad. Inside the mouse, the rubber ball presses against two rollers that are perpendicular to each other. The motion of the rolling ball is converted into two separate rolling motions that indicate movement in the X or Y direction. The computer uses an analog to digital (A to D) converter to turn this continuous motion into a series of binary numbers that the computer then uses to control the position of the pointer on the screen.

The rollers inside a mouse often get lint or fibers wrapped around them, which causes the pointer to behave erratically. Most newer mice use reflected beams of light instead of rollers to eliminate this problem, as shown in Figure 2.3. Such a mouse is called an ***optical mouse***. It does not need a mouse pad for traction, but the surface upon which it moves must have some variation in color or texture that would affect the reflected beam of light.

FIGURE 2.3
Underside of an
optical mouse.

Tatiana Popova / shutterstock.com

Using a mouse involves a combination of moving the body of the mouse to control the position of the pointer on the screen and clicking a button. Because mouse actions are so common, instruction manuals usually abbreviate an entire process with a simple word or phrase. See Table 2.2 for a list of simple instructions, a full description of the process, and common mistakes and problems.

TABLE 2.2

INSTRUCTION	DESCRIPTION	COMMON MISTAKES/POSSIBLE PROBLEMS
Click	Move the mouse on the desktop to move the tip of the on-screen pointer to the desired location. Hold the mouse stationary—usually by resting the heel of your hand on the desktop or mouse pad—and then press and release the button on the left side of the mouse.	The tip of the pointer is not on the desired object.
Double-click	Move the mouse on the desktop to move the tip of the on-screen pointer to the desired location. Hold the mouse stationary—usually by resting the heel of your hand on the desktop or mouse pad—and then press and release the button on the left side of the mouse two times in rapid succession.	The mouse moves slightly between clicks or too much time elapses between clicks.
Right-click	Move the mouse on the desktop to move the tip of the on-screen pointer to the desired location. Hold the mouse stationary—usually by resting the heel of your hand on the desktop or mouse pad—and then press and release the button on the right side of the mouse.	• An instruction such as "click the right mouse button" could be misinterpreted to mean to click the "correct" mouse button. • The right mouse button is disabled in some laboratories for security reasons. • The right mouse button is used much less than the left, and readers often misread the instruction and use the left mouse button.
Drag	Move the mouse on the desktop to move the tip of the on-screen pointer to the desired location. Press and hold the button on the left side of the mouse. Move the mouse on the desktop to drag the pointer to a new location. Release the mouse button.	The mouse button is accidentally released during the motion of the mouse and then pressed again, resulting in two separate drag operations.

Another pointing device is the trackball, shown in Figure 2.4. It is similar to a mouse turned upside down, and you move the ball directly. Some people prefer trackballs because you control them using just your fingers, not your arm. Trackballs are sometimes used with notebook computers because you do not need much space to use them. A trackball has right and left mouse buttons like a standard mouse. Some portable computers use a small trackball, sometimes referred to as a ***thumb mouse***.

FIGURE 2.4
The ball in a trackball is manipulated directly by the user while the rest of the device remains stationary.

Jorgen Udvang / istockphoto.com

To use the mouse

Refer to Table 2.2 and practice using the mouse.

1 **Click the Start button** ⊕**.** The Start menu displays.

2 **On right side of the Start menu, click Control Panel.** The Control Panel window opens. The blue bar at the top of the window is the *title bar*, even though there is currently no title in this window.

3 **Double-click the title bar.** The Control Panel window switches between full screen and a floating window.

4 **Double-click the title bar, if necessary, so that the Control Panel window does not fill the screen.** See Figure 2.5.

FIGURE 2.5
Control panel window.

5 **Move the pointer to the middle of the Control Panel title bar. Click and hold down the left mouse button while dragging the window to another location on the screen.**

6 **Click the Start button, click All Programs, click the Accessories folder, and then in the list of programs, click Snipping Tool.** This feature is available only in Windows Vista and later Windows operating systems.

7 **In the Snipping Tool dialog box, click the New Snip button arrow** ✂**, and then click Full-Screen Snip.**

8 **Near the top of the Snipping Tool dialog box, click the Save Snip button** 🖫**. In the Save As dialog box, navigate to the folder where you store your files. In the File name box, type** U1Ch02ControlStudentName **substituting your name as indicated, and then click Save.**

9 **Right-click the title bar.** A shortcut menu displays.

10 **On the shortcut menu, click Close. Submit your snip as directed.** The Control Panel window closes. Alternatively, at the right side of the title bar, click the Close button ❌.

Mouse Alternatives for Notebook Computers

A pointing stick, as shown in Figure 2.6, is a small knob on some notebook keyboards that responds to sideways pressure. It controls a pointer on the screen like a mouse does. Right and left buttons are located elsewhere on the keyboard.

FIGURE 2.6
Pointing sticks are used in some notebook computers to save space.

Pierre Yu / istockphoto.com

A ***touch pad*** is a small, rectangular, flat area below the space bar on many notebook computers, as shown in Figure 2.7. It senses the position of your finger when you touch it, and it can be set to interpret a brief touch as a mouse click. Care must be taken not to accidentally touch this pad while typing. Right and left buttons are located near the touch pad.

FIGURE 2.7
Touch pads are common on portable devices and are usually placed below the space bar on the keyboard.

René Mansi / istockphoto.com

A ***click pad*** combines a touch pad and a single-button mouse. The pad itself can be depressed to indicate a mouse click. Some Apple laptop computers use a click pad.

Keyboard

The most commonly used piece of input hardware is the keyboard, shown in Figure 2.8. Each keystroke is converted into a binary number that the computer understands. Keyboards have function keys at the top that can be programmed to perform special functions. There are other special function keys on some keyboards that start a browser or open the Start menu in Windows. Some keys are intended for use with other keys. The ***Control key*** Ctrl, the ***Alternate key*** Alt, and the ***Shift key*** ⬆Shift may be used in combination with other keys for special commands. Desktop computer keyboards typically have a numeric keypad at the right that can double as navigation keys; these keys are labeled with a number and an arrow or a navigation term. The ***Num Lock key*** Num Lock at the top of the numeric keypad toggles the numeric keys' function between the navigation arrows and numbers. There is usually a status light on the keyboard that comes on to indicate when the keypad is in numeric mode. On a notebook computer that does not have a separate numeric keypad, the numbers are on letter keys and are toggled on and off using the (Fn) button.

Mashe/fotolia.com

Macintosh computer keyboards are slightly different, as shown in Figure 2.9. They have keys that are similar to Control and Alternate, called the **Command key** and **Option key**. On a Macintosh keyboard, the key with the apple on it is the Command key, which may be used in combination with other keys or mouse clicks to provide alternative functions and screen menus. Most Macintosh computers use a mouse with only one button. If you are running software on a Macintosh that was designed for a mouse with right and left buttons, use Command in combination with a mouse click to emulate a right-click of the mouse.

Tim Graham / Alamy

Instruction manuals indicate the use of combinations of keys by writing a plus sign between them; for instance, (Ctrl) + (C) means to press and hold (Ctrl) and then press the (C) key. Because there is also a key with a plus sign on it, this instruction is easily misinterpreted. If a program stops responding while you are running Windows, you can press and hold both (Ctrl) and (Alt) and then press (Delete) to bring up the Task Manager dialog box that enables you to close the unresponsive program and continue working. Similarly, if a program stops responding while you are running a Macintosh computer, hold down both (⌘) and (Option), and then press (Esc). Most notebook computers have a **Function (Fn) key** that provides another possible combination of keys.

There are several ways to connect the keyboard and mouse to the main system unit in a desktop computer. Older models used dedicated ports with round plugs. Newer models use USB connectors or wireless connection. Keyboards and mice that are connected via a USB wire are powered by the main system unit through the USB wire. Wireless peripherals must have their own batteries to provide power. When these batteries run low on power, the keyboard or mouse may behave irratically or simply stop working. Replacing the old battery with one that is fully charged will usually resolve the problem. If the keyboard or mouse does not work immediately, look for a button on the back of the keyboard or mouse labeled *Connect* that will force the system to check for its presence.

If a program ever freezes and pressing Ctrl + Alt + Delete doesn't bring up a dialog box in Windows, you can check to see if the computer is still communicating with the keyboard. To find out if the keyboard is being recognized by the computer, press Num Lock a few times to see if the indicator light goes on and off. If not, the keyboard isn't being recognized and you will have to turn the computer off using the power button.

Optical Discs

Media used to store information using magnetic methods are called *disks*, whereas similar media that store data using optical methods are called *discs*. Information is stored on a *compact disc (CD)* as binary numbers by burning a *pit* and leaving the surface between pits unmarked (called a *land*). A reflective layer is deposited on the pitted surface and the pits become reflective bumps. The reflective bumps represent ones and the spaces between represent zeros. A laser beam scans the disc as it turns, and the reflection is picked up by a sensor that converts the flickering reflection into binary numbers, as shown in Figure 2.10. Optical drives, in which you play or record optical discs, come in two categories: read-only and writable. Read-only drives can read the data on the disc but cannot alter the content or write data on a blank disc. Writable drives can write to writable optical discs.

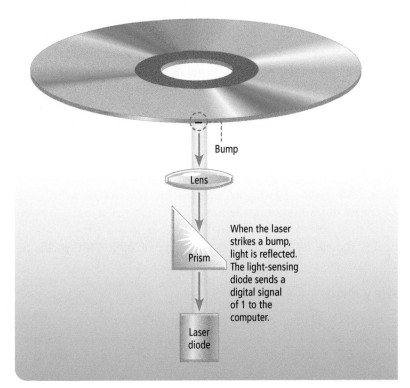

Bump

Lens

Prism

When the laser strikes a bump, light is reflected. The light-sensing diode sends a digital signal of 1 to the computer.

Laser diode

There are three types of optical discs: CD, DVD, and Blu-ray. Each of these types may come in versions that are read-only, recordable one time, or can be erased and recorded many times.

CD-ROM

The oldest and most common optical disc is the **CD-ROM**. ROM stands for *read-only memory*. This type of disc comes with information or music already written on it. The optical disc drives commonly found in personal computers can read this type of disc. When you buy software in a box, it probably comes on a CD-ROM.

CD-R

If you purchase a blank **CD-R**, you can record on each part of the disc one time and read it as many times as you like. These discs are comparable in price to an old removable disk but hold approximately 400 times as much data. Many people simply keep recording onto an unused part of a CD-R instead of using a removable disk that can be erased and rewritten. The drive must be able to write to a CD to use this type of disc. The process of writing data to an optical disc is often referred to as *burning* the disc.

CD-RW

A **CD-RW** is rewritable like a magnetic disk—it can be written to and erased over and over. A CD-RW is more expensive than a CD-R, but the drives that are able to write to this type of CD are common on new computers. CD-Rs and CD-RWs hold about 650 megabytes of data.

DVD

Another type of optical disc for recording data is called digital video disc (DVD)—also referred to as a digital versatile disc (DVD). Recording on DVDs can be done on two different layers and on both sides of the disc. DVDs can hold approximately 4.7 gigabytes (or 4,700 megabytes) on a single-sided single-layer disc and up to 17 gigabytes on a double-sided double-layer disc. A DVD can hold up to 133 minutes of 30-frames-per-second, full-screen video. Read-only DVDs are also known as *DVD-ROM*.

Recordable DVD

Like CDs, DVDs come in two other versions, one that may be written to once (DVD-R) and one that may be erased and written to many times (DVD-RW). There are competing standards for the format used with these types of DVDs, which may cause some not to work in older DVD drives or may require that you use rerecordable discs that are compatible with specific drives.

Blu-Ray Disc

A new type of DVD using *Blu-ray* technology enables you to store 25 gigabytes on a single-layer disc and 50 gigabytes on a double-layer disc. Like DVDs, Blu-ray discs come in three types: *BD-ROM* (read-only), *BD-R* (write once), and *BD-RE* (can be erased and recorded many times).

Flash Memory

RAM stores data using special integrated circuits that are fast enough to keep up with the processor. The biggest drawback to most RAM is that it requires constant power to function. Another type of memory that uses integrated circuits is *flash memory*. Flash memory is not as fast as RAM, but it does not require constant power.

Flash memory is built into small cards or devices that plug into computers, cameras, or other devices to provide compact storage without moving parts, as shown in Figure 2.11. *CompactFlash cards* are typically used to store images in cameras. *Secure Digital (SD) cards* and *microSD cards* are used in cameras, cell phones, smartphones, PDAs, and similar devices.

FIGURE 2.11
Flash drives are used as external storage for computers and for digital cameras and smartphones.

Silvia Ganora / istockphoto.com

For computers, flash memory has become the most popular way to store and transport files from one computer to another, replacing the older magnetic removable disks; most newer computers do not even come with removable disk drives. Flash memory that is used for computer storage plugs into a USB port. These storage devices are called *flash drives*, *thumb drives*, or *USB drives*.

Recent improvements in flash technology have resulted in some manufacturers creating *flash hard drives*, sometimes referred to as solid state drives (SSD). The advantage of these drives is that they contain no moving parts and therefore break down less frequently. They are especially useful in notebook computers, where they can withstand impact and also do not use as much energy as magnetic hard drives.

External Hard Drive

Most personal computers come with a **hard drive** built into the computer—the **internal hard drive**—that is the main storage unit. Some computers use large capacity flash memory instead of a hard drive. **External hard drives** are also available and are used as supplementary storage when the internal hard drive is nearly full and, more often, for backup of important data files. External hard drives, one of which is shown in Figure 2.12, are readily available in storage sizes from 80 gigabytes to 1 terabyte and even larger.

FIGURE 2.12
External hard drives are used for supplemental storage to back up computer files.

mbbirdy / istockphoto.com

The physical size of external hard drives also varies from drives that will fit in a pocket to larger sizes that are less portable. External hard drives connect to computers using either a USB port or a FireWire port. (FireWire will be discussed later in this chapter.) Most of these drives come with backup software that enables you to automatically back up your data files on a scheduled basis. They are also very convenient for moving large quantities of information (e.g., digital pictures, audio, or video) from one computer to another.

Printers

Printers place ink on paper in patterns that resemble text or pictures. Early printers employed type-writer technology in which a metal rod struck an ink-infused ribbon, and the impact transferred the ink to the paper to make a dot. Printers that use this method are called **impact printers**. In one type of impact printer, a group of tiny rods are arranged in a rectangular bundle, or matrix, and the computer activates selected rods to produce patterns of dots that form text characters. This type of printer is called a **dot matrix printer**. Impact printers are rarely used with personal computers now, but businesses may need them to print duplicate copies using older, multilayer forms.

The impact printer was noisy and slow. It was replaced in many commercial applications such as cash registers, gasoline pumps, and automated teller machines with a printer that uses heat to make dots on temperature-sensitive paper. Because it uses heat to change the color of the special paper, this type of printer is called a **thermal printer**.

The copying industry developed a method of transferring powdered ink to paper in the shape of text or pictures and then heating the ink to make it stick to the paper. This technology was adapted for use in computer printers called ***laser printers***, shown in Figure 2.13. In a laser printer, a laser beam traces the shapes to be printed, producing an electrostatic charge on the paper. The powdered ink, known as ***toner***, is attracted to the static electricity, and a hot drum then melts the ink into the paper. Many laser printers print only in black and white, but prices have dropped enough to make color laser printers affordable even for home use.

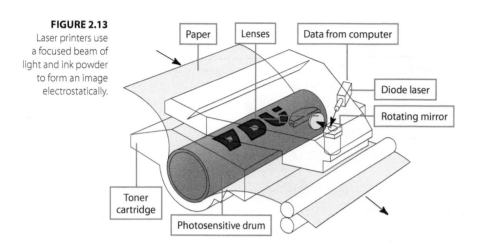

FIGURE 2.13
Laser printers use a focused beam of light and ink powder to form an image electrostatically.

Paper
Lenses
Data from computer
Diode laser
Rotating mirror
Toner cartridge
Photosensitive drum

Another method of producing high-quality printouts uses liquid ink that is fed through a special device that separates the flow of ink into separate tiny droplets that are directed to the paper using electric fields. This type of printer is called an ***ink-jet printer***. Ink-jet printers usually have four colors of ink: black, magenta, cyan, and yellow. The magenta, cyan, and yellow inks are used in combination to produce all the other colors. Higher-end, photo ink-jet printers have many more ink colors, stored in individual cartridges.

Speakers

Computers are capable of playing music or videos, producing sound effects with games, or speaking the content of documents. A pair of external speakers is provided with many computers, and some monitors have built-in speakers. More expensive systems include a larger speaker called a ***subwoofer*** to play low bass notes. Most computers have a small speaker inside the system unit; when there is a significant hardware problem with the computer that may prevent the monitor from working, this speaker may beep several times in a code that can inform a technician of the nature of the problem.

Microphones

Microphones pick up sounds, such as our voices, and convert them into analog signals. The computer uses an A to D converter to change the sounds into binary numbers. You can use computer programs that recognize voice commands to control the computer. Other programs translate what you say into text for use in a document or e-mail. This process is called ***voice recognition***. You can also use a computer microphone to play online multiplayer games, to participate in online conference calls, or to record comments that can be attached to an e-mail. Microphones can be very small and built into laptop computers, Web cameras, and monitors. When a microphone is used for voice recognition, it works better if it is placed within a few inches of the speaker's mouth and off to one side. Microphone headsets are often used to pick up the speaker's voice to improve quality. Laptop computers often have a small camera and microphone built in to facilitate video conferencing, as shown in Figure 2.14.

Video camera

Supri Suharjoto / shutterstock.com

Lesson 2 ▶ Identifying Specialized Input Devices

There are many other ways to provide input to a computer in addition to using a keyboard, a mouse, or a microphone.

Game Controllers

Controlling the action in a computerized game requires a specialized input device that combines several modes of input simultaneously, as shown in Figure 2.15. Game controllers come in various shapes and sizes. The most common is the ***gamepad***, sometimes referred to as a *joypad*. The gamepad is held in both hands, and a combination of buttons and control sticks are used to play the games. Another type of game controller uses a ***joystick*** and several buttons that are programmed for specific actions in the game. A joystick uses the same technology as a mouse or trackball, but the rotating ball is inside the case and the user moves an attached rod. The stick often has a button near the top and several others on the side for controlling game action.

Another type of game controller—used by the Nintendo Wii—is a wireless device that comes in different shapes that enable you to play virtual golf or the guitar, dance, or participate in role-playing games, competing against the computer or against another person.

FIGURE 2.15
A game controller is used for specialized computer games.

Paul Matthew Photography / shutterstock.com

Digital Cameras: Still and Video

In a digital camera, a lens focuses an image on an array of light-sensitive detectors that convert the image into electrical signals that are analogous to the brightness of the light at each detector. These signals are fed into an A to D converter that produces a number that represents the brightness of the image for each detector. The digital numbers are recorded on a removable storage medium—usually flash memory. The resolution of the image taken by a digital camera is measured in *megapixels* (millions of pixels). A higher number of megapixels generally means better resolution and larger picture sizes when you print the image. An image that is 1,280 pixels wide by 960 pixels high is a 1.2-megapixel image, while a picture taken at 4,000 × 3,000 pixels is a 12-megapixel image.

There are several options for transferring image files into your computer. Some cameras use cables that connect to USB ports, some use a *docking station* where the camera sits, and some transfer the images using a wireless connection. Most digital cameras use flash memory on small SD cards, or CompactFlash cards, that may be removed from the camera and placed in a card reader that is either built into the computer or connected by a wire to a USB port on the computer.

Digital cameras that take photographs usually fall into one of two categories. The smallest, lightest, and least expensive is a *point-and-shoot camera*. Point-and-shoot cameras are commonly used with automatic focus and automatic shutter speeds determined by a microprocessor in the camera, although many of the newer models give the user some manual control over the process. Semiprofessional and professional cameras are *digital single lens reflex (DSLR)* cameras, as shown in Figure 2.16. These cameras are more expensive than point-and-shoot models, are usually much larger and heavier, and use interchangeable lenses. They give the photographer complete control over the camera settings, in addition to automatic settings. Many digital cameras have built-in video features for creating videos.

FIGURE 2.16
Digital SLR camera.

Inhabitant / shutterstock.com

Digital video cameras are like digital cameras, except that they take several pictures each second. The number of pictures they take is measured in *frames per second*. It takes 30 frames per second to simulate smooth motion. Most video cameras that are attached to computers are used for videoconferencing or monitoring a scene. If the video is intended for transmission over the Internet, a rate of 30 full-screen images per second is more than most connections can handle. In that case, video cameras use 15 frames per second, and the picture does not have enough pixels to fill the screen so it displays in a small window. Video cameras that are attached to a computer and intended for videoconferencing or monitoring, like the one shown on the left in Figure 2.17, are called *Web cams*. Handheld digital video cameras, like the one shown on the right in Figure 2.17, are typically more expensive than Web cams and are capable of recording full-screen motion at 30 frames per second with sound. Some video cameras are designed to capture video and sound and then upload the video over a wireless connection to a social media site. Many cell phones also include very basic digital cameras and video cameras.

FIGURE 2.17
Digital Web
camera (left)
and digital
video camera
(right).

Scanners

The process of converting an image into digital data is called *scanning*. The device that performs this task is called a *scanner*—shown in Figure 2.18. Using a scanner is a great way to input pictures into a computer or to use OCR software to convert printed documents into electronic text documents. Scanners are relatively easy to use, and their prices have fallen drastically in the last few years. Scanners that work with individual sheets of paper or books are called *flatbed scanners*. They have a pane of glass and a bright fluorescent lamp that travels the length of the glass. The light reflected from the picture or document is detected and converted to numbers using an A to D converter as the lamp moves down the glass. These numbers are assigned to pixels. The image quality of scanners is rated using a measurement that is common in the graphic reproduction industry: *dots per inch (dpi)*. The higher the number of dots per inch, the smaller the pixels and the more detailed the image, which results in larger file sizes.

FIGURE 2.18
Flatbed scanners can
scan pages of bulky
books as well as
individual pictures or
pages of text.

Multifunction machines, like the one shown in Figure 2.19, can copy, scan, print, and fax. They can scan many sheets of paper sequentially or use a flatbed scanner to scan books or small pieces of paper such as receipts.

FIGURE 2.19
A multifunction
copier, printer,
scanner, and fax.

If you want to convert printed documents into text that your word processor can use, you need a computer program that can recognize the image of a character and convert it to its ASCII or Unicode number. Programs that do this are called *optical character recognition (OCR)* programs. Some companies bundle an OCR program with a scanner. Look for this feature when you purchase a scanner, because the OCR program can cost as much as the scanner if purchased separately.

Graphics Tablets

Architects, mechanical engineers, photographers, and animation artists are among the people who use graphics tablets to assist them when they create drawings or process photographs. A *graphics tablet*, also known as a *digitizing tablet*, has a flat surface with an array of crossed wires built into the surface that can sense the vertical and horizontal position of a pointing device, as shown in Figure 2.20. When the user touches the tablet with a special pointing device, the array of crossed wires senses its position and determines the X and Y coordinates.

FIGURE 2.20
A graphics tablet enables an architect to assemble complex drawings from a library of predefined parts.

kryczka / istockphoto.com

A program running on the computer may define certain areas at the top or side of the tablet to represent standard shapes like doors, windows, electrical outlets, walls, or cartoon characters. These areas appear on the screen as menus of buttons or icons. When the user touches the tablet in one of those areas, the program looks up how to draw that object. Next, the user touches the tablet where the object should go and the computer draws the object at a corresponding location on the screen. The user assembles a drawing quickly by selecting standard objects and placing them in the drawing. Digitizing tablets are also frequently used by photographers to process photographs while they use graphics editing programs.

Bar Code Reader

Bar codes consist of a series of parallel dark lines and white spaces. When a narrow beam of light passes across these lines, the reflection flickers. A *bar code reader*, shown in Figure 2.21, has a narrow beam of light and a sensor. The sensor converts the flickering reflection into binary numbers the computer can use to identify the item. Bar codes are used to identify a variety of objects such as groceries, clothes, music CDs, railroad cars, overnight delivery packages, and bulk mail. Bar code readers are used in conjunction with a database for pricing and inventory control.

Radio Frequency Identification (RFID)

A *radio frequency identification (RFID)* device uses radio frequencies to remotely retrieve data. These devices are often used for inventory control, but are most visible in automobiles on tollways. An RFID device is attached to the windshield; then, when the car passes through a toll gate, the signal is read from the device, the car is identified, the user's account is checked to confirm that the account has enough money in it, and the toll is subtracted from the user's account—all in seconds.

Touch Screen

Touch screens are monitors that are designed to act as input devices. When you touch the screen, the location of your touch is translated into X and Y coordinates. A program that is running on the computer may display buttons, menus, pictures, or icons, and when you touch the screen at a location that corresponds to one of these, the touch becomes input. Touch screens are used in some large stores to allow customers to check out without the direct aid of a clerk. They are also used to provide information in public kiosks. Most smartphones, tablets, and game consoles use a touch screen and sometimes use a *stylus*, a penlike device that is used to tap the screen.

Sensors and Probes

A *sensor* detects the status of something and responds to changes in a predictable manner. Many sensors produce an electric signal that changes in a manner that is analogous to changes it senses. An A to D converter can change the electrical signal into a series of zeros and ones that the computer can interpret. *Probes* are sensors that are used to explore places that are not conveniently accessible. Sensors provide input the computer can act upon. For example, the oxygen sensor in the exhaust pipe of an automobile provides information that is used to adjust the fuel-to-air mix in the engine, and a series of probes in remote locations sense ground movement that can be used to help study—and even predict—earthquakes and volcanic eruptions.

Remote Controls

Remote controls are wireless devices that are often used as input devices for appliances such as music CD players, televisions, or computer media centers. Remote controls usually have a series of buttons that typically include a numeric keypad. Pressing a button produces a binary number that is transmitted to a receiver on the appliance. Many remote controls use *infrared light* to transmit the number; others use radio waves. Infrared light is invisible to the human eye but behaves like a beam of visible light that flashes to represent the zeros and ones of a binary number. You have to point the remote control at the infrared sensor on the appliance like you would point a flashlight. If the remote control uses radio waves, you do not have to point the remote control at the sensor. The radio waves spread out in all directions and pass through some objects.

Security Devices

Some computers that contain sensitive data are protected by special security devices. The most basic security device is a password. Swipe card readers can be installed on a computer for extra security. For security at a higher level, **biometric devices** can be used to match unique characteristics of each user, such as fingerprint, voice, or retinal scans. Biometrics applies statistics to biology. A biometric device can match a user's biological information with patterns stored in a database to confirm the identity of authorized users.

Specialized Input Devices

There are a number of input devices designed for special applications and **adaptive computer devices** for use by people with different types of special needs, like the keyboard shown in Figure 2.22. There are also miniature keyboards that require very little hand strength or reach but work with very slight hand or head movements; keyboards with tactile surfaces, which can be used by the visually impaired; and one-handed keyboards. There are even input devices that use eye control and breath control to activate on-screen keyboards. Most people with a visual impairment can use a standard keyboard, but they need special software that uses speech synthesis to indicate which menu items were selected and which characters have been typed.

FIGURE 2.22
Adaptive devices like this enhanced keyboard enable people with special needs to use computers.

ZUMA Wire Service / Alamy

Lesson 3 ▶ Identifying Specialized Output Devices

In addition to printers and monitors, other specialized output devices include projectors, voice synthesizers, plotters, and robots.

Projectors

Computers are often used to create presentations that are projected on a screen for group viewing. **Projectors** that work with computers, like the one shown in Figure 2.23, are really monitors that are designed to project images. A projector has a very bright lamp, and the brightness of the light coming from the projector is rated in **lumens**. To display a computer slide show to a group of 20 people in a classroom or conference room with some of the lights on, the projector should have a rating of at least 2,000 lumens. Brighter lamps can project pictures on larger screens or in brighter rooms.

FIGURE 2.23
LCD projectors
can be small and
lightweight but project
a bright image in
a lighted room.

Rich Legg / istockphoto.com

The most common projectors use metal halide lamps that pass light through three liquid crystal display (LCD) panels, one for each color (red, green, and blue). Another technology, ***digital light processing (DLP)***, developed by Texas Instruments, uses thousands of tiny mirrors that are controlled by the computer. The mirrors do not absorb light as the LCDs do, so this technology can produce brighter images from similar lamps. Computer projectors also accept input from video players and other sources such as digital video cameras.

Plotters

A ***plotter*** is a device that draws designs on paper. Plotters usually create drawings that are much larger than ordinary printers can handle. They are often used in design and manufacturing operations and to create architectural blueprints.

There are two basic types of plotters. A ***pen plotter***, shown in Figure 2.24, uses individual pens and different colored ink to create line drawings. Pen plotters tend to be slow and cannot be used to print graphics. An ***electrostatic plotter*** uses toner and can print photographs or other graphics in much the same way as laser printers do. Commercial plotters can print on paper up to about 6 feet in width and use rolls of paper so that the length of the printout is limited only to the length of paper on the roll.

FIGURE 2.24
Pen plotters use pen
and ink to draw large
diagrams.

Alexander Dunkel / istockphoto.com

Voice Synthesizers

A computer can communicate information by producing sounds through the speakers that correspond to human speech. Many companies that do business by telephone use computers that respond to voice commands and synthesize spoken responses to commonly asked questions. *Voice synthesizers*—sometimes called *speech synthesizers*—are also used in computers to assist people with visual or reading disabilities.

Control Devices/Robots

Computers are also used as the "brains" of control devices and robots. A *robot* is a mechanical device that is programmed to perform specialized functions. At the lowest levels, computers assist in controlling such things as robot arms, used in everything from medical research to handling toxic materials to performing functions in space that could not be performed by astronauts.

Robots—like the one shown in Figure 2.25—are used extensively in manufacturing to perform tasks that are dull, repetitive, or dangerous. Many of these robots are programmed to adjust themselves and learn to perfect the tasks they are programmed to perform. Although robots in manufacturing can work 24 hours a day, 7 days a week without needing breaks or time off, their use poses serious social implications because they have eliminated a number of manufacturing jobs.

FIGURE 2.25
A manufacturing robot performs repetitive tasks.

gerenme / istockphoto.com

Vehicles like the moon and Mars rovers, used in space programs, are also a type of robot; they are controlled remotely but also have the ability to make decisions based on the environment. Unlike the robots shown in movies, most robots do not resemble humans; however, some humanoid robots have been developed, including ASIMO, a robot developed by Honda (shown in Figure 2.26). This robot was named after Isaac Asimov, one of the authors who popularized the concept of the humanoid robot.

FIGURE 2.26
ASIMO is a humanoid robot developed by Honda.

LISA POOLE / Associated Press

Lesson 4 # Connecting Devices to a Computer

Most computers consist of a system unit with several other devices connected to it. These devices are called *peripherals*, and most of them connect through a *port* on the back of the system unit. Most peripheral devices now use USB ports. If you set up a new desktop computer or have to move an existing one, you need to know enough about the connectors and the ports to reconnect the peripherals to the system unit. *Port* is a general term for the connectors into which wires are plugged. Determining which plug goes into which port can be easy on some computers and challenging on others. Some computer makers label the ports and use matching colors on the plugs and ports to make it easier, but many computers do not have labels or colors.

Connection Devices

Universal Serial Bus

To reduce the number of different ports on the system unit, the ***Universal Serial Bus (USB)*** port was designed to accept a variety of devices. USB ports may be used to attach the keyboard, mouse, printer, scanner, digital camera, speakers, and other devices such as docking cradles for cameras, digital recorders, and flash memory modules. The ports also provide a small amount of electrical power so that some small peripheral devices do not need their own power supplies. This connection method facilitates assembling and moving a computer because it provides one type of port that works for many different peripherals. The symbol for a USB connection is shown in Figure 2.27.

FIGURE 2.27
USB symbol.

kenjito / shutterstock.com

Most computers come with several USB ports at the back and one or two at the front of the case. There are four common shapes, which are shown in Figure 2.28. Most computers use ports that have a *type A USB* plug. The connection uses a key to ensure that the plug fits in only one orientation. If a wire is used that plugs into another device such as a digital camera, another shape plug and port is used. Large devices, such as printers, have a *type B USB* port in them. Smaller devices, like cameras, use a *mini* or a *micro* plug.

FIGURE 2.28
USB connectors come in several shapes. From left to right: type A, type B, mini, and micro.

trevorb / shutterstock.com. robootb / shutterstock.com. Pawel Bartkowski / istockphoto.com. lexan / shutterstock.com

USB 3.0

The first version of USB that was introduced in the mid-1990s had a relatively slow data transfer rate of about 12 megabits per second. It was replaced in 2000 by *USB 2.0*, which is also called *Hi-Speed USB*. This had a much higher data transfer rate of 480 megabits per second. A newer, faster standard named *USB 3.0* or *SuperSpeed USB* was introduced in 2008 and has a data transfer rate of about 5,000 megabits per second or 5 gigabits per second.

The USB 3.0 standard allows for two-way communication and has more connecting wires that are attached to the ports and plugs. The USB 3.0 ports are designed to also accept the older USB 2.0 type A plug and will operate older devices. Newer peripheral devices such as external hard drives or video cameras that need fast data transfer rates might have USB 3.0 ports that require USB 3.0 plugs, which are not compatible with USB 2.0 ports in older devices. The USB 3.0 plugs are shown in Figure 2.29.

FIGURE 2.29

USB 3.0 plugs.

Tom K Photo / Alamy

Andrew Kitching / Alamy

USB Hub

A connection device called a **USB hub** can be used to provide multiple USB ports. USB hubs may be plugged into each other to increase the number of ports available for connecting devices. Up to 127 devices may be connected to a computer using USB hubs. USB devices are **hot-swappable**, which means you can safely plug them in or remove them without shutting down the host computer. Some USB hubs also provide additional power to supplement the small amount of power provided by the host computer.

Wireless Devices

Some keyboards and mice are wireless, which means they are not directly wired to the system unit. Most wireless mice and keyboards use radio waves to bridge the gap between the keyboard or mouse and a receiver. The receiver is plugged into the computer using a USB plug. Wireless keyboards and mice require batteries that need to be replaced periodically. Some wireless peripherals use infrared light instead of radio waves. The flashing infrared light conveys the data, but the light source must remain pointed at the receiver.

There are two wireless standards: **wireless fidelity (WiFi)** and **Bluetooth**. WiFi is a wireless standard that works on nearly all computers and enables several computers and some peripheral devices such as printers to be networked together without the use of cables. Bluetooth is a newer standard used for very short distances. The most common use for Bluetooth is to connect cell phones and smartphones to special hands-free headsets, as shown in Figure 2.30, or to connect MP3 players and headphones. Bluetooth connections are also used in some wireless keyboards and mice. If a computer does not have Bluetooth built in, a **dongle**, which resembles a USB drive, is required to connect the computer to the wireless device.

FIGURE 2.30
A hands-free headset
uses a Bluetooth
wireless connection.

Szymon Apanowicz / shutterstock.com

FireWire

USB has become the new standard for connecting peripherals, but two competing connection methods are still available. Some computers use a connection system called *FireWire*, which is Apple Computer's version of the Institute of Electrical and Electronics Engineers (IEEE) standard 1394 for a high-performance serial bus. FireWire is very similar to USB, but it has some advantages for use with devices that require very high rates of data transfer or for enabling devices to communicate directly with each other without a host computer. A FireWire connection is often found where people want to work with digital video cameras. FireWire initially had a data transfer rate of 400 megabits per second, which was a significant advantage over USB 1.1, but USB 2.0 has a similar data transfer rate. An 800-megabits-per-second FireWire connection is now common, and a connection is planned that will go up to 3.2 gigabits per second. However, because USB 3.0 has a speed of 5 gigabits per second, few computer manufacturers other than Apple provide FireWire ports.

An older connection method uses a *Small Computer System Interface (SCSI)* bus, pronounced "scuzzy." It has been around since 1986 and may be used to connect to some older scanners or external hard drives. Recent versions have speeds of 1,280 megabits per second. There are several variations of SCSI connectors. A SCSI bus needs a device called a *terminator* at the end of the bus.

The *Device Manager* provides a list of the internal and external devices that are connected to the computer and tells you if any of them are having a problem. You can open the Device Manager through the Windows 7 Control Panel.

To review a list of connected devices

1. **On the left side of the taskbar, click the Start button** ⊛**.** The Start menu displays.

2. **On the right side of the Start menu, click Control Panel.** The Control Panel window opens.

3. **If necessary, change the View by option to Small Icons. Click the Device Manager icon.** The Device Manager window displays. The expand arrow ▷ to the left of an item indicates that there is another level to the list.

4. **To the left of the DVD/CD-ROM drives, click the expand arrow** ▷**.** The Device Manager window displays a list of DVD and/or CD-ROM drives on your computer.

⑤ Click the expand arrow ▷ to the left of the System devices. The Device Manager window displays a list of system devices. Your list will differ somewhat from the one shown in Figure 2.31.

FIGURE 2.31
The Device Manager displays a list of the devices on your system.

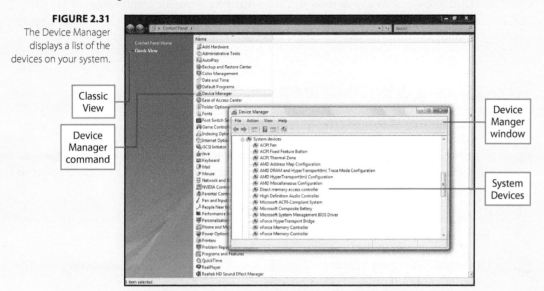

⑥ Use the skills you practiced previously to start the Snipping Tool program and do a Window snip of the Device Manager window. Save a copy of this window to the folder where you store your files. Name the file U1Ch02SystemStudentName **substituting your name as indicated.**

⑦ In the Device Manager window, click the Close button [×] in the upper-right corner. Use the same method to close the Control Panel. The Device Manager window and the Control Panel are closed.

⑧ Submit your snip as directed by your instructor.

Making Connections

It is helpful to remember a few tips when you connect components:

- You probably will not be able to make a mistake that will damage the computer.
- Some plugs have screws on either side to hold the connection firmly in place. Using the screws is optional but will reduce problems caused by loose connections.
- On older computers, the ports for wired keyboards and mice are round with a plastic key. Look at the end of the plug to see where the key is to align it with the hole in the port. If the keyboard and mouse use wired connectors, be sure to check the colors or labels to get them into the correct port.
- USB ports are interchangeable, but if you connect several USB devices that depend on the USB for power, use a USB hub with its own power supply.

Installing Device Drivers

Most peripheral devices—such as printers, flash drives, scanners, and digital cameras—require programs that tell the computer how to control the devices and how to communicate with the devices. These programs are called **drivers** or **device drivers** and are written for a specific combination of operating systems and devices. The disc that comes with the device will have drivers for most of the common operating systems such as Windows 7, Vista, and XP; Mac OS X; and Linux.

To update a device driver

1. **On the left side of the taskbar, click the Start button 🟦.** The Start menu displays.

2. **On the right side of Start menu, right-click Computer, and then from the shortcut menu, click Properties.** The Control Panel System window opens. This is a shortcut to get to the System commands from the Control Panel menu.

3. **Under Control Panel Home, click Device Manager.** Notice that the same list of devices displays as when you opened the Device Manager through the Control Panel.

4. **To the left of Display adapters, click the expand arrow ▷. Right-click the item listed under Display adapters. If there are two, choose either one.**

5. **On the shortcut menu, click Properties. In the displayed dialog box, click the Driver tab and examine the information.** See Figure 2.32. The information on your screen will be different.

FIGURE 2.32
Driver information.

6. **Use the skills you practiced previously to start the Snipping Tool program and do a Window snip of the Properties window. Save a copy of this window to the folder where you store your files. Name the file** U1Ch02DriverStudentName **substituting your name as indicated.**

7. **At the side of the dialog box, click Update Driver.** Notice that a dialog box asks if you have the driver on your computer, or whether you want the program to search the computer and the Internet for the newest driver.

⑧ **In the Update Driver Software dialog box, click Cancel.** Because updating drivers occasionally causes problems, you should wait until you learn how to set and use a Restore Point in Chapter 5.

⑨ **Close ☒ all open dialog boxes and windows.**

⑩ **Submit your snip as directed by your instructor.**

Using an Installation Disc

If you have a new peripheral device, read the installation manual. Some devices, particularly printers and digital cameras, require that you install the software before you connect the device. If that is the case, insert the disc provided with the device and follow the directions that appear on the screen. Some peripheral devices, such as USB drives, do not come with installation discs.

Using Automatic Detection and Installation

If you do not have an installation disc, you may not need it. Some operating systems include drivers for popular peripheral devices. If your operating system is newer than the device, the driver for your device may already be available as part of the operating system. When you connect the device for the first time and turn on the computer, or plug in a device to a USB port when the computer is turned on, the operating system checks its connections. If it finds a device for which it already has a driver, it will install the driver automatically. This feature is called *plug-and-play* in Windows operating systems.

Installing Hardware Without an Installation Disc

If you do not have an installation disc with a driver for your operating system, you can often go to the manufacturer's website and download the driver you need. In some cases, amateur programmers have written drivers for combinations of less common devices and operating systems. You may find these drivers by searching the Internet. Once you have the driver, you may run a program that is part of the operating system to install the driver.

Summary

You learned how to identify common and specialized input and output devices. You also learned how to install peripheral devices using a CD or plug-and-play.

You can extend your learning by reviewing concepts and terms and by practicing variations of skills presented in the lessons.

Key Terms

adaptive computer device *(p. 56)*

Alternate (Alt) key *(p. 44)*

backlight *(p. 40)*

bar code reader *(p. 54)*

BD-R *(p. 48)*

BD-RE *(p. 48)*

BD-ROM *(p. 48)*

biometric device *(p. 56)*

Blu-ray *(p. 48)*

Bluetooth *(p. 61)*

burn *(p. 47)*

cathode ray tube (CRT) *(p. 40)*

CD-R *(p. 47)*

CD-ROM *(p. 47)*

CD-RW *(p. 47)*

click pad *(p. 44)*

Command key *(p. 45)*

compact disc (CD) *(p. 46)*

CompactFlash card *(p. 48)*

Control (Ctrl) key *(p. 44)*

device driver *(p. 64)*

Device Manager *(p. 62)*

digital light processing (DLP) *(p. 57)*

digital single lens reflex (DSLR) *(p. 52)*

digital video interface (DVI) *(p. 40)*

digitizing tablet *(p. 54)*

disc *(p. 46)*

disk *(p. 46)*

docking station *(p. 52)*

dongle *(p. 61)*

dot matrix printer *(p. 49)*

dots per inch (dpi) *(p. 53)*

driver *(p. 64)*

DVD-ROM *(p. 48)*

electrostatic plotter *(p. 57)*

external hard drive *(p. 49)*

FireWire *(p. 62)*

flash drive *(p. 48)*

flash hard drive *(p. 48)*

flash memory *(p. 48)*

flatbed scanner *(p. 53)*

frames per second *(p. 52)*

Function (Fn) key *(p. 45)*

gamepad *(p. 51)*

graphics tablet *(p. 54)*

hard drive *(p. 49)*

Hi-Speed USB *(p. 60)*

hot-swappable *(p. 61)*

impact printer *(p. 49)*

infrared light *(p. 55)*

ink-jet printer *(p. 50)*

internal hard drive *(p. 49)*

joystick *(p. 51)*

land *(p. 46)*

laser printer *(p. 50)*

liquid crystal display (LCD) *(p. 40)*

lumen *(p. 56)*

megapixel *(p. 52)*

microSD card *(p. 48)*

micro USB *(p. 60)*

mini USB *(p. 60)*

monitor *(p. 40)*

mouse *(p. 41)*

Num Lock key *(p. 44)*

optical character recognition (OCR) *(p. 54)*

optical mouse *(p. 41)*

Option key *(p. 45)*

pen plotter *(p. 57)*

peripheral *(p. 59)*

pit *(p. 46)*

pixel *(p. 40)*

plotter *(p. 57)*

plug-and-play *(p. 65)*

point-and-shoot camera *(p. 52)*

port *(p. 59)*

probe *(p. 55)*

projector *(p. 56)*

radio frequency identification (RFID) *(p. 55)*

remote control *(p. 55)*

resolution *(p. 40)*

robot *(p. 58)*

scanner *(p. 53)*

scanning *(p. 53)*

Secure Digital (SD) card *(p. 48)*

sensor *(p. 55)*

Shift key *(p. 44)*

Small Computer System Interface (SCSI) *(p. 62)*

stylus *(p. 55)*

subwoofer *(p. 50)*

SuperSpeed USB *(p. 60)*

system unit *(p. 40)*

terminator *(p. 62)*

thermal printer *(p. 49)*

thumb drive *(p. 48)*

thumb mouse *(p. 42)*

toner *(p. 50)*

touch pad *(p. 44)*

touch screen *(p. 55)*

type A USB *(p. 60)*

type B USB *(p. 60)*

Universal Serial Bus (USB) *(p. 59)*

USB 2.0 *(p. 60)*

USB 3.0 *(p. 60)*

USB drive *(p. 48)*

USB hub *(p. 61)*

video graphics adapter (VGA) *(p. 40)*

voice recognition *(p. 50)*

voice synthesizer *(p. 58)*

Web cam *(p. 52)*

wireless fidelity (WiFi) *(p. 61)*

Checking Concepts and Terms

MULTIPLE CHOICE

Circle the letter of the correct answer for each of the following.

1. Which of the following has the largest storage capacity? [L1]
   a. DVD
   b. CD-RW
   c. CD-ROM
   d. CD-R

2. Which of the following is optical storage media? [L1]
   a. DVD-R
   b. Hard disk
   c. SD card
   d. Removable disk

3. Which of the following is not a common input device? [L1]
   a. Keyboard
   b. Microphone
   c. Voice synthesizer
   d. Mouse

4. Which of the following is a specialized input device? [L2]
   a. RAM
   b. CD-ROM
   c. Scanner
   d. Flash card

5. Which type of scanner can be used to scan books and magazines? [L2]
   a. Impact
   b. Smartphone
   c. Document
   d. Flat bed

6. Which of the following is used in conjunction with a database for pricing and inventory control? [L2]
   a. OCR software
   b. Bar code reader
   c. Adaptive computer device
   d. Dongle

7. Which of the following can print very large diagrams but not photographs? [L3]

a. Pen plotter

b. Impact printer

c. SCSI interface

d. Electrostatic plotter

8. The brightness of projector devices is rated in which of the following units? [L3]

a. Watts

b. Amps

c. Lumens

d. Ohms

9. Computer peripherals such as printers and scanners that do not use a wireless connection need to be plugged into which of the following? [L4]

a. Sensor

b. Device manager

c. Port

d. Subwoofer

10. Which of the following is a program that works with the operating system to manage a device? [L4]

a. Agent

b. Expansion slot

c. Interpreter

d. Driver

MATCHING

Match each term in the second column with its correct definition in the first column by writing the letter of the term on the blank line in front of the correct definition.

_____ **1.** Powdered ink used in a laser printer [L1]

_____ **2.** A projector technology that uses thousands of tiny mirrors [L3]

_____ **3.** The number of pixels displayed per inch on a screen [L1]

_____ **4.** The fluorescent light behind a flat panel monitor [L1]

_____ **5.** A common pointing device that uses reflected light instead of rollers [L1]

_____ **6.** Wireless standard often used for cell phone hands-free headsets and for MP3 player headphones [L4]

_____ **7.** An LCD display [L1]

_____ **8.** A sensor used to explore places that are not conveniently accessible [L2]

_____ **9.** Type of storage device that does not need constant power [L1]

_____ **10.** A feature that enables you to install peripheral devices without having an installation disc [L4]

A. Backlight

B. Bluetooth

C. Digital light processing (DLP)

D. Flash drive

E. Flat panel

F. Optical mouse

G. Plug-and-play

H. Probe

I. Resolution

J. Toner

Skill Drill

Skill Drill exercises reinforce chapter skills. Each skill reinforced is the same, or nearly the same, as a skill presented in the chapter. Detailed instructions are provided in a step-by-step format.

Each exercise is independent of the others, so you can do the exercises in any order.

1. Customizing the Keyboard's Ability to Repeat Characters

One of the many advantages of an electronic keyboard over a mechanical typewriter is that you may repeat the same character many times by holding down a key. The computer is programmed to recognize that when a key is held down for a certain time, you intend to repeat that character. You can adjust these settings through the Windows 7 Control Panel.

To view and adjust the Keyboard properties, follow these steps:

1. Click the **Start** button.

2. On the right side of the **Start** menu, click **Control Panel**.

3. If necessary, change the **View by** option to **Small Icons**. Click the **Keyboard** command. If necessary, at the top of the **Keyboard Properties** dialog box, click the **Speed** tab. The Speed tab displays the options for changing the character repeat rate and cursor blink rate.

4. Click in the **Click here and hold down a key to test repeat rate** text box. The insertion point will blink in the box. Hold down a key on the keyboard and observe the time delay before it starts to repeat and how fast it repeats the character. Release the key after about 10 characters.

5. Drag the **Repeat rate** slider to the right or left to a new location.

6. Click again in the **Click here and hold down a key to test repeat rate** text box. Hold down a key on the keyboard and observe how fast it repeats the character. Release the key after about 10 characters.

7. Drag the **Repeat rate** slider to its previous location.

8. Click the **Start** button, click **All Programs**, click the **Accessories** folder, and then in the list of programs, click **Snipping Tool**.

9. In the **Snipping Tool** dialog box, click the **New Snip** button arrow, and then click **Window Snip**. Point anywhere in the **Keyboard Properties** dialog box and click one time.

10. Near the top of the **Snipping Tool** dialog box, click the **Save Snip** button. In the **Save As** dialog box, navigate to the folder where you store your files. In the **File name** box, type U1Ch02KeyboardStudentName substituting your name as indicated, and then click **Save**.

11. In the upper-right corner of each open dialog box or window, click the **Close** button.

12. Submit your snip as directed by your instructor.

2. Adjusting Mouse Sensitivity

When you move the mouse, a pointer on the screen moves in a corresponding manner. If the pointer does not travel all the way across the screen with one movement of the mouse, you might need to lift the mouse to make a second motion. The ratio of movement of the pointer to the movement of the mouse can be increased so the entire screen can be traversed in one move. Alternatively, if you find it difficult to select small amounts of text or small objects because the pointer moves too much, the ratio of movement can be decreased to give more control of small details. You can adjust this ratio through the Windows 7 Control Panel.

To view and adjust the mouse properties, follow these steps:

1. Click the **Start** button.

2. On the right side of the **Start** menu, click **Control Panel**.

3. If necessary, change the **View by** option to **Small Icons**. Click the **Mouse** command. If necessary, at the top of the **Mouse Properties** dialog box, click the **Pointer Options** tab. This tab displays the option for changing the pointer speed, among other options.

4. Under **Select a pointer speed**, drag the indicator arrow to the far right or left. Move the mouse pointer to experience the difference.

5. Drag the speed indicator to a location that you like best for mouse speed.

6. Click the **Start** button, click **All Programs**, click the **Accessories** folder, and then in the list of programs, click **Snipping Tool**.

7. In the **Snipping Tool** dialog box, click the **New Snip** button arrow, and then click **Window Snip**. Point anywhere in the **Mouse Properties** dialog box and click one time.

8. Near the top of the **Snipping Tool** dialog box, click the **Save Snip** button. In the **Save As** dialog box, navigate to the folder where you store your files. In the **File name** box, type U1Ch02MouseStudentName substituting your name as indicated, and then click **Save**.

9. In the upper-right corner of each open dialog box or window, click the **Close** button.

10. Submit your snip as directed by your instructor.

3. Exploring Attached Computer Devices

You can check the internal and some external devices connected to your computer. You can also check to see if a device is working properly. Many computers have more than one optical drive.

To determine which CD and DVD drives you have connected to your computer, and whether they are working properly, follow these steps:

1. Click the **Start** button.

2. On the right side of the **Start** menu, right-click **Computer**, and then from the shortcut menu, click **Properties**.

3. Under **Control Panel Home**, click **Device Manager**.

4. Click the expand arrow to the left of **DVD/CD-ROM drives**.

5. Choose a drive and double-click it. In the **Device Properties** dialog box under **Device status**, check to see if the device is working properly.

6. Click the **Start** button, click **All Programs**, click the **Accessories** folder, and then in the list of programs, click **Snipping Tool**.

7. In the **Snipping Tool** dialog box, click the **New Snip** button arrow, and then click **Window Snip**. Point anywhere in the **Device Properties** dialog box and click one time.

8. Near the top of the **Snipping Tool** dialog box, click the **Save Snip** button. In the **Save As** dialog box, navigate to the folder where you store your files. In the **File name** box, type U1Ch02DVDStudentName substituting your name as indicated, and then click **Save**.

9. In the upper-right corner of each open dialog box or window, click the **Close** button.

10. Submit your snip as directed by your instructor.

4. Updating a Driver

Drivers may be updated to solve problems. You can find out the date of the drivers used for your devices through the Windows 7 Control Panel.

To determine the date of the driver for your monitor, follow these steps:

1. Click the **Start** button.

2. On the right side of the **Start** menu, right-click **Computer**, and then from the shortcut menu, click **Properties**.

3. In the **Control Panel System** window, under **Control Panel Home**, click **Device Manager**.

4. Click the expand arrow to the left of **Monitors**.

5. Choose a monitor and double-click it. In the **Monitor Properties** dialog box, click the **Driver** tab and notice the date of the driver for your monitor.

6. Click the **Start** button, click **All Programs**, click the **Accessories** folder, and then in the list of programs, click **Snipping Tool**.

7. In the **Snipping Tool** dialog box, click the **New Snip** button arrow, and then click **Window Snip**. Point anywhere in the **Monitor Properties** dialog box and click one time.

8. Near the top of the **Snipping Tool** dialog box, click the **Save Snip** button. In the **Save As** dialog box, navigate to the folder where you store your files. In the **File name** box, type U1Ch02MonitorStudentName substituting your name as indicated, and then click **Save**.

9. In the upper-right corner of each open dialog box or window, click the **Close** button.

10. Submit your snip as directed by your instructor.

Explore and Share

Explore and Share questions are intended for discussion in class or online. Look for information that is related to the learning outcomes for this chapter, as directed. Submit your answers as directed by your instructor.

1. Explore the use of Bluetooth in computer devices. Click the Start button and then click Help and Support. Search for topics dealing with Bluetooth and locate information about setting up a Bluetooth-enabled device. Use the **Snipping Tool** to copy a window that shows how to add a Bluetooth-enabled device, and then save it as U1Ch02BluetoothStudentName Prepare to share what you learned about setting up a Bluetooth-enabled device. Submit your answer and the file as directed by your instructor. [L4]

2. Explore voice (speech) recognition options available with Windows, and then reflect on the possible future of speech recognition. Open the Windows **Control Panel** in **Small Icons** view and double-click **Speech Recognition**. Locate and click the link to **Take Speech Tutorial** and watch the demo. When you are through, consider the following: As computer performance increases, the ability of the computer to recognize and translate speech improves. In what situations would speech recognition be useful to you or a family member? List situations where speech recognition is currently used, and then try to envision what might be done with speech recognition in the next 5 to 10 years. Will speech recognition improve to the point where input devices such as keyboards and mice are no longer needed? Record and share your thoughts as directed. If you are recording your thoughts using a word processor, save the document as U1Ch02SpeechStudentName and then submit as directed. [L2]

3. Explore text to speech options available with Windows, and then reflect on the uses of text narration. Open the Windows **Control Panel**. In the **Search Control Panel** box, type **Narrator**. Under **Ease of Access Center**, locate and click the link to **Hear text read aloud with Narrator**. Click **Start Narrator**. In the Microsoft Narrator dialog box, review the options for narrating keystrokes, messages, and scroll notifications. Close the dialog box and exit Narrator. Click the **Start** button and then click **Help and Support**. In the **Windows Help and Support** dialog box, search for help on **Narrator**. Explore the use of Narrator by reading several of the topics related to its use. When you are through, consider the following: If you could not see the screen, do you think you could learn to use the Narrator feature to work on your computer? How much longer do you think it would take to do your normal tasks if you had to rely on Narrator, even when you became accustomed to it? Record and share your thoughts as directed. If you are recording your thoughts using a word processor, save the document as U1Ch02NarratorStudentName and then submit as directed. [L2]

4. Computer sensors, probes, and robots are often used to perform tasks that are repetitive, difficult, or dangerous for humans to perform. List some of the tasks you can think of that would require the use of these devices. On a computer with an Internet connection, open a browser, search for the term *weather probe* and then add some of the weather-related probe activities to your list. If you are writing your list using a word processor, save the document as U1Ch02ProbeStudentName. Prepare to share your list, and submit your file as directed. [L3]

In Your Life

In Your Life questions are intended for discussion in class or online where you can share your personal experience. Restrict your answers to the topics described in each exercise. Submit your answers as directed by your instructor.

1. Some desktop computer makers provide models that combine the monitor and system unit in the same case. Have you used a combined unit? What advantages and disadvantages do you perceive in this approach? [L1]

2. Do you find the variety of wires and plugs intimidating when you consider moving a computer? Would it be easier to move a desktop computer if more of the devices used wireless connections? What problems can you envision with wireless connections? [L4]

3. If you have used a game controller, describe to the group how many types of inputs there are on the controller and what features distinguish a high-quality controller from basic units. [L2]

4. You probably take pictures or videos, or record and save music. Which type(s) of storage do you use to store your files? Which type(s) of storage do you use to back up these files? Do you envision changing your backup storage in the near future to a newer storage technology than the one you are currently using? [L1]

5. Does your computer have a video card with a second port? Do you have the desk space for a second monitor, and would the extra screen space help with the tasks you perform? [L1]

Related Skills

Related Skills exercises expand on—or are somewhat related to—skills presented in the lessons. The exercises provide a brief narrative introduction, followed by instructions in a numbered-step format that are not as detailed as those in the Skill Drill section.

1. Trying Different Pointer Schemes

The mouse is an important input device. There are several options for configuring it and the pointer it controls on the screen.

To change the pointers that are controlled by the mouse, follow these steps:

1. Click the **Start** button.

2. From the **Start** menu, click **Control Panel**.

3. If necessary, change the **View by** option to **Small Icons**. Double-click **Mouse**.

4. At the top of the **Mouse Properties** dialog box, click the **Pointers** tab. The Pointers tab displays the options for customizing the look of the pointer.

5. Under **Scheme**, click the menu arrow at the right end of the box.

6. Click **Windows Inverted (large) (system scheme)** and then click the **Apply** button. Your pointer changes to a large black pointer. If your system does not have this option, choose one of the others.

7. Click the **Start** button, click **All Programs**, click the **Accessories** folder, and then click the **Snipping Tool** in the list of programs.

8. In the **Snipping Tool** dialog box, click the **New Snip** button arrow, and then click **Window Snip**. Point anywhere in the **Mouse Properties** dialog box and click one time.

9. Near the top of the **Snipping Tool** dialog box, click the **Save Snip** button. In the **Save As** dialog box, navigate to the folder where you store your files. In the **File name** box, type U1Ch02PointerStudentName substituting your name as indicated, and then click **Save**.

10. In the Mouse Properties dialog box under **Scheme**, click the arrow at the right end of the box, and then click **Windows Aero (system scheme)** to return the pointer to the default scheme. Click **Apply**.

11. In the upper-right corner of each open dialog box or window, click the **Close** button.

12. Submit your snip as directed by your instructor.

2. Adding Mouse Trails to the Pointer

If you have a mouse, trackball, or other pointing device attached to your computer, you can customize several of its features such as its sensitivity to motion, speed of double-clicks, scroll rate if it has a scroll wheel, style of screen pointer, or even reverse the right and left mouse buttons.

In this exercise, you will add a feature called *mouse trails* that makes it easier to see the pointer as it moves. A mouse trail is a series of images of the mouse pointer that appear behind the pointer as it moves across the screen, leaving a trail of pointer images that fade away.

To turn on the mouse trails feature, follow these steps:

1. Click the **Start** button.

2. From the **Start** menu, click **Control Panel**.

3. If necessary, change the **View by** option to **Small Icons**, and then click **Mouse**.

4. At the top of the **Mouse Properties** dialog box, click the **Pointer Options** tab. The Pointer Options tab displays the options for customizing pointer properties. Three types of pointer options are available: Motion, Snap To, and Visibility.

5. Under **Visibility**, select the **Display pointer trails** check box. Below the check box, if necessary, drag the slider to the far right to make longer trails.

6. At the bottom of the **Mouse Properties** dialog box, click the **Apply** button. Move the mouse around the screen and observe the pointer trails feature.

7. Click the **Start** button, click **All Programs**, click the **Accessories** folder, and then in the list of programs, click **Snipping Tool**.

8. In the **Snipping Tool** dialog box, click the **New Snip** button arrow, and then click **Window Snip**. Point anywhere in the **Mouse Properties** dialog box and click one time.

9. Near the top of the **Snipping Tool** dialog box, click the **Save Snip** button. In the **Save As** dialog box, navigate to the folder where you store your files. In the **File name** box, type U1Ch02TrailStudentName substituting your name as indicated, and then click **Save**.

10. Under **Visibility**, click the arrow at the right end of the box, and then clear the **Display pointer trails** check box. Click **Apply**.

11. In the upper-right corner of each open dialog box or window, click the **Close** button.

12. Submit your snip as directed by your instructor.

3. Trying Different Screen Resolutions on the Monitor

The resolution of the screen depends upon the capabilities of the monitor and the video card. Most monitors and video cards offer several options.

To increase the resolution by increasing the number of pixels displayed on the monitor, follow these steps:

1. **Close** all windows. In any clear area of the desktop, right-click. From the shortcut menu, click **Screen Resolution** to display the **Screen Resolution** window.

2. If more than one monitor displays, click the monitor icon that is labeled **1**. Note the resolution, which is width times length, given in the number of pixels. Click the **Resolution** arrow. Drag the pointer up or down to choose a different resolution.

   In the next step, you change the resolution of the screen, which may cause it to go dark temporarily or flicker. This is normal; do not be alarmed.

3. At the bottom of the window, click the **Apply** button. Observe the effect of changing the resolution. If a message displays asking if you want to choose this new resolution, click **Revert**.

4. Repeat Steps 2 and 3 to try a few other resolutions and to see which one you like best.

5. Click the **Start** button, click **All Programs**, click the **Accessories** folder, and then in the list of programs, click **Snipping Tool**.

6. In the **Snipping Tool** dialog box, click the **New Snip** button arrow, and then click **Window Snip**. Point anywhere in the **Display Settings** dialog box and click one time.

7. Near the top of the **Snipping Tool** dialog box, click the **Save Snip** button. In the **Save As** dialog box, navigate to the folder where you store your files. In the **File name** box, type U1Ch02DisplayStudentName substituting your name as indicated, and then click **Save**.

8. In the upper-right corner of each open dialog box or window, click the **Close** button.

9. Submit your snip as directed by your instructor.

Discover

Discover exercises give you general directions for exploring and discovering more advanced skills and information. Each exercise is independent of the others, so you may complete the exercises in any order.

1. Using the Control Panel to Learn About Accessibility

There are several ways to modify the inputs and outputs of your computer to make it more accessible to people with special needs. Click the **Start** button, and then display the **Control Panel**. Click **Ease of Access Center**. In the **Control Panel Ease of Access Center** window, under **Explore all settings**, click on each of the seven links and read about the options for using input and output devices in ways that are easier for people with special needs. Write a short paragraph on this topic that answers the following questions: (a) Do you know someone who has special needs who also uses a computer? (b) If so, which accessibility devices or software options do they use? (c) If not, which accessibility options might be useful if you could use only one hand? Close the dialog box and window and submit your answer as directed.

2. Using the Control Panel to Manage Sound

There are several options for playing sounds when certain events occur as well as for muting background sounds when using a microphone. Click the **Start** button, and then display the **Control Panel** in Small Icons view. Click **Sound**. In the **Sound** dialog box, click on each of the tabs and read about the options for playing different sounds for program events and for muting other sounds while using the microphone for communication. Try a few options by selecting and then clicking the **Test** button. Write a short paragraph on this topic that answers the following questions: (a) Is there a sound that you tried that you prefer for a particular event? (b) If so, what is its name? (c) If not, which alternatives did you try and why do you prefer the default sound? Close the dialog box and window and submit your answer as directed.

Evaluating, Purchasing, and Maintaining Computer Equipment

Why Would I Do This?

Buying a computer can be a bewildering task. There are many vendors and a wide variety of options. If you are buying computers for a company, cost may be more important than optional features. The opposite, however, may be true if you are buying a computer for your personal use.

Chapter at a Glance

Lesson	Learning Outcomes	Page Number	Related IC3 Objectives
1	Identify the different types of platforms that are available for personal computers	78	2.2.0
1	Identify the criteria for choosing a platform	80	2.3.1
1	Identify the criteria for deciding between a laptop computer and a desktop computer	81	2.3.1
2	Identify the relationship between processor word size and clock speed	83	2.3.2
2	Identify the role of multi-core processors	83	2.1.1
2	Identify the effects of RAM speed	84	2.3.2
2	Identify the effects of RAM capacity	84	2.3.2
2	Identify the role of RAM expandability	85	2.3.2
2	Identify hard drive factors in computer performance	85	2.3.2
2	Identify factors involved in selecting an LCD monitor	86	2.1.1
2	Identify video card factors in computer performance	86	2.3.1
2	Determine video RAM on a computer	87	2.3.2
2	Identify Internet connection speed variables	88	4.2.2
2	Identify network connection speed variables	89	4.2.2
3	Identify optical storage options	90	2.1.2
3	Identify the different methods of obtaining software	91	3.1.1
3	Identify fan noise level	91	4.3.0
3	Identify how to maximize computer performance/price ratio	92	2.3.1
4	Identify how to protect computers from theft	93	4.2.0
4	Identify how to protect a computer from overheating	94	2.2.0
4	Identify how to protect a computer from humidity and water	94	4.2.0
4	Identify how to protect a computer from magnetic fields	94	4.2.0
4	Identify how to protect a computer from power surges	95	4.2.0
4	Identify how to protect a computer from brownouts and power outages	96	4.2.0
4	Identify how to protect a computer from voltage differences while traveling	96	4.2.0
4	Identify how to protect a computer from static electricity	97	4.2.0
5	Identify maintenance issues that can be avoided by cleaning	97	4.2.0
5	Identify maintenance issues on the hard drive including use of disk management software	99	4.2.0
5	Identify how to remove unwanted files	100	3.1.2, 4.1.3
5	Identify maintenance that should be done by professionals	101	4.0.0
5	Identify the steps used to add or replace expansion or memory cards in the computer	101	2.3.2
5	Identify the steps used to add or replace optical or hard drives in the computer	102	2.1.2
6	Troubleshoot common problems associated with computer hardware	103	4.2.2
6	Identify the steps used to solve computer-related problems	106	4.0.0
6	Identify when and how to seek help	107	4.0.0
7	Identify the differences in hardware warranties	109	4.2.0
7	Identify the use of support agreements such as service contracts	109	4.1.0
7	Estimate the useful life of a computer	110	4.0.0
7	Identify how to dispose of old computer equipment	110	4.0.0

Visual Summary

In this chapter, you learn about the options and criteria used to select a personal computer that meets your needs or the needs of your organization, and how to protect and maintain the computer once it is purchased.

Figure 3.1 shows a picture of an office layout with several different computer systems.

FIGURE 3.1
A typical office setup.

Aleksandar Radovanov / Fotolia.com

List of Student Files

In most cases you will create files by capturing screens. You will add your name to the file names and save them on your computer or portable memory device. Table 3.1 lists the files you start with and the names you give them when you save the files.

TABLE 3.1

ASSIGNMENT:	STUDENT SOURCE FILE:	SAVE AS:
Lessons 1–7	none	U1Ch03VRAMStudentName U1Ch03DefragmentStudentName U1Ch03DVDStudentName
Skill Drill	none	U1Ch03InternetStudentName U1Ch03RecycleStudentName U1Ch03CleanStudentName
Explore and Share	none	none
In Your Life	none	none
Related Skills	none	U1Ch03OfficeStudentName U1Ch03CostStudentName U1Ch03VirusStudentName
Discover	none	none

Lesson 1 ▶ Identifying Criteria for Selecting a Personal Computer

Before you get into the specific details of selecting a personal computer, it is a good idea to identify some general criteria that will provide a framework for later decisions.

Identifying Tasks for Which the Computer Will Be Used

Buying a computer is like buying a truck. You need to consider what type of work needs to be done (see Figure 3.2). For instance, if you want to use a computer to do homework for an interior design class where you work with large images of detailed floor plans, you do not pick a computer with a small display. Instead, you pick one with a large, high-resolution display and the computing power to redraw the plans quickly as you make changes.

Images.com

The tasks for which you plan to use your computer are reflected in the type of software you intend to use. Most software packages give specific requirements for processor speed, memory, storage, and screen resolution on the side of the box or on the company's website. If you know the type of software you are likely to use, buy a computer that meets its requirements.

Graphic programs, video editing, and gaming tend to require computers with lots of resources, whereas word processing, surfing the Internet, and reading e-mail do not.

Identifying Personal Computer Platforms

The software that enables application software to work with specific types of hardware is called the *operating system*. The combination of the operating system and hardware is a ***platform***. Three platforms commonly in use on personal computers are Windows, Mac OS, and Linux.

Using Windows Running on an Intel or AMD Processor

Windows, shown in Figure 3.3, is an operating system that works with a processor from Intel or a compatible processor from another manufacturer such as AMD. The combination of Windows and one of these processors is a common platform that will run over 90% of software applications available for personal computers. When IBM PCs were dominant in the 1980s, they popularized platforms that use Intel processors and operating systems from Microsoft, such as PC-DOS and Windows. This platform was also known as ***IBM compatible***. The platform now is often referred to as *PC* for *personal computer*, even though the other platforms are also used for personal computing.

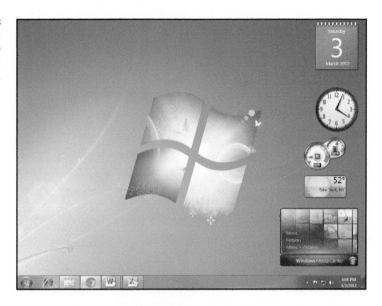

Using Mac OS Running on an Intel Processor

This platform is usually called *Macintosh* or *Mac*. Mac *OS X*, shown in Figure 3.4, is an operating system from Apple Corporation that works with processors made to its specifications. Early processors for Macs were made by Motorola and later by IBM. Apple is now using Intel processors for Apple computers, such as the iMac and the Mac Pro. Because Macintosh computers now use Intel processors, they can run Microsoft Windows as well as the Apple OS. A program named *Boot Camp* gives the user a choice of which OS to start when the computer is first turned on. To use Windows on a Macintosh, a second set of application programs made for Windows must be installed.

FIGURE 3.4
Apple computers now use Intel processors.

Michael Weber / imagebroker / Alamy

Using Linux Running on an Intel or AMD Processor

A third platform that works with the same Intel-compatible processors as Windows and Macs uses the *Linux* operating system (Figure 3.5). The Linux operating system is free, and the code is *open source*—that is, the source code for the core operating system is available to anyone for use or modification.

FIGURE 3.5
Linux operating system
runs on the same hardware
as Windows.

Realimage / Alamy

Other Platforms

IBM and Sun Microsystems are companies that have platforms that are mostly used on mainframe and server computers. IBM's POWER processor is used with UNIX, IBM i, and Linux operating systems, and is also the source of the derivative processors used in popular gaming systems such as Playstation 3, Nintendo Wii, and Xbox 360. Sun Microsystems has a platform that uses Sun's Sparc processor with the Solaris operating system. Some software, as described in the following section, will run on the Sun Microsystems platform as well as other PC platforms. If your company uses a Sun Microsystems platform on its larger computers, it may influence your choice of a platform for company PCs.

Choosing a Platform

To choose a platform, consider five criteria: application software requirements, cross-platform compatibility, backward compatibility, availability of drivers for peripherals, and cost.

Considering the Software Requirements

Application software is written for a particular platform, and it may not work on different platforms. The software you plan to use must be compatible with your computer's platform. For example, Microsoft sells a common suite of application software known as *Microsoft Office*. One version is available for PCs, and a different version is available for Macintosh computers, but there is no version currently available for Linux. An alternative suite of office applications, named ***OpenOffice***, runs on Linux as well as other platforms. OpenOffice uses an interface that resembles older versions of Microsoft Office. It is available for free download from OpenOffice.org and is available in many languages, as shown in Figure 3.6.

FIGURE 3.6
OpenOffice works on
several platforms in many
languages.

Welkom bij
OpenOffice.org

Stuwdamdorp / Alamy

Considering File Management Across Platforms

Some application software is designed to save files in formats that may be used on other platforms. For example, many software programs written for the Mac or Linux platforms create files that may be used on a Windows-based computer.

Considering Backward Compatibility

Operating systems and hardware are regularly updated with new versions. If a platform is designed to run older versions of software, it is **backward compatible**. Older versions are also called **legacy** software. Some platforms are backward compatible with older software but not older hardware. For example, the Windows 7 operating system will run software that is 10 years old, but it may not work with a scanner that is 2 years old. Newer Mac platforms may not run older Mac software applications.

Considering Availability of Drivers for Peripheral Devices

To communicate between the platform and peripheral devices such as printers, scanners, cameras, and smartphones, your computer needs programs called **drivers**. If no driver has been written for a specific platform and peripheral device combination, the device will not work properly. This factor favors the most popular platforms because device manufacturers always write drivers for the popular platforms first.

Considering Cost

The cost of hardware has decreased dramatically, to the point where software can easily cost more than hardware. The cost of operating system software for Windows and Mac platforms has not decreased significantly. However, the Linux operating system is either free or very low cost. Many people expect the Linux platform to become the dominant platform in countries where the cost of a computer and its software is a critical factor in choosing a computer.

In summary, choose an affordable platform that will run the software and peripheral devices you intend to use, and will enable you to exchange files with your coworkers and friends.

Choosing Between a Desktop and a Portable Computer

A personal computer must be moveable without specialized assistance. The degree of portability is another consideration when choosing a computer. Personal computers that consist of a system unit and several peripherals are called *desktop computers* because they tend to be larger, heavier, and used on a desktop. Personal computers that are designed so that all of the components fit into a single unit about the size of a large book are called *notebook*, *laptop*, or *portable computers*. Portable computers have batteries and can run for hours without an external electrical power connection. They are much more portable and take up less desk space than a desktop computer. However, they typically cost more and are more likely to be stolen or damaged during transport than a desktop computer.

A portable computer is a better choice if you plan to use it in several different locations within a short period of time, if you travel a lot on business, or if you have very limited desk space. If lower cost and security are important, a desktop computer is the better choice.

Determining the Relationship Among Task, Software, Platform, and Location Factors

It helps to make a list of the tasks you expect to perform to ensure that the computer you purchase meets your needs. Because software often costs as much as the computer, consider the software you already own or that you could install under your employer's license, and then look at the platform used by that software. Next, consider where you plan to perform the tasks. This information will help you determine how portable the computer must be.

To compare task, platform, and portability factors

1 **Create a table that looks like Table 3.2.** You can draw the table on paper with a straightedge or use a program like Microsoft Office Word or Excel to create the table.

TABLE 3.2

NAME:

CLASS:

CHAPTER 3, LESSON 1

TASK	SOFTWARE	PLATFORM	LOCATION
Word Processing			
Analyze Numeric Information (spreadsheet)			
Present Information to a Group			

2 **Fill in the first column with tasks you want your computer to perform. List at least five additional tasks.** The first three tasks—word processing, analyze numeric information (spreadsheet), and present information to a group—are already entered because these tasks have been identified as key applications that every user should know. Some examples of additional tasks are playing games, writing e-mail, editing digital video, social networking, or surfing the Internet.

3 **Fill in the second column. List the software that is already available to you without additional expense and that can perform the task. Enter *None* if you do not have the software.** You do not have to use this software, but because the cost of buying new software may exceed the cost of the computer, you should make an informed choice.

4 **Determine which platform each software package uses. Write *PC, Mac, Linux,* or *Other* in the Platform column.** You may enter more than one platform for a particular software application.

5 **Determine where you will perform the task. Write *Work, Home, Travel,* or a combination of those three in the Location column.**

6 **If you are using a computer to create the table, save and print the table.**

Lesson 2 ▶ ## Identifying Factors That Affect Computer Performance

Some tasks may be performed more quickly if your computer has expensive, high-performance hardware, whereas other tasks do not require that type of hardware. In some cases, a single, slow component will determine the maximum performance of your computer, and spending more money on other components will be a waste of resources. In order to understand where to spend your money on performance-enhancing hardware, you first need to know which factors affect performance for particular tasks.

Identifying Processor Word Size and Clock Speed

As discussed in Chapter 1, processors work with groups of binary numbers. Each step of a process is initiated by an electric pulse. The amount of work that a processor can do in a given amount of time depends on the size of the group of numbers, how fast the pulses occur, and how efficiently the processor handles the numbers. It is easier to compare numbers that rate the size of the group of binary numbers, or the rate at which the pulses arrive, than it is to rate the efficiency of a processor in accomplishing a goal.

Identifying Word Size

Recall that a processor works with binary numbers that consist of zeros and ones. Each digit of the number is called a *bit*. The unit of data that a processor can work with is called a *word*. Early processors worked with 8 bits at a time, which means they had an 8-bit word length. This size word is also called a *byte*, which is a common measurement unit for data. One of the biggest differences between early personal computers and mainframe computers is the word size. Most personal computers now have processors that use 32-bit or even 64-bit words. Although these processors have the potential to perform some tasks faster, the software must be written to take advantage of that potential. This currently limits the effectiveness of 64-bit processors to special applications. The main advantage of 64-bit versions of programs is memory management. The larger word size allows for more memory addresses. The 32-bit version of Windows can directly access up to 4 gigabytes of RAM, but the 64-bit version can directly access up to 128 gigabytes of RAM.

Extend Your Knowledge

IMPLICATIONS OF USING BIG WORDS

When personal computers were able to work with only 8-bit words, they were very limited in the number of characters they could use in an alphabet. Now, most personal computers have processors that use 32-bit words, which can represent over 4 billion different characters. This is enough capacity to assign a unique number to all the characters in every known language. To learn more about representing the world's written languages on computers, go to the Unicode website at http://unicode.org/standard/WhatIsUnicode.html. Use capital letters as shown.

Identifying Clock Speed

As discussed in Chapter 1, the term *clock* refers to a circuit on a computer chip that emits pulses. The processor performs an action with each pulse. Recall that clock pulses are measured in *hertz*, with 1 hertz equaling 1 pulse per second. The first IBM personal computer used a clock speed of 4.77 megahertz, or just under 5 million pulses per second. Current processors have clock speeds that are measured in gigahertz (GHz, billions of pulses per second), and more recent computers have clock speeds over 3 GHz (3 billion cycles per second). Because of efficiency differences, direct comparison between clock speeds is not exactly accurate, but clock speed remains a good measure of the general speed of the processor.

Identifying the Impact of Multi-Core Computers

A recent improvement to the performance of personal computers is the result of multi-core computing. To create a ***multi-core processor***, two or more microprocessors are built on a single integrated circuit chip—as shown in Figure 3.7. The work is divided among the processors and each one does part of the work, increasing the performance of the computer. Multi-core processors have been used on high-end workstations and servers since the mid-1990s, and multi-core processors are now available on personal computers. This makes it a bit more difficult to generalize about speed based on clock speed, because the tasks might be shared among several cores. If the task can be divided into smaller tasks that can be done at the same time on different cores, a multi-core processor could get the whole task done quicker than another single-core processor running at a higher speed.

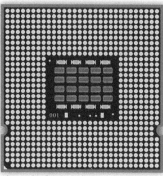

FIGURE 3.7
Multi-core chips divide the workload among several processors.

Alexander Strela / Alamy

Identifying Effects of RAM Speed and Capacity

The speed and capacity of a computer's random access memory interact directly with the computer's processor. This is a critical factor that affects the computer's speed if there is not enough memory to perform all the tasks required of the computer.

Identifying Effects of RAM Speed

The processor speed and number of cores are only two of the factors that determine a computer's performance, because its effective speed can be limited by the other components. The processor loads data from RAM, processes the data, and then stores the output in RAM. RAM is measured by its response time in nanoseconds (ns) and the quantity of data it can store in gigabytes. The higher the clock speed on the processor, the lower the response time of the RAM. RAM that is too slow to keep up with the processor may malfunction and cause errors. As mentioned in Chapter 1, DDR SDRAM is very fast, and it is sufficient to keep up with all but the fastest multi-core processors.

Identifying Effects of RAM Capacity

RAM is used to store instructions from the operating system, software applications, and all of the text, pictures, video, and data of files that are open. If you want to use several applications at the same time, or use very large files, you need enough RAM to make them readily available to the processor.

If you run out of RAM, the operating system will start using the hard drive. For example, if you are running five programs at the same time and you do not have enough RAM, the operating system will designate part of the hard drive as ***virtual memory***. If you are not currently using a program and its files, they are placed on the hard drive. When you want to switch to that program, it will take much longer to retrieve it from the hard drive than if it were available in RAM. If you find that your computer is slow to switch between programs and the indicator light on the hard drive is flashing while the computer switches programs, it is likely that you need more RAM to speed up this process.

Identifying RAM Expandability Factors

Most computers come with available slots where additional RAM can be added. When you view the specification for a computer's RAM memory, look for terms such as "2 gigabytes expandable to 4 gigabytes." RAM comes on cards that fit into slots located on the motherboard, as shown in Figure 3.8. Some cards contain more RAM than others, and many computers require that the cards all have the same amount of RAM. If all of the slots are filled with low-capacity RAM cards, it would be necessary to replace every card in order to increase the computer's amount of RAM. This would cost more than simply buying extra RAM and inserting it into an empty slot. Be sure to find out if "expandable" means that the computer has empty slots for additional RAM.

FIGURE 3.8
RAM is used to store data that is being actively processed by the computer.

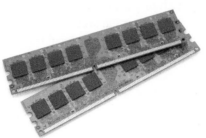

Norman Chan / Shutterstock.com

Identifying Hard Drive Factors

Inside the system unit is the *hard drive*. The hard drive is a complete unit with devices—known as *heads*—that read and write data in magnetic form on a stack of thin, rigid metal disks called *hard disks* (shown in Figure 3.9), hence the name *hard drive*. The disks are sealed in a metal box, so you do not see the hard disks themselves when you look inside the system unit. The rate at which the disks spin, and the speed with which the heads can move back and forth, determine how fast the data can be written to the disk and how fast it can be retrieved. The speed of rotation is measured in *revolutions per minute (rpm)*. Faster rotation rates indicate faster performance. Many hard drives hold more than 1 terabyte of data, which is approximately 1 million megabytes, and many higher-end computers come with several terabytes or more of hard disk storage.

FIGURE 3.9
Hard disk drives use a stack of individual disks with small coils that detect and create magnetized spots on the disks.

Tyler Boyes / shutterstock.com

Many desktop computers have the capability of housing multiple hard drives. Instead of buying a 2-terabyte drive, for example, you might install two 1-terabyte drives. This gives you backup capabilities in case the main hard drive (the one with the operating system installed) crashes.

Identifying Monitor and Video Card Factors

The screen on the monitor is divided into tiny picture elements called pixels that emit light to form an image. The picture elements are tiny rectangles with sharp corners. When the screen displays curved objects, the rectangular pixels at the edge give the object a ragged appearance. If the screen is divided into smaller, more numerous pixels, the corners of the pixels are smaller and less apparent. These images have higher resolution, which means that curved lines are smoother and toolbar buttons, which are a fixed number of pixels in size, appear smaller. For example, a 32 × 32 pixel toolbar icon will appear much smaller on a high-resolution monitor than on a low-resolution monitor. High-resolution monitors might display 1920 × 1080 pixels, whereas lower-resolution monitors might display 800 × 600 pixels.

The early standard for video connection between computers and monitors—*a video graphics array (VGA) port*—used an analog signal for each of the primary colors. Some video cards include an older type of port—*S-Video port*—that uses two analog signals and is limited in resolution. Monitors now have processors built into them that can translate the digital signal from the computer into images without creating and then decoding an analog signal. Most video cards now provide a *digital video interface (DVI)* port. The DVI port can be used to transfer the digital signal directly from the PC to the monitor. All three types of connections are shown in Figure 3.10.

FIGURE 3.10
A video card can contain VGA, DVI, and S-Video ports.

Sebalos / shutterstock.com

The standard DVI port also includes the analog VGA signals to assure backward compatibility. Adapters, like the ones shown in Figure 3.11, can be used with the DVI port to connect to a VGA plug. Many multimedia devices like DVD players use a *high definition multimedia interface (HDMI)* port to transfer digital image data. An adapter can connect the digital data pins of a DVI port to create an HDMI port.

FIGURE 3.11
An adapter can be used to convert a DVI port into a VGA port.

vetkit / fotolia.com

Identifying Response Time, Contrast Ratio, and Brightness

The *response time*—sometimes referred to as the *response rate*—of an LCD monitor is the amount of time it takes to change the color of a pixel. Faster response times result in smoother moving images, which is particularly important if you are going to use your computer for playing games or watching videos. The ***contrast ratio*** is the range between the darkest black on the screen and the brightest white. A higher contrast ratio is usually best, although tests have shown that advertised contrast ratios can be quite inaccurate. Brightness is a measure of luminous intensity—the higher the number, the brighter the screen. Contrast ratio and brightness are particularly important when you are considering a laptop computer that might be used in bright light conditions.

Identifying Video Card Factors

Another factor that affects the performance of a monitor is the amount of memory dedicated specifically to the display. ***Video RAM (VRAM)*** is dedicated video memory. It can be integrated on the motherboard with the CPU or it can be housed on its own card in a separate slot on the motherboard. Most high-end computers have at least 256 MB of dedicated VRAM. If you are going to play games or watch videos on your computer, purchasing a new graphic card that has more VRAM than your current card would be a good idea. On some low-end computers, the video card shares RAM with the computer, resulting in slower video and game performance. Figure 3.12 shows a computer that has a small amount of built-in system video memory, some shared RAM from the system, and no dedicated video memory, even though the computer advertisement did not mention that the majority of video memory was shared.

FIGURE 3.12
Some computers use a combination of dedicated video memory and system RAM.

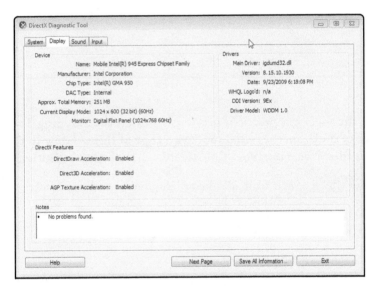

To determine video card RAM

1. **Close all programs and display the desktop. Click the Start button .**

2. **At the bottom of the Start menu, click All Programs.** A list of folders and programs displays.

3. **In the list of folders, click Accessories, and then in the Accessories menu, click Run.** The Run dialog box displays. This dialog box allows the user to run special diagnostic programs.

④ **In the Run dialog box, type** dxdiag **and then click OK. Click Yes to grant permission to use the Internet to gather information, if necessary. In the DirectX Diagnostic Tool dialog box, click the Display tab.** Your computer may have more than one display device. If so, choose Display 1. The dialog box will display the name of the video card. To the right of *Approx. Total Memory* it will display the amount of video RAM used by the card. See Figure 3.13. This procedure is something you can do when shopping for a computer to see what type (or types) of video memory is available on the computers you are evaluating.

FIGURE 3.13
The amount of video
RAM available.

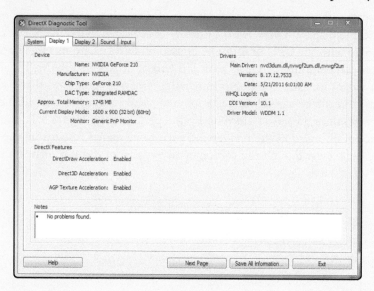

⑤ **Use the skills you practiced previously to start the Snipping Tool and create a Window snip of the Properties window. Save a copy of this window to the folder where you store your files. Name the file** U1Ch03CleanStudentName **substituting your name as indicated.**

⑥ **Close** [X] **or exit from all open dialog boxes and windows.**

⑦ **Submit your snip as directed by your instructor.**

Identifying Connection Speed Factors

Processors are often capable of working with data at a faster rate than can be transmitted between computers. As a result, the connection speed is often the limiting factor when a computer is used to surf the Web or exchange data with another user. When you are evaluating a computer for purchase, a faster computer might not increase the speed at which you use the Internet if your connection speed is the limiting factor.

Identifying the Internet Connection Speed

If you are using a normal telephone voice line to connect to the Internet from home, it will be the slowest part of the system. Faster connections that are always active—called *broadband*—are about 30 times faster. These connections are available from telephone, satellite, and cable television. A faster connection that uses the same wires as the telephone company is called an *asynchronous digital subscriber line (ADSL)*, commonly called a DSL line. Its range, however, is limited to within a few miles of the company's switching station. Your phone company or cable television provider can tell you if broadband service is available in your area. Several cell phone service providers offer a data service that can be used as an Internet connection. Another broadband option is direct satellite connection that uses a dish antenna to send and receive signals from a satellite in orbit above the earth. This type of connection is available throughout North America but is expensive and generally slower than cable television or DSL lines. Some cities and counties also provide wireless connections for anyone in a covered area.

Identifying the Network Connection Speed

If your computer will be connected to a network of other computers, then you will also need to consider the network speed. Networks typically transmit data at high speeds. Common network interface devices operate at 100 megabits per second (Mbps). Company networks may use devices that can transfer data at up to several gigabits per second (Gbps), or even higher speeds if there are numerous computers using the network or if the computers transfer large amounts of data. Higher speed connections require more specialized and expensive connection devices. Computers might be connected by wire or wireless radio. To connect using a wire, the computer needs an *Ethernet* port, which connects to a plug that is a larger version of the type of plug used to connect to a telephone line. A wireless connection might be built in or it can be added using a device that plugs into a USB port.

To match hardware and software

1 **Create a table that looks like Table 3.3.** You may draw the table on paper with a straightedge or use programs like Microsoft Office Word or Excel to create the table.

TABLE 3.3

NAME:

CLASS:

CHAPTER 3, LESSON 2

TASK	PROCESSOR WORD SIZE AND CLOCK SPEED	RAM	HARD DRIVE	VIDEO CARD AND MONITOR	INTERNET CONNECTION
Word Processing					
Analyze Numeric Information (spreadsheet)					
Present Information to a Group					
Picture Editing					
Video Editing					
Gaming					

2 **Fill in the first column with the tasks you identified in Lesson 1.**

3 **Rate the importance of spending extra money on high-performance hardware to accomplish each task. Fill in each box of the table with one of the following letters: H for High, M for Medium, or L for Low. Assume your resources are limited. Use a mix of all three ratings.** If your resources are limited, this table will provide an indication of which hardware enhancements would affect the most tasks.

Identifying Other Factors to Consider When Purchasing a Computer

Once you have identified the tasks you want to perform and which ones would benefit from spending more money on high-performance hardware, there are additional factors that need to be considered.

Identifying Optical Data Storage Options

A personal computer usually comes with a hard disk drive. If you want extra storage space, you can pay more and get a disk drive with higher capacity or get two hard drives. If you plan to use the extra space on a larger capacity drive to store documents, pictures, music, or videos, you run the risk of losing the stored information if the hard drive fails. Rather than put all of your data on one device, you should store copies of the data on a different device or make portable backup copies.

Optical discs provide inexpensive storage for large amounts of data that can be kept in a separate, more secure location. Optical disc drives are less than an inch thick and about 5" wide, as shown in Figure 3.14. The technology used to store data on optical discs uses a laser light and lenses that focus the laser on narrow tracks of data that reflect the light to a detector.

FIGURE 3.14
A DVD drive enables you to write data to DVD or CD discs.

Sinisa Botas / shutterstock.com

In general, newer drives that use smaller wavelength laser beams can read older format ROM discs because the smaller waves can fit in the older, wider tracks, so a DVD drive can read a CD-ROM and a Blu-Ray drive can read a DVD-ROM and a CD-ROM. To record discs, the drive must be designed to vary the strength of the laser light and you must buy the matching discs. For example, if you want to record data or music on a DVD, you need to have a drive labeled DVD-R/RW and purchase DVD discs that are also labeled DVD-R or DVD-RW.

Identifying Needed Software and Sources for Software

In Lesson 1, you identified the tasks you want to perform and the software that you already have. This lesson also identified the software you need to obtain. Software is usually licensed rather than sold, and it may not be copied without permission. You have several options for obtaining software legally. You need to consider the cost of software while evaluating a computer purchase.

Using Site-Licensed Software

Some organizations like schools or companies pay an annual fee that permits them to install multiple copies of a software program on a group of computers. If your organization has such an arrangement, you can get a legal copy of the program for no additional fee or for a very small fee. These licenses often have time limitations, and the software is disabled after the time period has expired.

Using Prepackaged Software

Some computers are provided with software already installed. This is typically included in the price of the computer. It is common for personal computers to come with operating system software installed. Many PCs come with a copy of Microsoft Starter, which consists of limited functionality versions of Microsoft Word and Microsoft Excel. They are intended for home use by people who do not need the full-function versions of Word or Excel. The file formats used in the starter versions are compatible with corresponding applications in Office.

Using Freeware, Shareware, and Trial Versions

Some software, called *freeware*, is available for use without charge. Another option enables you to use the software and pay a fee voluntarily if you like it and plan to continue using it. This type of software is *shareware*. Many companies allow you to use *trial versions* of their software for a limited period of time, after which the program stops working. Some surprisingly high-quality software products are available as freeware or shareware, such as OpenOffice, which is a suite of applications similar to Microsoft Office, or Microsoft Security Essentials antivirus software.

Using Student Discounts

If you are a student, you can obtain software at a significant discount from many software companies. Your campus bookstore may sell these discount-priced packages or you can buy them online.

Using Retail Software

If you cannot find software to handle the task using one of the lower-cost methods, you can purchase the software from a retail store or online. If you buy the software online, in some cases the software may be downloaded directly to your computer if you have a broadband connection. Otherwise, you can order the program on CD to be delivered by traditional means.

Identifying Fan Noise Level

One of the factors that is seldom considered before a purchase is how much noise the system unit makes. Most of the noise is produced by the cooling fans that blow air over the *heat sink* (radiator) fins attached to the processor (see Figure 3.15). If the fins are large, a slower fan speed will do the job. This produces less noise. If you plan to place the system unit on the desk next to your telephone, it may be too noisy to allow you to use your speakerphone option. If you plan to place numerous

FIGURE 3.15
An internal fan is used to
cool the processor.

Your lucky photo / Fotolia.com

computers in the same room, such as a computer lab, the noise may interfere with quiet conversations. Unfortunately, few manufacturers list the noise level of the system unit in their product specification. If reduced noise level is an important criterion, you may need to do more research to find a quieter PC, but the search may be worth it. Many higher-end personal computers have multiple fans, and some are water-cooled, using much the same principle as the radiator in an automobile. Water-cooled computers typically use no fans and are much quieter, but they can be very expensive.

Maximizing the Performance/Price Ratio

Computers continue to double in performance every year or two while simultaneously falling in price. Choosing a computer that provides the best performance for your money is different than for most other purchases. Because new computers double in performance for the same money every year or two, it does not make sense to pay for extra performance now if you don't need it. If your needs change, you will probably be able to buy a new computer 3 years from now that costs less than the extra money you were thinking of spending to anticipate those needs! If your tasks do not demand the fastest computers available, do not spend the extra money for them. You can always add RAM or more hard drive storage; you can even update the video card or processor at a later date if your needs change. The top-of-the-line computers always command a premium price.

Complying with Organizational Standards for Hardware, Software, and Procedures

If you are specifying a personal computer that will be paid for by your organization, you may find that the organization has already developed a list of approved computer models and standard software packages. If that is the case, your job is to identify the tasks you need to accomplish with the computer and determine the model for which you qualify. If you need a computer that is more powerful than your job classification normally qualifies for, you may use the tables you have created to justify an exception in your case. You also need to determine your organization's policies and rules regarding software installation, backup procedures, and communicating with other people in the company or using the Internet.

Lesson 4

Protecting Your Computer from Theft or Physical Damage

If someone stole your computer or it was damaged by fire or a natural disaster, what effect would it have on you? The cost of replacing the computer might be much less than the value of the time it would take to re-create the files on the computer. To secure your computer and its files from theft or disaster, you need to consider the physical security of the system unit and the files in it.

Protecting Computers from Theft

To help deter theft, especially in a lab environment, special antitheft devices such as cables with locks can secure the computer to its physical location (see Figure 3.16). Companies or educational institutions may have a policy that requires locked doors and limited access to rooms containing computer equipment. If a computer is stolen and then recovered by the police, you must be able to identify it as your property. One way to do this is to have a unique identifying tag affixed to the computer or a number inscribed into the metal of the case. Another option is to record the serial number of the system unit in another location.

Portable computers make a convenient target for theft. Vigilance is required when traveling to prevent simple theft, particularly at airports. You can also install tracking software from a security service on your computer. When the computer is used on the Internet, it will send the IP address of the user's Web service to the tracking company's website, which may then be used to identify whoever is using the stolen computer, or at least to pinpoint the computer's location.

FIGURE 3.16
Security often compromises convenience.

O.Bellini / shutterstock.com

Identifying Factors that Damage Computer Hardware or Media

You need to consider the environment and other conditions in which your computer and its peripherals operate and protect them from extremes of heat and humidity and from other possible sources of damage. Some of these factors are unique to certain climates, whereas others are universal.

Protecting a Computer from Overheating

Computers use integrated circuits that are extremely small and densely packed into tiny packages. These circuits use electricity to function, and the electricity turns into heat as the processor and other circuits perform their tasks. Higher clock speeds cause the processors and other circuits to consume more power and generate more heat. If the components get too hot, they will malfunction or fail.

As mentioned earlier, to cool the components, the system unit is equipped with fans to move outside air through the case and over the components. Critical components have heat sinks and dedicated fans attached. Large computers in corporations have special rooms with dedicated air conditioning units that circulate cool air underneath raised floors and up through the computer cases. To protect your computer from overheating, be sure that air can circulate through the system unit. Check to make sure that airflow to system unit fans is not blocked. A common mistake is to place a computer in an enclosed space where the heat is trapped. This often happens with home computers that are stored in desk cabinets or armoires and with network servers that are placed in closets that have no air vents.

Protecting a Computer and Its Peripherals from Humidity

If you bring a computer from a cool environment into a hot, humid environment, water may condense on the inside of the computer just as it does on the outside of a glass of ice water. It is advisable to allow the computer to warm up to an ambient temperature before you turn it on, to allow the condensation to evaporate. Computer peripherals, such as printers that work with paper, are very sensitive to humidity. Paper changes size when it absorbs water from the air or when it dries out, and sheets may stick together when the humidity is high. A printer that operates in a humid room may experience frequent paper jams.

Protecting Storage Media from Magnetic Fields

Magnetic fields can influence the flow of electricity. This is the reason why most system units are made of metal—even portable computers where the weight of metal is a liability. Magnetic fields can affect the beam of electrons in a CRT monitor and distort the picture. The component that is most sensitive to the influence of magnetic fields is a magnetic disk, such as the old floppy disks or a computer hard drive. Magnetic fields can come from permanent magnets, like those in refrigerator magnets and the cones of speakers, or from electric currents like those in powerful motors or sparks. If the magnetic field from any of these sources passes through a magnetic disk, the data on the disk may be erased.

Protecting a Computer from Physical Damage

Another source of damage, particularly to portable computers, is damage sustained during travel. Portable computers should always be carried in protective cases, which will minimize the chance of damage from vibration during transport, or from rough handling or dropping.

Protecting Computer Components from Electrical Damage

Computer components operate on low-voltage direct current, which they get by converting higher-voltage alternating current provided by local utilities. When the utilities built their power systems, they did not design them to provide power to sensitive computers. It is up to the computer's owner to buy additional equipment to protect the computer from damage. It is also important to understand that the power supplied by utilities may differ in voltage and frequency from one country to another.

Protecting from Surges

Computer systems need a constant supply of power to function well. Most computer systems have several devices that require power from a wall outlet. Because most outlets have only two receptacles, an extension cord with a box of additional receptacles—called a **power strip**—is often used. Many of these power strips have a small red button on the side that indicates the presence of a **circuit breaker**. The circuit breaker cuts off power to the computer in case of a short circuit in the equipment, helping to eliminate a potential fire hazard.

Computers need protection that is more sophisticated. The electronic parts of a computer are so small and close together that a sudden surge of voltage in the building can damage the circuits. Lightning can also induce very short but high-voltage pulses that travel along the power lines for miles and can damage a computer. These surges and pulses are not stopped by a simple **plug strip** with a circuit breaker.

Many plug strips include devices that limit the relatively slow surges of power that may be visible to the eye when lights dim and also block the lightning-induced spikes of transient voltage. These types of plug strips are called surge protectors. Many surge protectors, like the one shown in Figure 3.17, offer guarantees against lightning damage. If you use a dial-up modem, be sure to get a surge protector that also has receptacles for the telephone plugs to block lightning-induced pulses from entering the computer via the telephone lines.

FIGURE 3.17
Surge suppressors block sudden changes in voltage and often function as plug strips.

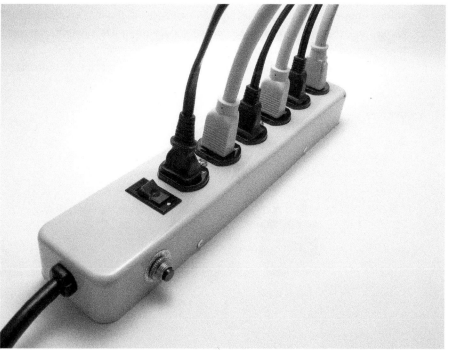

Anthony Berenyi / shutterstock.com

Protecting Against Power Brownouts and Power Outages

A lightning strike can cause the safety equipment in the power lines to shut off power for a moment, or electric motors starting up on the same circuit can cause the voltage to drop below the minimum required by the computer. In either case, there may be too little power to run the computer, causing it to freeze up or lose information stored in RAM. Units with batteries provide temporary power during brief power shortages or give you enough time to save your work and shut down your computer if the power goes out for longer periods. This type of unit (shown in Figure 3.18) is an ***uninterruptible power supply (UPS)***. A good UPS includes the functions of a plug strip with surge suppression—providing one set of outlets for noncritical devices and another set of receptacles with continuous power for critical devices such as the monitor and the system unit.

FIGURE 3.18
An uninterruptible power supply (UPS) continues to provide power when the utility power goes out.

vetkit / fotolia.com

Protecting from Voltage Differences While Traveling

Utilities in Europe provide electricity at 220 volts that alternates the direction of flow 50 times per second. North American utilities provide electricity at 110 volts that alternates the direction of flow 60 times per second. Fortunately, computers and most of their peripherals do not use alternating current; their power supplies convert it into direct current that flows continuously in one direction. The difference in voltage may be overcome by using a ***transformer*** that can convert one voltage into another. In desktop computers, the transformer in the power supply often has a switch that sets it to work with either voltage type, or a power cord with the correct plug for each type of system is provided. For portable computers, you need an adapter kit that includes a transformer and plug adapters, as shown in Figure 3.19.

FIGURE 3.19
Conversion kits adapt to different voltages and plug shapes.

pixinity / shutterstock.com

Protecting Components from Static Electricity

Static electricity is characterized by very small currents at very high voltages. If you have ever jumped a spark from your finger to a doorknob, voltage in that spark was about 20,000 volts per inch of spark. For a quarter-inch spark, that is about 5,000 volts! When you have the case of the system unit open, the voltage from the wall socket is confined inside the metal box of the power supply. The rest of the components use direct current at voltages from 1 to 6 volts.

A 5,000-volt spark from your finger is more than enough to destroy the tiny circuits in an integrated circuit. You do not even have to jump a spark to cause damage. The presence of a static charge on your fingers can induce a similar charge in nearby components and cause damage. To protect the sensitive components in your system unit, your hands and body must be the same charge as the system unit case. This is accomplished by touching the case before you reach into the system unit. Repair technicians often attach a wire that connects a cuff around their wrist to the system case to make sure they do not cause damage.

Lesson 5 ▶ Identifying Maintenance Issues

To get the most out of your computer and to minimize interruptions due to equipment failures, you need to perform routine maintenance and occasionally replace parts. You should be aware of the types of problems that are caused by lack of routine maintenance and what you can do to prevent them. If parts must be replaced, you need to know which parts can be replaced by a knowledgeable user and which parts require a professional's expertise to replace.

Identifying Common Problems That May Be Avoided by Regular Cleaning

Accumulation of dust, lint, and animal hair can cause problems that are not always easy to recognize or solve. These problems can be prevented by cleaning regularly.

Overheating Due to Dust Accumulation

Accumulation of lint or dust on the fan intakes or cooling fins of the processor, as shown in Figure 3.20, can cause overheating. If your processor is overheating, it may signal the problem before permanent damage occurs by sending out beeps through the system unit speaker. A symptom of overheating is that problems occur after the system has been running for a while and then disappear after the computer is allowed to cool down.

Dust may be blown out of the fans and cooling fins with compressed air or another pressurized gas. If the gas is a liquid in the can that turns into a gas under pressure when you spray it, the gas might be very cold. Read the label on any compressed air product to be aware of the dangers of use and disposal.

FIGURE 3.20
Accumulated dirt can cause a processor to overheat.

Dmitriy Goncharenko / fotolia.com

Sticky Keyboard

The keycaps on the keyboard are attached to rods that move up and down. If a small object has fallen between the keys or if a key is sticking in one position, you can usually pry the keycap from the rod and remove the object or clean any sticky material from the rod. Keyboards are not very expensive compared to other components, so it may be easier to replace the keyboard. If you dispose of an old computer whose keyboard still works well, keep the keyboard as a spare.

Malfunctioning Mouse or Trackball

The ball in a mouse, like the one shown in Figure 3.21, or trackball may pick up lint, string, or hair that is transferred to the XY rollers. The accumulated lint wraps around the rollers and interferes with the operation of the mouse or trackball. If your mouse or trackball is erratic while controlling the pointer on the screen, you can usually fix it yourself by removing the retaining ring that holds the ball and then removing the lint that is wrapped around the XY rollers.

FIGURE 3.21
A nonresponsive mouse pointer may result from dirty XY rollers.

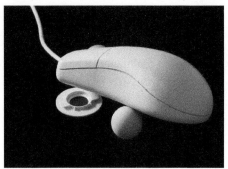

Manoj Valappil / shutterstock.com

A wireless mouse or trackball might become erratic if the battery is low on power, or it might stop working. Replace the battery with one that is fully charged. An optical mouse senses motion when a beam of light reflects from the surface below it. If the surface has no pattern or texture or is transparent, such as a glass table top, the mouse might not sense movement well. Avoid such surfaces when using an optical mouse.

Printing Problems Due to Clogged Ink Jets or Dirty Rollers

If you have an inkjet printer that produces blank rows on printouts, it may be due to a clogged nozzle. Read the printer's manual and follow its directions to initiate a cleaning cycle that clears the nozzles. If the paper does not advance properly or jams often, the rubber rollers that pull or push the paper may be dirty or worn smooth. Read the printer's manual and follow its directions for cleaning the rollers. If they are worn smooth, you probably need a new printer.

Identifying Common Filing Problems on the Hard Drive

The hard drive stores files that you choose to place on it, as well as files that are stored there as part of the function of software programs. To get the best performance from your hard drive, there are some maintenance procedures you can perform.

Avoiding a Full Drive

When the disk drive is empty, the first files are placed on the disk near the outside edge, with little wasted space between them. Like a child's merry-go-round, the outer edge of the disk moves faster than areas near the center, so data may be read and written fastest from the outer edge of the disk. As the disk fills up, files are written nearer the center where it takes approximately twice as long to read or write the data. This results in slower start-up of software programs and slower access to data files.

To minimize this problem, you should move unused files to secondary storage discs and delete software (for which you still have the installation discs) that is not used.

Optimizing Placement of Commonly Used Programs

If a program that you use often was installed after the disk was mostly full, its files may be near the center of the disk where it is slow to load.

To minimize this problem, you can run an optimizing program that tracks how often you use each program. After it creates a history of use, it can move the programs you use most often to locations near the edge of the hard disk and other programs closer to the center.

Reducing Fragmentation

As time goes on, some of the original files are deleted and newer files are written to the same locations. The new files are rarely the same length. If the new files are slightly shorter, empty gaps start to appear. If the new files are longer, they are broken up and placed in whatever space is available. When files are broken up and stored in different places on the disk, they are *fragmented*. When the processor tries to upload the file into RAM, it takes longer for the heads of the drive to move back and forth to find the fragments.

To reduce the number of fragmented files, as well as the time it takes to load those files, you can run a *defragmenting* program on the hard drive. The hard drive must have some empty space—usually about 10% of the total drive space—to use as temporary storage while it moves the files around. This process can take hours. Programs that defragment the hard drive are often combined with programs to optimize its use so that both functions are performed at the same time.

To defragment your hard drive

1. **Close all programs and display the desktop. Click the Start button** ⊕ .

2. **At the bottom of the Start menu, click All Programs.** A list of folders and programs displays.

3. **In the list of folders, click Accessories, and then in the Accessories menu, click the System Tools folder.** A list of system tools displays below the System Tools folder.

4. **In the System Tools folder, Click Disk Defragmenter. Compare your screen with Figure 3.22.** Your screen will show different dates and degree of fragmentation.

FIGURE 3.22
The Disk Defragmenter.

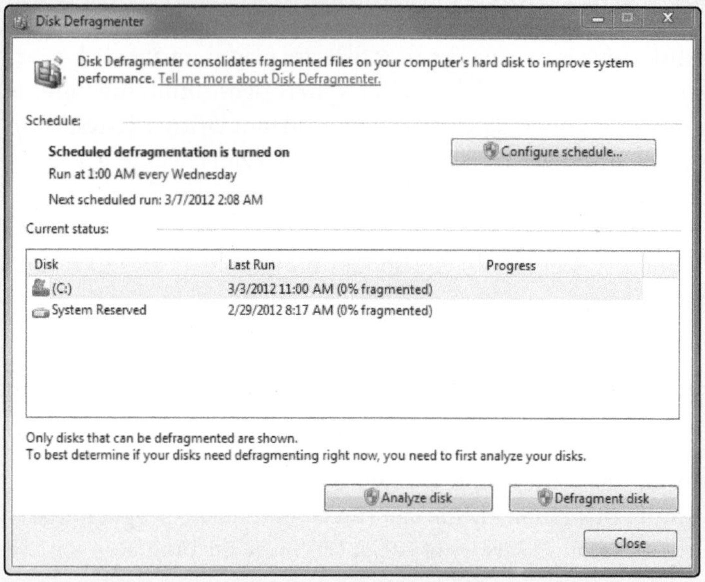

⑤ Use the skills you practiced previously to start the Snipping Tool and create a Window snip of the Disk Defragmenter window. Save a copy of this window to the folder where you store your files. Name the file U1Ch03DefragmentStudentName substituting your name as indicated.

⑥ Decide whether you want to analyze or defragment your hard drive at this time. This process could take up to several hours. If you decide to proceed, click Analyze disk and then, if necessary, click Defragment disk; otherwise, close 🔲 all open dialog boxes and windows.

⑦ Submit your snip as directed by your instructor.

Clearing Stored Files Such As Web Pages and Wastebaskets

Your Web browser often stores copies of Web pages on your computer so that when you ask for the page, it loads it from your hard drive rather than through your Internet connection. If you do not delete these files regularly or set your browser to limit the amount of disk space used for this purpose, hundreds or even thousands of Web pages may be stored that you rarely use. To reduce the disk space used by stored Web pages and files marked for deletion, you can delete stored Web page files by going into Internet Explorer and selecting Tools, and then Internet Options. Other browsers have similar methods for removing stored Web pages.

When you delete a file from the hard drive, the data is not actually erased; it is placed in a wastebasket called the Recycle Bin. (For a guide to emptying the Recycle Bin, see Skill Drill 2.) The areas of the disk on which the deleted file is stored are made available for use. The data is not erased until another file is written to that area of the disk. If you have enough empty disk space, the computer writes new files to the unused portion of the disk, which is probably nearer the center and is likely to load more slowly. There are utility programs that will optimize a hard drive by placing frequently used files near the outer edge of the disk.

Identifying Maintenance That May Need to Be Done by Experienced Professionals

Personal computers were created by hobbyists who loved to build computers from component parts. You can still buy all the parts for a PC system unit and build one yourself if you know how and want to save some money. However, do not open the case of a computer you do not own without the owner's permission. If you work on the inside of a system unit, be prepared to take responsibility for any mistakes you make—up to, and including, replacement of the unit. If you are unsure of what you are doing, take the unit to an experienced technician. In this discussion, the term *system unit* refers to a desktop personal computer system unit that does not have a monitor built in; it does not refer to portable computers. Other than inside the power supply, the electric voltage inside a system unit is as safe to you as handling a 9-volt battery. The static electric charge from your fingers is a greater danger to the components of a system unit than the low-voltage direct current is to you. Be sure the system unit is unplugged from a source of electric power before you open the case.

Replacing the Power Supply

The power supply is the device that handles the relatively high voltage from the utility company. It is not designed to be opened or serviced by hobbyists. If you suspect the power supply has failed, it should be tested and replaced by someone who is trained to do it safely. Do not attempt to open the case of the power supply.

Replacing or Adding Expansion Cards

Replacing or adding expansion cards, such as sound or video cards, should be done by professionals unless you feel confident that you have the skills to perform the task. If you decide to try to replace or add a card, carefully follow the directions that come with the expansion card for installation of the software and hardware. Be sure the system unit is unplugged from a source of electric power before you open the case. You may need to install software before you install the card.

Expansion cards, like the one shown in Figure 3.23, plug into slots on the **motherboard**—the main circuit board of the computer where the CPU is located. One end of the card has a plate with ports. To install an expansion card, you remove a metal plate at the back of the computer that is in line with the slot. The plate is usually held in place by a single screw. Position the expansion card so that one edge fits into the slot on the motherboard, and the adjacent side—with the ports—fits in the space left by the plate. With gentle but firm pressure, you can rock the expansion card into the slot. The single screw that held the plate is replaced to hold the expansion card. Keep the plate. If you remove an expansion card, you will need to replace the plate. Otherwise, dust or even insects may enter the unit through the opening.

FIGURE 3.23
Expansion cards should be replaced by professionals unless you are confident of your skills.

kastianz / shutterstock.com

Replacing or Adding RAM

Replacing or adding RAM cards should be done by professionals, unless you feel confident that you have the skills to perform the task. RAM cards fit into slots on the motherboard (see Figure 3.24). You should get some advice from the retailer when you buy the cards because they come in different sizes, capacities, and speeds. When you go online or to the store to buy RAM, you will need a description of your computer that includes the processor model and clock speed as well as the make and model of the computer.

FIGURE 3.24
RAM cards press and lock into slots on the motherboard.

charistoone-images / Alamy

Slots for RAM cards often have snaps on each end to hold the cards firmly in place. The card has a notch on the bottom edge so that it only fits in one direction. Different types of cards have the notches in different locations to prevent voltage mismatches. The first time you install a RAM card, it may be a good idea to have someone who has done it before show you how. Some types of RAM cards do not mix with others, and some must be installed in pairs. Check with the retailer to see if this applies to the type of memory you plan to buy.

Replacing or Adding an Optical Drive

Most system units have bays that hold optical drives, where the front of the drive sticks out the front of the system unit. The drives are held in by screws. Two cables connect the optical drive to the rest of the computer. One cable comes from the power supply and the other one is a ribbon cable or SATA cable that connects the drive to the motherboard (see Figure 3.25).

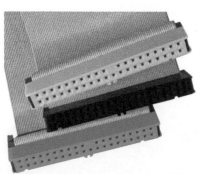

FIGURE 3.25
Ribbon cable connects a drive to the motherboard.

Kaspri / shutterstock.com

If you are replacing an existing drive with a ribbon cable, be sure the system unit is unplugged from a source of electric power before you open the case. Read the directions carefully. Before you disconnect the old drive, check the ribbon cable to see which edge is marked with a separate color and which side that color is on when the cable is plugged into the device. You may have to install software before you install the drive. Check the installation guide that comes with the drive for details. Next, unplug the cables from the power supply and the motherboard and remove the screws. The old drive slides out and you can slide a new one in. The power supply plug is normally keyed so that it only plugs in one way, but the ribbon cable can be plugged in backward on some computers. Check the markings on the back of the drive to determine which end of the port is the zero wire. Plug in the ribbon cable so that the zero wire on the cable plugs into the zero wire on the drive. Replace the screws to hold the drive in place.

Replacing or Adding Hard Disk Drives

The process of replacing a defective hard disk drive or upgrading to a larger capacity unit is physically similar to replacing an optical drive, but it is more challenging. If you have files or programs on the old hard drive that need to be transferred to the new drive, it takes some training and additional equipment to do this. If you do it incorrectly, you could lose valuable files. This is a task that is worth paying an experienced technician to do. Adding a second hard drive is easier than—and similar to—installing an optical drive. On the new drive, you will need to set the switches or *jumpers* on the back of the drive (see Figure 3.26). Jumpers have to be set to identify the new drive as the second drive. Follow the directions that come with the drive. Do not attempt to open the case of the hard drive itself.

FIGURE 3.26
Jumpers must be set before installing a new drive.

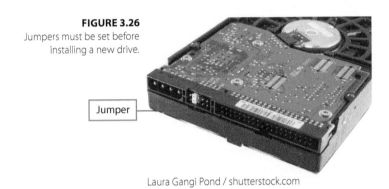

Jumper

Laura Gangi Pond / shutterstock.com

Replacing the Processor

Processors fit into sockets or slots, and they must be replaced carefully. This is a job for an experienced technician who can match the new processor's capabilities to the existing motherboard, bus, and RAM. It is often easier and more cost effective to buy a new computer than it is to try to upgrade the processor on an old unit.

Working on Peripherals Such As Printers, Monitors, or Scanners

Unlike the system unit of a PC, most peripherals are not designed to be opened by hobbyists. Laser printers contain hot drums and high voltage. CRT monitors have transformers that increase the utility company voltage and a picture tube that stores a dangerous static electric charge. Both CRT and LCD monitors should never be opened except by repair professionals.

Lesson 6 — Troubleshooting Hardware Problems

When a piece of hardware does not work, it could be an electrical problem, a mechanical problem, or a software problem. (Software problems will be discussed in Chapter 4.) Some of the components of a computer have no moving parts except the electricity that flows through them. These electrical components can fail because they overheat and cause some of the elements to melt, crack, or behave differently than they were designed to behave. Other components have moving parts that may break, jam, or run out of consumable supplies. All the components are controlled by the processor, which depends on software called a driver. This software enables the processor's commands to be carried out by the device. The driver may be the incorrect one for the platform or it could be damaged.

Some types of hardware failures are preceded by symptoms, but other failures happen without warning. You must assume that some part of your computer will fail at some time. It is a good idea to have an older system as a backup or know where you can use a computer at a local library or college. If your computer fails to turn on the next time you try to use it, how much trouble would that cause you? If contemplating this question gives you a sinking feeling, you need to make backup copies of your most valuable files to secondary storage right away. If your most valuable files are backed up and you have an alternative computer to use while yours is being repaired, you can work on fixing your computer with less urgency and panic.

Troubleshooting Common Problems and Selecting the Proper Actions

Some problems happen more often than others, and if you know how to recognize them and apply known remedies, they can be resolved quickly.

Nothing Happens

If the system unit or one of the peripherals is completely unresponsive and no indicator lights come on, check the supply of power by backtracking.

- Start at the back of the unit and check to see that the power cord is plugged all the way in. Sometimes these cords work loose.
- Check the plug strip, surge protector, or UPS to see that the device is plugged in and turned on and that a circuit breaker has not tripped. (The circuit breaker is usually a red button that pops out when it shuts off.)
- Most plug strips, surge protectors, or UPSs have an indicator light to show that they are getting power. If they do not have power when they are turned on, check where they plug into the wall or into an extension cord. Plug a lamp into the wall outlet to determine if the wall circuit has power.

System Becomes Erratic

If a device performs well for a while after startup but then becomes erratic, the problem might be caused by heat buildup. Check the fans, heat radiators, and airflow passages in the device to be sure that they are not blocked so the parts remain cool during operation. Another option is to replace elements of the system with devices from another system that are known to work well.

Keyboard or Mouse Do Not Work

If the keyboard stops working, check the connection cable if it is a wired keyboard. If it is a wireless keyboard, replace its batteries. If that does not resolve the problem, use the mouse to close and save files, close programs, and restart the computer.

If the mouse stops working, check the connection cable if it is a wired mouse. If it is a wireless mouse, replace its batteries. If that does not resolve the problem, you can perform many of the same functions from the keyboard in order to close and save files, close programs, and restart the computer. Most programs have keyboard shortcuts that perform the actions you commonly perform using a mouse. If you press (Alt), the current program's menu becomes active. You can then move between menu headings and drop-down menu items using the arrow keys, and then select the menu item by pressing

←Enter). To restart the computer, press and hold Alt and Ctrl and then press Delete. Restarting the computer will reload the device driver for the mouse and keyboard and they might operate normally.

If the computer is unresponsive to the mouse or keyboard, press and hold the power button for about 10 seconds to force a shutdown and then press the power button to start the computer.

The System Unit Makes a High-Pitched Whine

If the whine is from a floppy, CD, or DVD drive, it will stop when the drive is not in use. If the whine does not stop until the computer is turned off, it could be a fan bearing or a bearing in the hard drive. The hard disk inside the system unit spins very rapidly. It is attached to a post that rests on a bearing. If the bearing starts to wear out, it can make a high-pitched whine that comes and goes as the bearing heats up from the friction. When this bearing fails completely, the disk will not turn and your computer will not boot. Before the drive completely stops working, move all of your important files to secondary storage and take the system unit in for repair. Before the hard drive fails completely, have a technician replace it so that the installed programs can be moved to a new hard drive. If the cause of the whine is a fan bearing, the noise may go away when the fan fails, but your processor may overheat. Have the system checked even if the whine goes away.

The System Unit Lights Come On and the Hard Drive Runs Normally, but the Screen Remains Blank

Check the monitor. It may be turned off, unplugged, or have a loose connection to the system unit. If you have an old backup computer, turn off the computer, plug in the old monitor, and start the computer. If the monitor is the problem, it probably needs to be replaced.

The System Unit Lights Come On, but the Screen Remains Blank and Nothing Happens with the Hard Drive

The boot process uses instructions stored in ROM. If the ROM is damaged, or other integrated circuits on the motherboard are damaged by lightning or static electricity, you need to take the system unit in for repair. You may need a new system unit.

Another explanation is that the hard drive has failed. The bearing may have seized or the read/write head may have scratched the surface of the disk. The hard drive needs to be replaced by a technician. If the drive has vital company information on it, some of the data may be recovered by a specialist, but the process is expensive.

The Image on the Monitor Is Distorted or Off-Center

Some monitors have a set of controls—usually located on the front of the monitor or behind a cover—to adjust the location of the image on the screen. Some LCD monitors are controlled by software, and you have to run a program to adjust the screen. These controls vary considerably between manufacturers, and you may need the instruction manual to figure out how to use them. CRT monitors can be affected by magnetism, and some of their parts may become magnetized. Most CRT monitors have a small button with an icon that looks like a horseshoe magnet combined with the international symbol for No. If you press this button, the monitor will send a pulse through its components in an effort to demagnetize them. The image will distort temporarily and return to normal if this is the problem.

A New Peripheral Device Does Not Work Properly

If you connect a new peripheral device or upgrade the operating system, the device may not work properly. The driver for this platform and device combination may not be present. This can happen if you were supposed to install the software drivers before you connected the device. Use the Control Panel to uninstall the device, and then start over by first installing the software from the disc that comes with the device.

If the operating system is newer than the device, the CD that came with the device might not have the right driver for that operating system. If this is the case, you can go to the company's website and download a driver. In some cases, no driver has been written by the company for the old device. Use a search engine like Google to search for a driver for your device and the new operating system. If you are lucky, some enterprising amateur has written a driver that you can use for free. If not, you may have to buy a new device that works with your new operating system.

Loss of Connectivity

If you lose your connection to a network or to the Internet, there are a few steps you can take that might solve the problem. If you are connected to the Internet with a cable modem and the connection is lost, disconnect the power to the modem for a minute or so, and then reconnect the power. This may reboot the modem and solve the problem. If your network connection is lost, you can open the Control Panel, click Network and Sharing Center, and then click Troubleshoot Problems. If these solutions do not work, check with your network administrator or Internet provider to see if the network is functioning properly.

Identifying Steps Required to Solve Computer-Related Problems

If the problem is not one of the common problems described in the previous section, you may still be able to solve it using one of the following procedures. Even if you are not successful, make note of what you have already tried so that you can provide vital information to a repair technician.

Isolating the Problem

A desktop computer system has several components. If you have another working computer, you can use some of its parts to determine which component is malfunctioning. If you suspect the keyboard, mouse, or monitor to be the problem, you can switch these components one at a time between computers. If the problem goes away or transfers to the other computer, you have determined which component is faulty and needs to be fixed or replaced. This method is not recommended for sensitive components on the motherboard, like RAM, where the malfunctioning computer could damage the replacement part.

Restarting the Computer

Most of the components of the computer system go through a self-diagnostic when they start up and load a new set of operating instructions into RAM. A lot of problems can be resolved by turning off all of the components and starting them up again. Be sure to turn the system unit completely off. This may require turning off the power at the back of the unit or pressing the On/Off button for 4 or 5 seconds. If you are connected to the Internet by a modem, turn it off and unplug it. If you use an uninterruptible power supply, you will need to unplug your system from that. When you turn the devices back on, using the correct sequence may be important.

- If you are connected to the Internet through an external modem, restart the modem first. Watch the indicator lights to see when the modem has reestablished communication with the server over the Internet.
- Turn on the monitor.
- Turn on the system unit and wait until it starts completely.
- Turn on the peripheral devices.
- Start the software application programs.

Using the Troubleshooting Guide

If you have trouble with a peripheral device, check the manual for a section on troubleshooting problems. Common problems most users encounter are described there, along with suggestions for resolving the problems.

Seeking Help

If basic procedures do not resolve the problem, you need outside help. Before you contact someone, you need to have detailed information you can provide to them to show that you have already tried some of the basic remedies. It is embarrassing to take up other people's time only to find out that the computer was unplugged.

Reproducing the Problem

Identify the steps you take that create the problem. If you follow those same steps, does the problem always occur? Problems that happen sporadically are hard to fix, especially if they will not happen in front of someone else. If you have a problem that you cannot reliably reproduce, determine if it is more likely to happen after the device has been in operation for a while. This could be a clue that the problem is related to overheating.

Documenting the Problem

Write down the steps you take to produce the problem and describe the symptoms. If the symptoms manifest themselves on the screen, you can capture an image of the screen or write down any error codes or explanations that display.

To manage devices

1. **At the left end of the taskbar, click the Start button ⊕, and then click Control Panel.**

2. **On the Control Panel, change the view to Small Icons, if necessary, and then click Device Manager.** A list of device categories displays, as shown in Figure 3.27. Your list of options may vary.

3. **Locate DVD/CD-ROM drives, and then click the arrow to the left.** The DVD or CD drive in your computer is displayed as shown in Figure 3.27. Your screen will differ from the one in the figure.

FIGURE 3.27

The DVD drives on a computer.

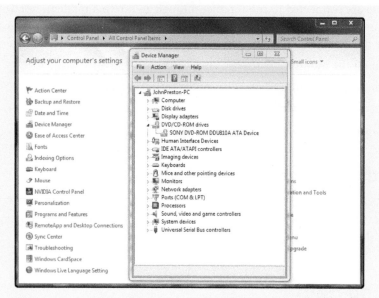

If You Have Problems

If you are using a notebook computer, it might not have a built-in DVD or CD drive. If your computer does not have a DVD or CD drive, display the Processor or Network Adapter devices.

④ **Use the skills you practiced previously to start the Snipping Tool and create a Window snip of the Device Manager window. Save a copy of this window to the folder where you store your files. Name the file** U1Ch03DVDStudentName **substituting your name as indicated.**

⑤ **Submit your snip as directed by your instructor.**

Finding Help

The first place to try to find help is your network of friends and family who are computer users. They may recognize the symptoms of your problem and relate a remedy that they found useful. (Be prepared to render similar service when they have trouble.) If that doesn't work, try using the Internet to search for information on the problem you have encountered. If free advice fails, you need to seek professional help. This may be available by telephone or e-mail through your company's help desk, the computer manufacturer's help line, or a repair technician. You may benefit by establishing a relationship with a local repair shop where you buy your hardware. You may also purchase service contracts where a technician will come to your home.

Providing Specific Information

Be prepared to relate a history of the problem, with specific information about the symptoms and what remedies you have already tried. People often spend time seeking sympathy for their plight. This may be appropriate for a discussion with your friends, but professionals who earn a living doing this type of work appreciate it if you get to the point of the problem.

Using a Repair Shop

If you have to take the system unit in for repair, get an estimate of minimum charges and when the unit will be repaired. Get a receipt that proves that the company has the computer and contains the date on which you left it. When you pick it up, ask for a demonstration that the problem has been resolved, if practical. Ask the repair technician if he or she an idea of what caused the problem and if you can do anything to reduce the likelihood of its recurrence.

Confirming the Problem Has Been Fixed and Avoiding a Recurrence

When you have solved a computer problem, it is always a good idea to test the computer using the same conditions that existed when the problem first occurred. If the problem was related to overheating, for example, let the computer warm up, and then try to re-create the problem. If your computer was taken to a repair shop or fixed in your home or place of business, have the repair technician demonstrate that the problem has been solved.

Always note the steps that you took to solve the problem, and if possible avoid the conditions that caused the problem in the first place. For example, if overheating was the problem, be sure the system unit has good airflow and regularly remove dust buildup. If the problem was the result of too little hard disk space, file fragmentation, or viruses, be sure you regularly remove unnecessary files, run disk management software, and have current antivirus software installed.

Lesson 7 ▶ # Identifying Consumer Rights and Responsibilities

You have to assume that something will go wrong with the computer eventually. If it happens soon after your purchase, you need to know the length of time in which you can return the computer for a full refund. If something breaks and needs to be fixed, you should find out who will fix it, how much you will have to pay, and how long it will take. You also need to assume that at some point in the not-too-distant future, your computer will be outdated; you will need to replace some or all of the old computer and dispose of at least some of its parts.

Identifying Hardware Warranties

All computers come with a warranty, but all warranties are not the same—even warranties that appear to last for the same amount of time. Check the warranty carefully to find out if someone will come to your house or place of business to fix the computer, if you have to take it back to the store for repairs, or if you have to ship it back to the manufacturer. Also, check to see if the conditions of the warranty remain the same throughout the life of the warranty—some warranties provide full coverage for a short period of time and then limited coverage for the remainder of the warranty period.

Identifying Support Agreements

In some areas, you can buy service contracts (sometimes called *maintenance contracts*) to supplement the manufacturer's warranty. Like warranties, service contracts are not all equal. Some provide for a technician to come to your home or place of business and perform various types of service for a period of time—usually 2 or 3 years—beyond the end of the warranty. Some service contracts require that you take any malfunctioning equipment to a store for repair. Some manufacturers sell service contracts that are honored through stores in national chains.

There is some disagreement among computer professionals about whether service contracts are worth the extra money—they are usually quite expensive. If you travel a lot and take a laptop computer with you, a service contract might be good insurance against accidental damage—provided accidental damage is covered in the contract! When considering a service contract, be sure to ask questions, and then be sure to read the contract to verify the services that it provides.

Estimating the Useful Life of a Computer

Estimating the useful life of a computer always depends on how the computer is being used. For a power user who does a lot of video editing or image processing, or a gamer who plays the latest computer games, the useful life of a computer might be less than two years. For someone who uses the computer a lot but doesn't have special needs, a computer is probably useful for two to four years. For a person who only uses the computer to read and send e-mail and use basic word processing features, the useful life of a computer might be five years or more.

Many colleges and universities have a policy of replacing about a third of their computers every year, resulting in a useful computer life of three years. One rule of thumb that you can follow is that when it is easier and/or less expensive to buy a new computer than to fix an old one, the useful life of the old computer is probably over. However, when you replace a computer, you may not have to replace all of the components; for example, the LCD monitor and printer may still be in fine shape, in which case all you would need to replace is the system unit.

Disposing of Computer Equipment

There are several considerations when you decide to dispose of a computer. The first is how to handle the hard drive. Even if you delete all of your personal files, those files can still be recovered fairly easily. Also, when you fill out forms or make purchases online, some of your personal information may well be stored on your hard drive, and people who know where to look can find that information. Some organizations that deal with sensitive information remove the hard drives and keep them in a safe area. Others hire service companies to wipe all magnetic information from the hard drives. Some people remove their old hard drives and destroy them with a hammer! Finally, there are free programs on the Internet that wipe hard drives clean by writing over all the information in each of the disks contained in the hard drive.

The Environmental Protection Agency suggests that old equipment be taken to a site that recycles computer components. The metal can be sold for scrap, and there are often recoverable quantities of precious metals and base metals on the printed circuit boards and in the wiring. Most communities have recycling centers that will accept old computers, although some charge to dispose of them. Many states have passed legislation making it illegal to dispose of a computer in a landfill.

If the computer is old but still usable, you might consider donating it to a local charity or school. However, if the computer is too old, most organizations will not accept it. If you think your computer might be of use to an organization, call first and describe the computer to see if it is interested.

When you get rid of an old computer, it is often a good idea to keep the keyboard and mouse. Nearly all new computer systems come with these components, but they are the devices that fail most often, and having a backup is always a good idea. You might even want to keep the old monitor as a backup to test the video card if your new monitor stops working.

 How Do You Feel About It?

ELECTRONIC WASTE

Many computers or other electronic devices contain valuable metals that can be reclaimed and reused. The process of reclaiming those metals can release some of them into the air and water if it is not done carefully. Some of this recycling is done in poor countries where there are few environmental controls. Use an Internet search program and find out about e-waste and how reclaiming metals from old electronic devices is impacting third-world countries. Will this information affect how you dispose of your old computer or monitor? Think about what you learned in your search and explain your reasons.

Summary

You learned how to identify factors that affect the performance of a computer, and then you learned how to protect a computer from theft and damaging conditions. You learned how to identify computer problems and what to do once you know what is wrong. Finally, you learned about the rights and responsibilities of computer ownership.

You can extend your learning by reviewing concepts and terms and by practicing variations of skills presented in the lessons.

Key Terms

asynchronous digital subscriber line (ADSL) *(p. 88)*

backward compatible *(p. 81)*

Boot Camp *(p. 79)*

broadband *(p. 88)*

circuit breaker *(p. 95)*

contrast ratio *(p. 87)*

defragment *(p. 99)*

digital video interface (DVI) *(p. 86)*

driver *(p. 81)*

Ethernet *(p. 89)*

fragmented *(p. 99)*

freeware *(p. 91)*

hard disk *(p. 85)*

hard drive *(p. 85)*

head *(p. 85)*

heat sink *(p. 91)*

high definition multimedia interface (HDMI) *(p. 86)*

IBM compatible *(p. 78)*

jumpers *(p. 103)*

legacy *(p. 81)*

Linux *(p. 79)*

Macintosh (Mac) *(p. 79)*

motherboard *(p. 101)*

multi-core processor *(p. 83)*

open source *(p. 79)*

OpenOffice *(p. 80)*

OS X *(p. 79)*

platform *(p. 78)*

plug strip *(p. 95)*

power strip *(p. 95)*

response time *(p. 86)*

revolutions per minute (rpm) *(p. 85)*

S-Video port *(p. 86)*

shareware *(p. 91)*

transformer *(p. 96)*

trial version *(p. 91)*

uninterruptible power supply (UPS) *(p. 96)*

video graphics array (VGA) port *(p. 86)*

video RAM (VRAM) *(p. 87)*

virtual memory *(p. 84)*

Checking Concepts and Terms

MULTIPLE CHOICE

Circle the letter of the correct answer for each of the following.

1. Which of the following is the least important criterion for selecting a personal computer? [L1]

   a. Platform

   b. Available software

   c. Ability to run new software in 5 years

   d. Portability

2. Which of the following is likely to be the most restrictive performance factor when you are using the Internet? [L2]

   a. Connection speed

   b. Processor speed

   c. Web page server speed

   d. Hard disk speed

3. Which of the following are types of low-cost computer software? [L3]

   a. Retail, student discount, trial version

   b. Freeware, shareware, student discount

   c. Student discount, shareware, retail

   d. Trial version, retail, freeware

4. Which of the following protects your computer from pulses of higher-than-normal electric voltage? [L4]

   a. Circuit breaker

   b. Surge suppressor

   c. Plug strip

   d. Grounded outlet

5. Which of the following is a device with a battery that continues to supply constant power even during brownouts or power outages? [L4]

   a. Plug strip

   b. Surge suppressor

   c. Uninterruptible power supply (UPS)

   d. Circuit breaker

6. Which of the following refers to a maintenance problem that is *not* caused by dirt or dust accumulation? [L5]

   a. Erratic trackball response

   b. Overheating

   c. Disk fragmentation

   d. Sticky keyboard keys

7. Which part of a hard disk moves the fastest past the read and write heads and therefore is the most desirable location for commonly used files? [L5]

   a. Outer edge

   b. Halfway from center to outer edge

   c. Side A

   d. Near the center

8. If nothing happens when you turn on the computer or a device, what should you check first? [L6]

   a. Disk fragmentation

   b. Flash drive in USB port

   c. Monitor

   d. Supply of power

9. Which of the following should *not* be considered when you need to dispose of an old computer? [L7]

   a. Take the computer to a landfill.

   b. Donate the computer to a charitable organization.

   c. Take the computer to a recycling center.

   d. Keep some of the parts as backups for your new computer.

10. Which of the following is a relatively easy fix for many software and hardware problems? [L6]

   a. Call the manufacturer.

   b. Ask your friends.

   c. Turn off and restart the computer.

   d. Call the company help desk.

MATCHING

Match each term in the second column with its correct definition in the first column by writing the letter of the term on the blank line in front of the definition.

_____ **1.** Port on the video card that contains both digital and analog image signals [L2]

_____ **2.** The ability of a newer version of a program to open and display files that were created using an earlier version of the program [L1]

_____ **3.** Software that can be used for a trial period but may be paid for voluntarily if used regularly [L3]

_____ **4.** Rearranging data on a hard disk so that files are written on adjacent sectors [L5]

_____ **5.** Optical disc format that uses smaller wavelength laser light than red to record more data per disc [L3]

_____ **6.** More than one processor on the same chip [L2]

_____ **7.** The amount of time it takes to change the color of a pixel on an LCD monitor [L2]

_____ **8.** The source code for software that is available to anyone [L1]

_____ **9.** Derivative of UNIX, which is free and open source [L1]

_____ **10.** Space on a hard disk used to supplement physical memory [L2]

A. Backward compatibility

B. Blu-ray

C. Defragmenting

D. Linux

E. Open source

F. Multi-core

G. Response time

H. DVI

I. Shareware

J. Virtual memory

Skill Drill

Skill Drill exercises reinforce chapter skills. Each skill reinforced is the same, or nearly the same, as a skill presented in the chapter. Detailed instructions are provided in a step-by-step format. Each exercise is independent of the others, so you can do the exercises in any order.

1. Deleting Web Pages from the Cache

Your Internet browser is probably configured to save copies of Web pages you have recently visited. This practice is intended to speed up the process of Web surfing, but having too many of these files can slow down other processes. If you have these files in your cache, someone else can also determine where you have been surfing. The following instructions are for Internet Explorer version 9.0. Other browsers have similar options.

To delete the cache of stored Web pages in Internet Explorer, and then set the size of the cache to a lower setting, follow these steps:

1. Start **Internet Explorer**.

2. On the menu bar at the far right, click the **Tools** icon, and then from the menu, click **Internet Options**. The Internet Options dialog box displays. Click the **General** tab, if necessary. (Note: If the menu bar does not display, right-click in the bar across the top of the screen that contains the address box, and then click **Menu Bar**.)

3. Under **Browsing History**, click the **Delete** button. The Delete Browsing History dialog box displays.

4. In the **Delete Browsing History** dialog box, click to remove the check mark next to Cookies. The only check marks should be next to *Preserve Favorites website data*, *Temporary Internet files*, and *History*. Click the **Delete** button. If you have never done this, it may take several minutes to delete thousands of files.

5. In the **Internet Options** dialog box, under **Browsing history**, click **Settings**.

6. Use the **Disk space to use** spin arrow or type to change the disk space to use to **200** MB.

7. If necessary, under *Check for newer versions of stored pages*, click **Automatically**.

8. Use the skills you practiced previously to start the **Snipping Tool** and create a Window snip of the *Temporary Internet Files and History Settings* dialog box. Save a copy of this window to the folder where you store your files. Name the file U1Ch03InternetStudentName substituting your name as indicated.

9. Click **OK** two times to close the dialog boxes.

10. Submit your snip file as directed by your instructor.

2. Emptying the Trash from the Recycle Bin

Deleting a file is a three-step process in the Windows operating system. When you delete a file from the hard drive, it is simply removed from the list of active files that you can list in application programs. If you open the Recycle Bin on the desktop, you can restore the deleted file to its original location. The file still takes up space on the disk. If you delete the file from the Recycle Bin, the space on the disk that is occupied by the file is made available for writing, but the file is not actually erased. The next time a file is saved to the disk, the operating system may write the new file to the space occupied by the deleted file, at which time the data is actually erased. Between the time files are removed from the Recycle Bin and the time they are overwritten, they may be partially recovered by special techniques, but they are no longer available from most programs. If you are using a computer that is not your own, you should obtain permission from the owner of the computer or from your instructor to delete files from the Recycle Bin before you proceed with this exercise. You may do the exercise but skip the step where you actually delete the files if you choose.

To delete files from the Recycle Bin and check the Recycle Bin settings, follow these steps:

1. On the left side of the taskbar, click the **Start** button. The Start menu displays.

2. On the right side of **Start** menu, click **Computer**. In the **Computer** window, in the **Navigation** pane, under **Favorites**, click **Desktop**. On the right side of the dialog box, double click **Recycle Bin**. The files that have been deleted display in the Content pane. If your Content pane is empty, it means that there are no files to delete.

3. On the **Command** bar, click the **Empty the Recycle Bin** button. The Delete Multiple Items message box displays.

4. Use the skills you practiced previously to start the **Snipping Tool** and create a full-screen snip of the **Recycle Bin** window. Save a copy of this window to the folder where you store your files. Name the file U1Ch03RecycleStudentName substituting your name as indicated.

5. In the **Delete Multiple Items** message box, click **Yes**. All of the files are removed.

6. In the upper-right corner of the **Computer** window, click the **Close** button.

7. Submit your snip as directed by your instructor.

3. Using Disk Cleanup

Microsoft provides system tools to help you maintain your computer. One of the tools is Disk Cleanup, which enables you to empty your Recycle Bin, clear your temporary Internet files, and delete other unnecessary temporary files. If you are using a computer that is not your own, you should have permission from the owner of the computer or from your instructor to use Disk Cleanup before you proceed with this exercise. You may do the exercise but skip the step where you actually clean up the files if you choose.

To use Disk Cleanup, follow these steps:

1. Click the **Start** button, click **All Programs**, click the **Accessories** folder, click the **System Tools** folder, and then click **Disk Cleanup**.

2. If prompted, click *My files only*. If prompted, select your main hard drive to be cleaned up. The program takes a few moments to search the hard drive for files that are unnecessary and can be removed. When this search is complete, the Disk Cleanup dialog box displays.

3. In the **Disk Cleanup** dialog box, scroll down and look at all of the different types of temporary files that will be removed. Notice that there are check boxes to the left of each one that enable you to delete or not delete any of the file types. Also notice that near the top of the dialog box, the total amount of space that can be cleaned up displays.

4. Scroll back to display the top of the list.

5. Use the skills you practiced previously to start the **Snipping Tool** and create a Window snip of the **Disk Cleanup** window. Save a copy of this window to the folder where you store your files. Name the file U1Ch03CleanStudentName substituting your name as indicated.

6. If you are using your own computer and would like to clean up your hard drive, at the bottom of the **Disk Cleanup** dialog box, click **OK**; otherwise move to Step 7.

7. Click the **Close** button in the upper-right corner of the Disk Cleanup dialog box.

8. Submit your snip as directed by your instructor.

Explore and Share

Explore and Share questions are intended for discussion in class or online. Look for information that is related to the learning outcomes for this chapter as directed. Submit your answers as directed by your instructor.

1. Microsoft has developed a system that requires people to register their copies of Microsoft Office online to reduce the use of unlicensed copies. Using a Web browser, search for *activate Microsoft Office software* and find Microsoft's explanation of what activation is and why it does it. Do you think this policy will increase the number of people who use freeware or shareware software, such as OpenOffice? [L1]

2. If you have old computer equipment lying around, how could you dispose of it in your area? Use a Web browser and find recycling centers in your area—both commercial centers and local government centers. Are there charges to drop off computers? Are there some materials they will take and others that they will not take? Go to http://ngm.nationalgeographic.com/2008/01/high-tech-trash/carroll-text. Note: If this link does not work, open a Web browser and search for high tech trash. and locate an article that deals with this topic.

3. Go to the website of a company that allows you to customize a computer online, such as www.hp.com or www.dell.com. Assume that you have $1,000 to spend. Pick a basic desktop model that costs less than $1,000 and choose which of its basic components you would upgrade. While you are selecting each component, make a note about which components cost the least to upgrade the most in capability. When you complete your customization, take a look at what you chose to upgrade and what you chose not to upgrade. This will give you a feel for what components of a computer are most important for *your* computing needs. [L2]

In Your Life

In Your Life questions are intended for discussion in class or online where you can share your personal experience. Restrict your answers to the topics described in each exercise. Submit your answers as directed by your instructor.

1. When you see portable computers in use on television shows or in movies, what brand logos do you remember seeing? Does one brand seem to appear more than others? If so, what are the possible reasons? Does this influence your decision on which brand to buy? [L1]

2. If your computer were stolen, what would be the most difficult data to replace? What could you do to avoid losing the data? [L4]

3. How old is your computer? When was the last time the dust was blown out of the cooling fins around the processor? If you have never cleaned out the dust, would you feel comfortable opening up the computer? [L5]

Related Skills

Related Skills exercises expand on or are somewhat related to skills presented in the lessons. The exercises provide a brief narrative introduction, followed by instructions in a numbered-step format that are not as detailed as those in the Skill Drill section.

1. Learning About OpenOffice

OpenOffice is a suite of software that runs on the Intel/Windows platform as well as the Intel/Linux platform. It has many of the same features as Microsoft Office but it is free.

To answer some questions about OpenOffice, follow these steps:

1. Use your Web browser to go to **www.openoffice.org.**

2. Click **I want to learn more about OpenOffice.org**. Read the general information about OpenOffice.

3. Use a search engine to locate answers to the following questions about OpenOffice and make note of the answers:
   a. Will it exchange files with Microsoft Office Word, Excel, and PowerPoint?
   b. What file format does OpenOffice use to save its files?
   c. Is OpenOffice available for the Macintosh platform?
   d. Does OpenOffice have a database program? If so, what is it?

    e.   Does OpenOffice have a program like Outlook that manages personal information, contacts, and e-mail? If so, what is it?

    f.   Go to a retail outlet online such as **www.amazon.com,** and find out the price for Microsoft Office Professional.

4. Record your answers to these questions. Save your file as U1Ch03OfficeStudentName and submit it as directed.

2. Determining Student Discounts on Software

Students may purchase software at a discount rate from many software companies. Most colleges carry some of these programs in their bookstores, but you also can buy software online for a student discount.

    To determine student discount prices on software from several different companies, follow these steps:

1. Use your Web browser to go to **www.studica.com**.

2. In the menu at the left of the screen, click **Products**. In the *Browse by Company* screen that displays, click **Microsoft**.

3. Find the student price of Microsoft Office Professional Academic 2010 and write it down. (Hint: The program may be located near the top of the page in a *Featured Products* section.)

4. Using the same procedure as in Step 2, display the **AutoDesk Student** page.

5. Find the student price of a perpetual license of AutoCAD 2012 and write it down.

6. Using the same procedure as in Step 2, display the **Adobe** page.

7. Find the student price of Adobe Photoshop Elements and write it down.

8. Use your Web browser to go to an online retail software dealer such as **www.amazon.com** or **www.bestbuy.com**, and look up the prices of these three software packages and write them down.

9. Record your answers to these questions. Save your file as U1Ch03CostStudentName and submit it as directed.

3. Checking Out Free Antivirus Software

Antivirus software is necessary to protect us from unethical people who wish to place programs on our computers that may damage them or use them for unauthorized or illegal purposes. Because these people continue to create new virus programs, a good antivirus program needs to have regular updates with the latest remedies and prevention schemes.

    To examine a freeware antivirus program, follow these steps:

1. Use your Web browser to go to **Microsoft.com**.

2. At the top of the screen place your pointer over **Security**, and then click **Microsoft Security Essentials**.

3. Read about the product's key features and other benefits, and then answer the following questions:
    a.   What kind of threats does it protect against?
    b.   What does it cost to download or to update?
    c.   What are the minimum system requirements for running the software?

4. Write down your answers to these questions. Save your file as U1Ch03VirusStudentName and submit it as directed.

Discover

Discover exercises give you general directions for exploring and discovering more advanced skills and information. Each exercise is independent of the others, so you may complete the exercises in any order.

1. Discovering the World of Freeware and Shareware

Learn more about freeware. Go to **www.freewarehome.com** and **www.gnu.org,** and read about the philosophy of the people who support this effort with their time and creative energy. Describe some of the software that looks like it might be useful, and also write your impression of the philosophy behind these sites. Write and submit a one- or two-page essay and submit it as directed.

2. Learning About Antitheft Software that Reports on Your Stolen Computer's Activity

Portable computer theft can be a big problem for companies if their price lists and company secrets are lost along with the hardware. Go to **www.absolute.com.** Read about this approach to protecting and recovering stolen portable computers and protecting the data on those computers. Describe in a one- or two-page essay what types of things can be done to track a computer and to work on the computer from a remote location. If the site previously mentioned is no longer valid, use your Web browser to search for the term *track stolen computer.* Submit the essay as directed.

Chapter 4

Identifying Software and Hardware Interaction and Types of Software

Why Would I Do This?

Computers have several layers of software that enable us to use them even though they understand only zeros and ones. You need to understand how application software interacts with hardware through the operating system, how drivers recognize at what level problems may be occurring, and when it may be appropriate to upgrade your software.

If you understand the software development cycle, you can make more informed choices about adopting new software and know which types of problems to expect. If you are having software written for your company, you will better understand the role you can play in the process.

Software is upgraded often; therefore, making this change can be expensive and disruptive to your organization. You need to be able to decide if the upgrade is worth the potential problems that may occur during the transition.

We interact with our computers through application programs. There are hundreds of commonly used application programs from which to choose. Picking the right programs will determine your level of productivity when performing certain tasks. In order to pick the software that will be most productive, you need to know how to categorize the software by task to narrow your search, as well as what criteria to use when making your choices.

Chapter at a Glance

Chapter at a Glance

Lesson	Learning Outcomes	Page Number	Related IC3 Objectives
8	Identify audio and video software	138	3.3.7
8	Identify desktop publishing tools	139	3.3.3
8	Identify gaming software	139	3.3.6
8	Identify virtual reality software	139	3.3.6
8	Identify media storage formats	139	3.3.7
9	Identify the use of utility programs such as virus and malware protection, or system maintenance	140	3.4.1, 3.4.3, 3.4.4
9	Identify integrated software packages	141	3.3.0
9	Identify eLearning programs	141	4.1.0
9	Identify other types of software	141	3.3.3
9	Identify custom software programs	142	4.1.0
10	Identify the appropriate software for a given task	143	4.1.6
10	Identify common incorrect uses of software	143	4.1.0

Visual Summary

In this chapter, you identify the ways in which hardware and software interact. You learn about the steps used to create software. You learn how the development process influences decisions to make minor or major upgrades, and you learn about types of software available for a variety of common tasks (see Figure 4.1).

FIGURE 4.1
Hardware and software interact to create the computing experience.

Booka/Shutterstock

List of Student Files

In most cases you will create files by capturing screens. You will add your name to the file names and save them on your computer or portable memory device. Table 4.1 lists the files you start with and the names you give them when you save the files.

TABLE 4.1

ASSIGNMENT:	STUDENT SOURCE FILE:	SAVE AS:
Lessons 1–11	none	U1Ch04CorrectStudentName U1Ch04OfficeStudentName U1Ch04PaintStudentName
Skill Drill	none	U1Ch04WindowsStudentName U1Ch04ExcelStudentName U1Ch04UpdateStudentName
Explore and Share	none	none
In Your Life	none	none
Related Skills	none	U1Ch04OneDriveStudentName U1Ch04ReadmeStudentName U1Ch04EssentialsStudentName
Discover	none	none

Lesson 1 ▶

Identifying Hardware and Software Interaction

We interact with the computer through input and output devices and application programs that interpret our input. In this lesson, you identify how data is entered, different ways in which you issue commands, how software applies rules and performs prewritten operations, and how software communicates results.

Data Input

You are familiar with several input devices from the previous lessons on computer hardware, such as the keyboard, mouse, scanner, and microphone. Among other things, the keyboard is used for entering text and numbers, the mouse is used to select and reposition items, the scanner is used to convert photos and documents to digital files, and the microphone—along with a sound card—is used to input voice commands or text. The term *software* refers to programs that tell the computer what to do with the input. One of the important functions of the software is to interact with the user during the data input process. For example, when you use the keyboard to enter data, the word processing software displays what you type on the screen. The software also displays a vertical line called the *insertion point*, which indicates where the text will go when you start to type.

Software Commands

Software contains modules of instructions that may be activated by choosing *commands*. Commands are activated by clicking an option on a menu, clicking a button, pressing special keys on the keyboard, or by voice through a microphone. Any input device can be used to give commands. For example, when you click the Print button, the software performs a series of actions that result in a printed version of a file, selected data, or what displays on the screen.

Software Applies Rules and Processes

Software can be used to apply rules to data for making editing decisions. For example, using a spreadsheet Sum function activates an algorithm that adds the contents of two or more cells together. Some software even enables you to create your own rules; in Microsoft Office Word, you can use the AutoCorrect feature to recognize a typing error that you commonly make and substitute the correct word.

To create a rule in Word using AutoCorrect

1 **Click the Start button 🏁, and then click All Programs.** Programs like Word, Excel, PowerPoint, and Access may be found on the Start menu or in the Microsoft Office folder.

2 **Search the menu for Microsoft Office Word 2010 and click it.** The Word window opens.

3 **In the left end of the Word ribbon, click the File tab.** The File window displays.

4 **Near the bottom of the File window on the left side, click Options. In the left pane of the Word Options dialog box, click Proofing.**

5 **Under AutoCorrect options, click the AutoCorrect Options button.** The AutoCorrect dialog box displays.

6 **Under *Replace text as you type,* click in the Replace box, and then type** comptuer If the word is already there, it means someone else has used the computer you are using to complete this exercise.

7 **In the With box, type** computer

8 **Confirm that the *Replace text as you type* check box is selected.** The rule will be applied when you accidentally mistype the word *computer*. See Figure 4.2.

FIGURE 4.2
Software can apply a rule to replace a common typing error.

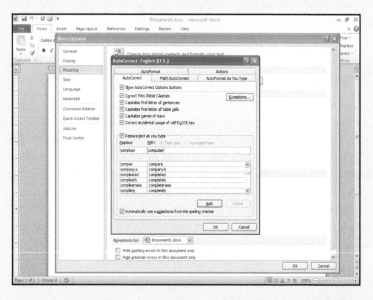

9 **Use the skills you practiced previously to start the Snipping Tool and create a Window snip of the AutoCorrect dialog box. Save a copy of this snip to the folder where you store your files. Name the file** U1Ch04CorrectStudentName **substituting your name as indicated.**

10. **In the AutoCorrect dialog box, click Add.** The rule is created and will be applied when you make this typing mistake.

11. **Close all dialog boxes including the Snipping Tool. In the blank Word document, observe the blinking insertion point in the upper-left corner of the document. Type** comptuer **and then press** Spacebar**.** The mistyped word is automatically corrected.

12. **From the File tab, click Exit. Click Don't Save when asked if you want to save your changes.** The file closes without being saved and the Word program closes.

Commands start processes that must be written precisely so that the computer can follow the instructions.

Software Communicates Results

The monitor is the most common output device, displaying text in a word processing document or numbers in a spreadsheet, but there are other types of devices the software can use for output. For example, you can use software commands to send a document to a printer in your office or to a printer down the hall in the copy room. In another example, software may be used to calculate the path of a robot's arm when it welds a car body, where the output is in the form of signals to the motors that control the arm.

Software Interacts and Shares Data

In some cases, when you input data into one application, it affects another (and different type of) application. For example, a word processing file might be linked to a spreadsheet file. When data is changed in the spreadsheet file, a chart based on that data is automatically updated in the word processing document. Similarly, data from the Internet, such as stock market information, can be linked to a spreadsheet file on your computer, and the spreadsheet file will be updated with current stock information every time it is opened.

Lesson 2 ▶ Identifying Steps in the Development Process

Creating software that works reliably and is easy to use is a process made up of several steps. The process is complex, but the major steps are listed as follows.

Planning

During the initial planning stages, the goals of the project are analyzed and the feasibility of the project is evaluated from economical, operational, and technical perspectives. Once the project is analyzed, the next step is to break it down into its component parts for further analysis. This stage also includes input from potential end users.

Programming

Computer instructions must be written in a language that can be understood by the computer. Unlike most human languages, computer languages are designed so that each word has only one meaning and the words are used in a very structured way to create commands and procedures that are not ambiguous.

Writing instructions in a computer language that accomplish a task is called **programming**. To develop software, a specific task is identified and one or more people are assigned to do the programming. If the task is large, it may involve many programmers and a management team to coordinate their efforts.

Debugging

If the programmers make a mistake, the software does not work properly. The malfunction in the software is called a **bug**. This is the same term used to describe hardware malfunctions. Programming languages include internal error checkers that catch simple mistakes such as misspelling a command word or using it incorrectly. Mistakes that involve faulty logic or failure to anticipate all the possible combinations of inputs are harder to catch and may go undetected by the programmer. The software may be reviewed by other team members to remove any errors they can find. Removing errors from the software is called **debugging**.

Beta Review

When the programmers have reviewed the first version of the software—typically called the **alpha version**, after the first letter in the Greek alphabet—and made appropriate changes, the second version of the software is ready for testing by a sample of users. The second letter in the Greek alphabet is *beta*, and this version of the software is called the **beta version** because it is the second stage in the development process.

The beta copy of the software is distributed to a sample of users called **beta testers**, who are asked to use it and report any errors they find. The beta testing stage may consist of more than one step—first a technical beta for a small group of experienced users, and then a general beta for a larger number of users. Beta testers are typically asked to sign a **nondisclosure agreement**, agreeing not to share the product's new features with anyone else. Once the software is ready for release, a **release to manufacturing (RTM)** version is produced and sent to the companies that process the product for distribution. This final copy is sometimes referred to as the **gold version** or *gold master*. The final step in the process is the release of the product to retail chains or making the software available for online distribution.

Instructions and Help Manuals

The beta copy also goes to the people who write the instruction manuals that accompany the software. These instruction manuals are written while the beta testing and final revisions are in progress. Instruction manuals used to be printed; now most manuals come on a CD or are available online. Beta versions of software are also sent to authors of textbooks and trade publications, to be sure that textbooks and reference books are available at or around the release date for the software.

Quality Control

The quality control team runs a series of tests on the software to find most of the errors before the program is released to the beta testers. After the beta test, the team collects comments from the beta testers and prepares a list of things to fix, which is returned to the team of programmers. The program is revised and given a version number. If it is the first version of the software, it is usually given a number that starts with a 1, such as *1.0*. Microsoft is using the year of the software's introduction as a way to indicate the version of some of its software.

It is particularly difficult to write computer programs that anticipate all the possible input conditions or work with all the different combinations of hardware. It is also challenging because the capability of computers changes so rapidly that the time available for development is often only a few months. If the software development takes too long, competitors will take market share or the software will become obsolete due to advanced capabilities available on new hardware.

The short development time poses a particular problem when trying to coordinate the writing of the manuals and the software. The programmers may continue to make changes to the software that are not reflected in the accompanying electronic or printed manuals. To adjust for this difference between the software and the manual, programmers often include a file called **readme** with comments about changes they have made that are not documented in the manual. This difference between the final version of the software and the manuals is also why many software companies are not including manuals in book form. Instead, they are providing manuals as help text within the software. The most up-to-date manuals and help files are typically found on the company's website. Microsoft Office software now includes the option to search the manuals on Microsoft's website as part of any search in Help.

| Lesson 3 |

Identifying Issues Related to Software Distribution, Installation, Updates, Upgrades, and Removal

Developing software is a continuous process that does not stop when the first version of the product is shipped to retailers. Programmers continue to fix problems that arise when the product is exposed to a greater variety of users. Software creators also continue to work on new features that would be useful in the next version.

Distributing Software

Software can be distributed in four ways: for single users, for users on a network, by license for employees or staff and students in an organization, or on the Web. A single-user license usually restricts the use of the software to one user at a time. The software program is copied from the vendor's website or from an optical disc to a drive where it can be accessed when needed. This process is called **installation**. Installation often involves adding several files to the computer and making changes to related files. This does not necessarily mean that when you buy software you can install it on only one computer. Most software publishers allow you to install a copy on your desktop computer and one on your notebook computer. You need to read the **End User License Agreement (EULA)** to find out what restrictions there are on your software; you are responsible for maintaining your license and using it in a manner allowed by the licensing agreement. If you remove software and then **reinstall** it or install it on another computer, you might need to obtain specific permission.

A **network license** enables anyone on the network to use the software. The software is installed on a server, and the desktop computers do not need to have it installed, although frequently a portion of the software is installed on the desktop computers. Some network licenses have restrictions limiting the number of users, or **seats**, who can access the software at any given time. Most licenses offer a volume discount for more seats.

A **site license** works differently from a network license because the software is installed on the desktop or notebook computer of each qualified user in the organization who requests it. Some site licenses even allow eligible employees to install the software on their home or personal notebook computers. Site licenses usually have time limits, and the license must be renewed (paid for) on a regularly scheduled basis—typically every year.

Some types of software are available online through an ***application service provider (ASP)***. This type of software tends to be specialty software and is paid for on a license basis or, more recently, on a per-use basis using a logon procedure. Some examples of ASPs include Web-hosting companies, ad management software for websites, and personnel and database management programs for businesses.

Office-type software—particularly word processors and spreadsheets—are available online. Some versions, such as Google Docs or Microsoft Office Web Apps, do not have as many features as the installed versions of Microsoft Word or Microsoft Excel, but they do the common tasks most people need. The advantages of using Web versions of software are cost, convenience, and continual upgrades; the obvious disadvantage is that it requires a reliable Internet connection. Some popular commercial sites, such as eBay, provide similar types of services to individuals who want to sell on the Web but who do not want to purchase the software required to set up an online store. As mentioned in Chapter 3, there are also several types of noncommercial software available, such as freeware and shareware. Trial versions of commercial software are available that may be used for a limited time without charge. Computers often come with some bundled software and many trial versions of other software.

Updates

Once the software is in the marketplace, users often discover additional errors or unusual combinations of input that cause problems. Also, some users will have hardware that does not work properly with the software. For these reasons, the current version of the software must be fixed. Revised versions are indicated with numbers like *1.1* or *1.2.1* to indicate that they are a variation of the first version. Users who bought the original version of the software may download a fix for the problem free of charge. This is called an ***update***, ***patch***, or ***service pack*** and it will fix some of the problems. Companies may also include minor improvements to features that were not ready when the first version was released.

Upgrades

After the software has been out for a year or so, changes in hardware and pressure from competitors may prompt the company to make more significant changes to the software. The company will go through the development process again to produce a new version of the software, which may be indicated by a version number such as *2.0*. Microsoft Office uses the year of the release as part of some of its product names to indicate the version, but it also has a version number. For example, Microsoft Office 2010 is also known as *Microsoft Office 14*. Changing to a new version is called an ***upgrade***. An upgrade is typically not free, but it usually costs less than buying the software for the first time.

To determine the version of Microsoft Office

1. **Click the Start button ⊕, and then locate and click Microsoft Office Excel 2010.**

2. **Click the File tab.**

3. **In the left pane of the File window, click Help. In the right pane, read the information listed under About Microsoft Excel.** The edition of Office displays, along with a version number, as shown in Figure 4.3.

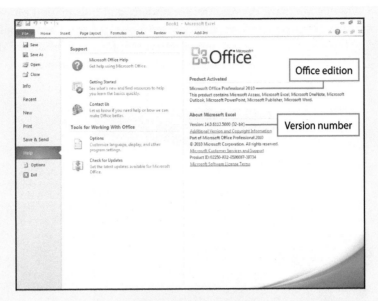

④ Use the skills you practiced previously to start the Snipping Tool and create a Window snip of the About Microsoft Office Excel information. Save a copy of this snip to the folder where you store your files. Name the file U1Ch04OfficeStudentName substituting your name as indicated.

⑤ Close ☒ all windows and dialog boxes. Submit the snip as directed.

Reasons to Update and Upgrade

If an update is available, it is probably a fix for some problem or a refinement of an existing feature. It is usually a good idea to take advantage of free updates unless the software company has added new features that require evaluation or training. Antivirus programs are a good example of software that should be updated regularly to keep ahead of new viruses.

Upgrades from one version to another require more consideration. The software often has drawbacks to consider, but probably also has benefits. When a company releases an upgrade, it usually stops selling the earlier version. If your organization buys some new computers and wants to install software, only the newest version will be available. If you do not upgrade the existing computers to the new version, you will have a mixture of versions in the organization, which could cause problems such as incompatible files.

Methods of Upgrading and Staying Up to Date

Most updates can be accomplished over the Internet by downloading a program that can make the changes. This type of program usually has the file extension .*exe*. This indicates that it is an executable file. Once the program is on your computer, you activate it by double-clicking the file name. This starts the program. It decompresses its files and makes the appropriate changes and replacements. Some programs may be set to inspect the software company's website at regular intervals to check for updates.

Upgrades require you either to purchase the program on a CD or to download it from a website. To assure that you are doing an upgrade rather than installing the software for the first time, the upgrade version of the software checks to see that the earlier version is present on the computer before it will install its programs. If your computer is on a network, the network administrator can often upgrade your computer's software over the network without visiting your office.

To be sure that you have the most recent updates and information on possible upgrades, you can visit the software company's website, subscribe to industry newsletters, or allow the company to send you notices. You can also run the program and check for ways to update the software, as shown in Figure 4.4. If there is not an update button visible, check the Help menu.

Benefits

The benefit of performing updates is to obtain a more functional version of the original software for no additional expense. One obvious benefit to updating antivirus software is that the updated definitions may catch a newly created virus that the older program would not have caught. The benefits of an upgrade may involve new capabilities, better ways of doing things, or solutions to technical problems with the software.

Drawbacks

Some new versions are not backwardly compatible with files created by earlier versions, although most are. If the user interface is significantly different, users may require additional training. Major upgrades of the software often require more advanced hardware and an additional cost for the software.

End of Life

At some point, software manufacturers will not only stop selling a version of their product, they will also stop supporting it. This means that there will be no further updates and often means that no online help will be available. You can continue to use nonsupported software—as long as you don't run into problems!

Identifying Fundamental Word Processing Concepts and Uses

The term *word processing* is used to indicate that you can do a lot more with the words in a document than simply type text on a page. When you use a keyboard as an input device on the computer, what you type does not go immediately on paper as it does with a typewriter; instead, it is stored in RAM and displayed on the screen. While it is in RAM, it can be manipulated according to the capabilities of the word processing software before the final copy is printed.

Identifying Basic Word Processing Concepts

When working with word processing software, a *document* is a file that exists in RAM or storage that can be printed, displayed on the screen, posted to the Web as a Web page, or used in many other ways. Because it is in electronic form, it may be *edited* or revised by simply changing the data stored in RAM. This process is far faster and easier than changing a typed version or retyping a document, which were the only choices when using a typewriter.

Another major advantage of word processing over manual typewriters is the ability to change the *format* of a document. The format is the appearance of the document, including the page orientation of the text and the size of the margins. Formatting also includes choosing the size, shape, and color of the text. A coordinated set of character designs is called a *font*, and word processing programs provide a variety of fonts, as shown in Figure 4.5.

FIGURE 4.5
Word processing programs offer a variety of formatting options.

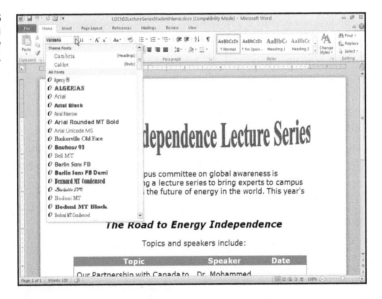

Identifying Types of Documents

Word processing programs can be used to create a variety of documents, from short memos and letters to entire books. Complex documents like reports and books may use advanced word processing features to create an index or a table of contents, add footnotes, insert a bibliography, or display the document in outline form.

Word processing programs can support graphics to produce flyers and brochures that were formerly handled by specialists at publishing companies. Creating documents with graphics and special formatting that are ready to be printed is called *desktop publishing*. Word processors can be used to create basic Web pages that can be saved in **Hypertext Markup Language (HTML)**, the language used to create Web pages for use on the Internet. Word processors can also be used to save documents in special file types that are used by other applications or to publish a document to a **blog**—an abbreviation of the word **Weblog**—on the Web.

Lesson 5 ▸ Identifying Fundamental Spreadsheet Concepts, Processes, and Uses

Spreadsheets are used primarily to display and manipulate numbers in cells, although text is often used, typically as column or row headers to help make the data understandable. They are different from tables in word processing documents because some of the cells have formulas that calculate values based on the values in other cells. Spreadsheets can also process and display the numbers in a variety of ways that make them useful in many different situations.

Identifying Basic Spreadsheet Concepts

Instead of using the general term *spreadsheet*, some popular spreadsheet programs, such as Microsoft Office Excel, use the terms **worksheet** and **workbook**. A worksheet is a single page of cells, and a workbook is a collection of worksheets. When you save a workbook file, you give it a name, and all the worksheets in that workbook are saved as a collection under that name.

The first 26 columns of a worksheet are designated by the letters of the alphabet. The next 26 columns are designated with two letters, the first of which is A. For example, the column to the right of Z is AA, followed by AB and AC. The naming convention for columns continues with BA–BZ for the next 26 columns, CA–CZ for the next 26, and so forth. The rows are numbered sequentially. An individual cell is identified by pairing the column and row designations. For example, the cell in the upper-left corner is identified as cell *A1*, and the one immediately below it is *A2*.

Spreadsheets use **formulas** resembling algebraic formulas, which use **cell references**—the locations of the numbers used in the calculations instead of the actual numbers typed in the cells. The formulas are one-sided. They always assume that the current cell reference is on the left side of the equals sign and the rest of the formula is on the right side. For example, if you want to add the contents of cells A1 and A2 and then place the result in cell A3, you would select cell A3 and type *= A1+A2*. You can write your own formulas or call up a library of prewritten formulas called **functions** (see Figure 4.6).

FIGURE 4.6
Spreadsheets have a library of special functions.

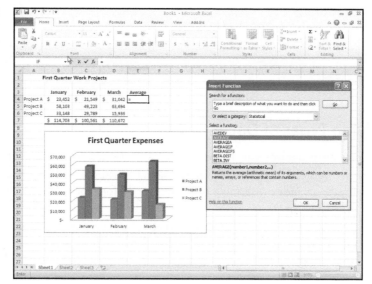

The formula in a specific cell appears to refer to other specific cells, but the spreadsheet program actually stores the cell references in the formula as their position relative to the selected cell. In the previous example, the formula is stored as an instruction to add the two cells immediately above cell A3. If you copy the formula into another cell, the specific cell references change with the formula, adding the contents of the two cells immediately above. This feature enables you to copy a formula—such as adding a column of numbers—across many columns without rewriting it each time.

Spreadsheets also have the ability to represent the data as charts. The charts are linked to the data, and changes to the underlying data are immediately displayed in the charts.

Identifying Spreadsheet Processes

Spreadsheets are also equipped with features that help analyze data. Charting data helps identify trends, proportions, and exceptions. You can also sort tables of data or *filter* the data to match criteria that you specify, hiding the data that does not match the filter criteria. The most important process for which spreadsheet software was originally created is performing *what-if analysis*, which could be used to test the difference in payments on a car loan with different interest rates and over different periods of time. If a sheet of numbers contains many formulas where the results of one formula are used as data in other formulas, changing the value of one cell causes a ripple effect throughout the sheet, thereby causing many other cell values to also change. You can try different values in critical cells to see what would happen if you made changes. The results of dozens of dependent calculations will immediately be apparent.

Identifying Types of Documents

Spreadsheets are used primarily to manage money, but they can also be used with other types of numbers. They are typically used to create and maintain budgets or to prepare expense reports. The what-if process may be used to examine the sensitivity of profits to changes in pricing when analyzing pricing models. Almost any table of numbers that involves calculations can be placed in a spreadsheet, from stock prices to student test scores.

Lesson 6 ▶ Identifying Fundamental Presentation Software Concepts and Uses

Communicating ideas to groups is facilitated by using visual aids. Computers can be used to create a series of images that are projected onto a screen or displayed on a computer display.

Identifying Basic Presentation Concepts

Visual aids are designed to support a live presentation by a speaker. They provide a focus for the eyes of the audience to reinforce points a speaker is making using short amounts of text. They also typically provide information in graphical form using pictures, clip art, and charts. Presentations can also be enhanced by the use of animation, where bulleted points appear one at a time, or each element of a chart appears individually. Individual elements could be a title, a list of talking points in a bulleted list, or a graphic. Each screen is called a *slide*. The slides may all use the same background color, graphic, and font. If so, these elements are located on a *slide master*, which is applied to the other slides.

A group of slides that is intended for use in the same presentation is called a ***slide show***. The presentation software is capable of printing several slides at a time on a page, along with space for notes to use as audience ***handouts***. The software can also record ***speaker notes*** with each slide and print them out with an image of each slide, or display them next to the slide on the computer screen but not on the projected screen. Figure 4.7 shows an example of a presentation created using PowerPoint.

FIGURE 4.7
Presentation software helps the speaker communicate important points.

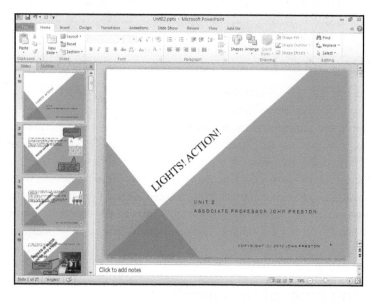

Identifying Purposes of Presentations

Presentation software can also save the presentation as a series of Web pages that can be saved on a Web server and viewed over the Internet. When used for this purpose, the content of the slides must be changed from supporting a speaker to a complete stand-alone presentation. The speaker notes can be displayed with the slide to give the complete text of the presentation.

Lesson 7 ▶ **Identifying Fundamental Database Concepts and Uses**

A collection of organized data is called a ***database***. Some software companies use this term to refer to the combination of data and the software used to manage it. Database software is used when the quantity of data becomes too large to manage with simple lists or tables in word processing software or in worksheets in a spreadsheet program.

Identifying Basic Database Concepts

The data in a database is stored in ***tables*** where the columns represent individual data values and the rows contain all related data about one individual person, transaction, or event. The data in a row is called a ***record***, and the data in a column is called a ***field***. The field that contains a unique identifier for each record is the ***primary key field***. An example of a key field would be a Social Security number or a student ID number.

If a table has many fields, all of the columns may not fit on the screen. To enter and review records one at a time, a ***form*** is used where the fields are arranged on the screen in any order or orientation. Additional text that is not stored in the table may be added to the form to explain how to enter data in certain fields. Database software provides users with the ability to create *queries*. A query is a set of criteria intended to extract the records and fields that would answer a particular question and display the table with only those records. The data may also be presented in structured pages intended for printing, called *reports*.

Database software has the ability to sort and filter tables of data. Spreadsheet software that can sort and filter tables of data is often used to store data. However, spreadsheet software has several limitations when used in place of database software. The amount of data a spreadsheet can store is limited by the RAM in the computer. Even though personal computers have hundreds of megabytes or even several gigabytes of RAM, databases can be much larger if the tables have dozens of fields and millions of records. Spreadsheets are not designed to allow many users to work with the tables at the same time, and they are not designed to link different tables together to reduce storage requirements and produce combined reports.

A database that separates the data into several tables that are related to each other is called a *relational database*, which reduces the amount of redundant data. See Figure 4.8. A database that can perform all of the tasks previously mentioned, and also provide data security, external and multi-user access, and a programming language that can be used to customize the tasks, is also referred to as a *database management system (DBMS)*.

FIGURE 4.8
Relational databases use tables.

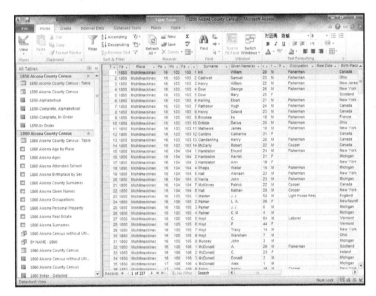

Identifying Examples of Databases

If you work for an electric utility and you are storing records of the monthly payments by customers for electric bills, you do not want to record the customer's home address and phone number each month in the same record with the date and amount of payment. You have one table for information about the customer and another table that records the details about each month's payments, and you relate them using the key field that has the customer's identification number. This is an example of a relational database.

Databases are typically used by large organizations such as utilities, banks, and government agencies, but they are also used by much smaller organizations like small stores, school organizations, and volunteer groups for inventory control, personnel records, or for names and addresses of clients or donors. Individuals can use databases for inventories for insurance purposes; collections of CDs, DVDs, or books; or even mailing lists. Most databases have built-in tools that enable you to merge the information from the database with form letters created in a word processor.

Large databases have recently begun to be used to support the functions of application service providers. All of the information on bidders, sellers, and items being sold on eBay, for example, are stored in a database. Genealogical databases made available online by the LDS church at FamilySearch.org contain census, birth, marriage, death, military, and other records that provide information on billions of names.

Identifying Unusual Use of Memory and Storage by Database Software

Storage capacity on a hard disk is much larger than the capacity of RAM. Normally this is not a problem unless you are running several application programs at once. However, database files can be much larger than other types of files. Designers of database software write their programs differently than other types of programs. Database programs do not necessarily load the entire file into RAM; instead, they just load parts of it at a time as needed. Using this method enables you to use larger database files, but it changes the way you do some basic file manipulation. For example, you do not save the database when you are done; you simply close it. Because it was on the hard disk all along, you do not save a copy from RAM to the disk. For this reason, the Save As option works differently in a database program such as Microsoft Office Access than it does for other Office applications.

Lesson 8 ▶ Identifying Fundamental Graphic and Multimedia Concepts and Uses

The ability of computers to display and transmit still images, sound, animations, and video is limited by processor speed, capacity of memory and storage, and connection speed. To get the most out of the available hardware, graphic software is used to create sophisticated images and video while keeping within the limitations of the hardware.

Identifying Types of Multimedia and Graphic Software

Graphics are common in many applications. Drawing tools are usually available in word processing, spreadsheet, and presentation software to draw basic shapes and arrows and to manipulate pictures. Many programs also have the capacity to display videos or play audio recordings, and these typically contain tools to transform the resulting files so that they can be distributed and played on the Internet.

Drawing and Painting Tools

Drawing tools are often built into other applications and are typically designed to work with lines and shapes. Lines can be straight, curved, or free-form. Line colors can be changed, two-dimensional objects can be filled with colors, and often graduated shading can be added. Some stand-alone drawing programs—such as CorelDRAW, Adobe Illustrator, and Autodesk AutoCAD—are very sophisticated and enable you to create blueprints, detailed diagrams, or even three-dimensional figures that can be rotated. Many of these programs are very expensive, but some powerful programs, such as Google SketchUp, are free (see Figure 4.9).

Painting programs enable you to create lines and shapes, but also enable you to use the pointer as a brush to create works of art. A basic painting program, Microsoft Paint, comes with the Windows operating system. Simple drawing and painting tools of this type are often used with children to help promote creativity.

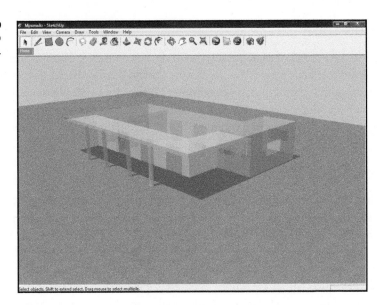

FIGURE 4.9
Google SketchUp
drawing program.

To open Microsoft Paint

1 **Click the Start button 🏐, and then click All Programs.**

2 **From the list of programs, click the Accessories folder, and then click Paint.** The Paint window opens to a blank window, as shown in Figure 4.10. You may draw in this window or import an image into the Paint program and edit it.

FIGURE 4.10
The Paint program opens
to a blank window.

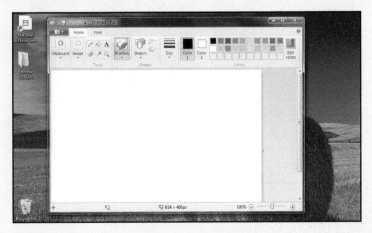

3 **Use the skills you practiced previously to start the Snipping Tool and create a Window snip of the Paint window. Save a copy of this snip to the folder where you store your files. Name the file** U1Ch04PaintStudentName **substituting your name as indicated.**

4 **Close 🗙 all windows and dialog boxes. Submit the snip as directed.**

Animation Tools

Animation is the process of making objects on the screen move. The simplest animation tools are built into other software. For example, in Microsoft PowerPoint, bulleted points can be animated to move onto the screen and then disappear, and graphic objects can be set to rotate, bounce, or move randomly across the screen. More sophisticated animation programs, such as Maya, Blender, or Adobe Flash, enable you to create the types of animated videos you might see on YouTube.

Graphic Editing Tools

The drawing and painting tools included as part of other programs typically provide very basic editing tools. These include tools for changing the contrast, color, and size of a graphic image and also enable you to *crop* an image—display only the portion of the image that you choose. More sophisticated programs, such as ArcSoft PhotoStudio, Adobe Photoshop, and Adobe Photoshop Elements, enable you to work on small portions of an image and to separate different elements of pictures into layers so that each layer can be edited separately to create sophisticated images. These programs also enable you to sharpen digital images, to bring out more detail or to blur an image, and even to move an object from one image to another. There are free graphic editing programs, such as Google Picasa, that enable you to adjust contrast and brightness, sharpen images, and organize your images, as shown in Figure 4.11.

FIGURE 4.11
Google Picasa is a simple graphic editing and organizing program.

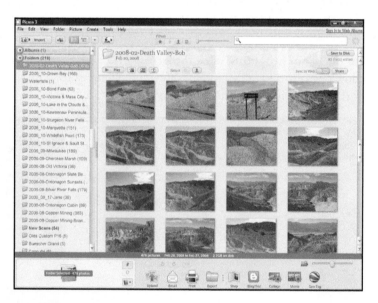

Audio and Video Software

Audio files can be inserted in files created by other applications, such as Microsoft PowerPoint, or can be played on their own using a *media player*—such as Apple QuickTime Player, RealPlayer, or Microsoft Windows Media Player—which will play audio or video files of many different formats, and enable you to organize your music, add special information to each file, and upload and download music to portable music players. To edit, download, upload, or create audio files, however, you need a special program, such as the open source Audacity or Adobe Audition. Many media players also enable you to download music from the Web and charge a nominal fee for each song downloaded.

Editing, downloading, and uploading video files also require special software, such as Adobe Premier Pro. For ease of editing, it is hard to beat Microsoft's Windows Live Movie Maker or Apple's iMovie. Windows Live Movie Maker, shown in Figure 4.12, can be downloaded free from the Microsoft website. With this software, you can drag and drop videos and pictures, add title screens and credits, and create animations between video elements. This software also enables you to organize your videos, add special information to each file, and upload and download videos to portable media players.

FIGURE 4.12
Windows Live Movie Maker
is a simple but powerful
video-editing program.

Desktop Publishing Tools

Most word processors contain rudimentary desktop publishing tools. However, if you need to create professional-looking flyers, brochures, posters, or advertisements, you will typically need to use a program designed for that purpose—a desktop publishing program. You can do basic desktop publishing using programs such as Microsoft Publisher, but if you need to do professional page layout and design, two programs—Adobe InDesign and QuarkXPress—are dominant in the field.

Gaming Software

Gaming software often requires a robust computer system, including a very good video card and monitor, a fast processor, plenty of memory, and good speakers. Games are available for individual use, for two players on the same computer, or for multiple players playing online. Recall from Chapter 2 that a special game controller is needed to play many of the popular games. Some of the interactive games use their own processor connected to a television—typically a high-definition television is recommended.

Gaming software is currently rated by the Entertainment Software Rating Board (ESRB). Its rating indicates the minimum recommended age of the audience for each game.

Virtual Reality Software

Virtual reality software is a developing three-dimensional software type that is also heavily dependent on video, audio, and other multimedia software. Virtual reality software can be used for an endless number of applications, from games to flight simulations, and from treatment of phobias to simulated travel. Most virtual reality applications require at least a headset and interactive wired gloves, and some even require a body suit that includes tactile information. Although much of the virtual reality software is still in a relatively primitive state, the recent rapid increase in computing power has made realistic virtual situations much more feasible.

Identifying File Formats

Pictures, sounds, animations, and video files can be very large, and working with them is limited by the capacity and speed of the hardware. For an image on the screen, 24 bits of data may be used to describe the color of each tiny element of the picture. If all this data is saved, the file format is called a **bitmap**, and the graphics file has the **.bmp** file extension. Using this format, a single image that fills the screen could take several megabytes of storage space, which would take several minutes to transmit over a slow Internet connection. One early method that reduced the file size by using only 8 bits of data for each picture element cut the number of possible colors to 256. This method uses *.gif* as the file extension, and files stored with this compression method are commonly known as ***Graphic Interchange Format (GIF)*** files. This method is still a good choice for images with blocks of simple colors. A more sophisticated method reduces the number of colors on a sliding scale, enabling the user to choose how much to compress the image file and to what extent to reduce the variations in color. This method uses *.jpeg* or *.jpg* file extensions and is commonly known as ***Joint Photographic Experts Group (JPEG)***. A graphic file format designed for the Web is ***Portable Network Graphics (PNG)***, which is used in newer browsers and is replacing GIF files. Files that are not compressed are called ***raw*** format.

Sound and video files face similar problems of managing file size. Four types of sound files are ***WAV***—which is uncompressed—and ***MP3***, ***AAC***, and ***WMA***—which are three of the most popular compressed formats. Video files are really a sequence of still images. Two popular compressed file formats for video files are ***QuickTime***, which uses the *.mov* file extension, and Windows media files, which use the *.wmv* extension.

Lesson 9 ▸ Identifying Other Types of Software and Their Uses

Some software programs may be used for a variety of tasks, whereas others are focused on doing one specific task well. Small programs that do one task are called ***utility programs***. Utility programs for tasks such as file compression, disk maintenance, or virus protection may be included with the operating system or provided by other companies.

Identifying Utility Programs

Most operating systems include some basic tools for maintaining a computer. These utility programs often include a disk defragmenter, similar to the one you used in Chapter 3, and file backup programs that come with the operating system or are included with external hard drives, as discussed in Chapter 3. They also often include a ***file compression program*** that reduces the disk space used by files. Some operating systems come installed with disk backup software, enabling you to regularly back up the files that you have modified. Other utility programs, such as a calculator, a calendar, a clock, and similar items, are available as gadgets in the Windows Sidebar in most versions of Windows 7, as shown in Figure 4.13.

FIGURE 4.13

The Windows Sidebar displays utility programs called *Gadgets*.

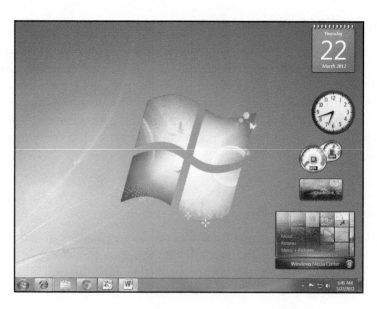

One type of utility program protects the computer from *malware*, which is a category of programs that are intended to do harm. The most common type of malware are viruses. *Virus protection software* protects your computer from malicious virus attacks, but usually must be purchased separately. Some virus protection software programs are available for free, such as Microsoft Security Essentials. *Adware protection software* helps protect you from advertising software that is installed on your computer, usually without your knowledge, and *spyware protection software* helps protect you against secretly installed software that can take partial control of your computer or intercept your messages or Internet interactions.

Identifying Integrated Software Packages

Several programs that are designed to complement each other are often sold together as a *suite*, as is the case with Microsoft Office. Some programs are referred to by one name—for example Microsoft Outlook—but are an integrated package of programs. Outlook is *personal information management (PIM)* software that handles contact information, appointments, task lists, and e-mail.

Identifying Electronic Learning Programs

Computer-supported *electronic learning (eLearning)* programs are becoming very common, especially in higher education. If you are taking this course online, you are probably using a *course management system*, such as eCollege, Blackboard, or Moodle. These programs deliver information such as a syllabus, lectures, assignments, a glossary, and links to other sites. Course management systems also offer a drop box to submit assignments, provide a grade book and chat room, and offer several other features; in many cases, students can take these courses entirely online, without ever attending a face-to-face class.

Many other software products are used to supplement classes. Podcasts are used to deliver information, conferencing programs enable students to participate in class discussions on a variety of topics, and *computer-based training (CBT)* is used to teach individual skills. Chat rooms, instant messaging, and even e-mail are used for class interaction.

Identifying Other Software Programs

There are many other types of programs that do one task well, including the following:

- Accounting software is used to manage the financial information for a business or for an individual.
- Income tax software helps a person fill out federal and state income tax forms and submit tax returns electronically.
- A Web browser enables people to surf the Internet, store and retrieve information, and sign up for special services such as online auctions and social networking sites.
- Web page authoring software helps create Web pages with advanced features, and then posts the pages to a Web server.
- Electronic mail (e-mail) software enables you to interact with friends, colleagues, and others.
- Project management software tracks and organizes complex tasks such as constructing a building or creating a business plan with others.
- Chat and instant messaging software enable you to interact with friends, relatives, and people with similar interests.
- Computer aided design (CAD) programs enable you to create two- and three-dimensional renderings.

- Web conferencing programs enable you to conduct meetings or make presentations over the Web.
- Collaborative software, also known as groupware programs, often consists of a bundle of other programs and enable a group of people to complete a job.

Programs designed to perform one function on a smartphone or tablet computer are simply called *apps*.

Identifying Custom Software Programs

Some applications require solutions that are not addressed by commercially available software, in which case programmers can create a program to meet a client's specifications. This may be the case if a company wants to offer services that are new in order to gain a market advantage. For example, the software used to manage PayPal did not exist; programmers had to write the software to manage sales and money transfer. The same would hold true for airline reservation software (see Figure 4.14), book inventory and sale software for a company like Amazon, the software used to operate a robot arm in a manufacturing plant, industrial quality control, or school information systems.

FIGURE 4.14
Specialized software is used to manage airline reservations.

David K. Crow / PhotoEdit Inc.

How Do You Feel About It?

FLY BY WIRE

When airplanes became too large to control by muscle power alone, or even with the help of hydraulic assistance, electric motors were used. This practice was called *fly by wire*. Many modern automobiles now use fly by wire technologies in which the steering wheel and gas and brake pedals are simple inputs into a computer. Mercedes developed a car that doesn't even have a steering wheel! Do you think a child who is learning to drive for the first time would be more comfortable driving a car that had a joystick or a game controller instead of a steering wheel? Do you think you could switch from a steering wheel with pedals to a joystick? How do you feel about trusting the computer entirely to control a car's speed and steering?

Identifying How to Select Software

Choosing software is similar to the process described earlier for choosing a computer. You start by identifying the tasks you want the computer to do, and then you look for software that can do the task. However, it is not always easy to tell which software is appropriate.

Identifying the Appropriate Software When Several Programs Perform Similar Tasks

If you have tables of data, it may not be apparent which software to use to manipulate the data, because word processing programs use tables, but so do spreadsheets and databases. You need to refer to the descriptions of each type of software provided earlier in this chapter and decide what kind of data is in the tables and how you want to use it. In general, a table in Word is used to provide information along with the text. If the data includes numbers and some cells of the table are calculated values using the contents of other cells, spreadsheet software such as Excel is a better choice. If you have large quantities of data that need to be available to numerous users at the same time, database software such as Access is the best choice.

Identifying Common Incorrect Uses of Software

Spreadsheet programs have some database management features, such as sorting and filtering, and the transition to database management software usually requires training. As a result, many people try to use their spreadsheet program to query data and produce reports. This is best performed in a database management program, especially when the size of the tables becomes large. Another common error is trying to use a table in a word processing program as if it were a spreadsheet. Word processing programs can sort a table and calculate a total for the bottom of a column, but they do not recalculate when a number is changed, which can result in errors. If necessary, you can move data between Excel and Word to take advantage of the strengths of each program.

Summary

You learned how to identify types of hardware and software interactions and how to make rules for the computer to follow. You learned about the software development process and how it produces different versions of the software. You also learned about the role of updates and upgrades to keep your software up to date.

You learned about the basic concepts and uses of word processing, spreadsheet, presentation, database, multimedia, and other types of software. You also learned about choosing between applications that appear to be similar and about some common mistakes people make by using software for the wrong task.

You can extend your learning by reviewing concepts and terms and by practicing variations of skills presented in the lessons.

Key Terms

AAC *(p. 140)*

adware protection software *(p. 141)*

alpha version *(p. 126)*

animation *(p. 138)*

app *(p. 142)*

application service provider (ASP) *(p. 128)*

beta tester *(p. 126)*

beta version *(p. 126)*

bitmap (.bmp) *(p. 139)*

blog (Web log) *(p. 132)*

bug *(p. 126)*

cell reference *(p. 132)*

command *(p. 123)*

computer-based training (CBT) *(p. 141)*

course management system *(p. 141)*

crop *(p. 138)*

database *(p. 134)*

database management system (DBMS) *(p. 135)*

debugging *(p. 126)*

desktop publishing *(p. 131)*

document *(p. 131)*

edit *(p. 131)*

electronic learning (eLearning) *(p. 141)*

End User License Agreement (EULA) *(p. 127)*

field *(p. 134)*

file compression program *(p. 140)*

filter *(p. 133)*

font *(p. 131)*

form *(p. 134)*

format *(p. 131)*

formula *(p. 132)*

function *(p. 132)*

gold version *(p. 126)*

Graphic Interchange Format (GIF) *(p. 140)*

handout *(p. 134)*

Hypertext Markup Language (HTML) *(p. 132)*

insertion point *(p. 123)*

installation *(p. 127)*

Joint Photographic Experts Group (JPEG) *(p. 140)*

malware *(p. 141)*

media player *(p. 138)*

MP3 (.mp3) *(p. 140)*

network license *(p. 127)*

nondisclosure agreement *(p. 126)*

patch *(p. 128)*

personal information management (PIM) *(p. 141)*

Portable Network Graphics (PNG) *(p. 140)*

primary key field *(p. 134)*

programming *(p. 126)*

query *(p. 135)*

QuickTime (.mov) *(p. 140)*

raw *(p. 140)*

readme *(p. 127)*

record *(p. 134)*

reinstall *(p. 127)*

relational database *(p. 135)*

release to manufacturing (RTM) *(p. 126)*

report *(p. 135)*

seat *(p. 127)*

service pack *(p. 128)*

site license *(p. 127)*

slide *(p. 133)*

slide master *(p. 133)*

slide show *(p. 134)*

software *(p. 123)*

speaker notes *(p. 134)*

spreadsheet *(p. 132)*

spyware protection software *(p. 141)*

suite *(p. 141)*

table *(p. 134)*

update *(p. 128)*

upgrade *(p. 128)*

utility program *(p. 140)*

virus protection software *(p. 141)*

WAV (.wav) *(p. 140)*

Web log (blog) *(p. 132)*

what-if analysis *(p. 133)*

WMA *(p. 140)*

WMV (.wmv) *(p. 140)*

word processing *(p. 131)*

workbook *(p. 132)*

worksheet *(p. 132)*

Checking Concepts and Terms

MULTIPLE CHOICE

Circle the letter of the correct answer for each of the following.

1. Database information is stored in which of the following? [L8]

    a. Reports

    b. Forms

    c. Queries

    d. Tables

2. Fixing a software problem is often called which of the following? [L2]

    a. Conflict resolution

    b. Centering

    c. Debugging

    d. Harboring

3. A person who uses early versions of software during the development process to find errors is which of the following? [L2]

    a. Guinea pig

    b. Freebie

    c. Beta tester

    d. Newbie

4. Which of the following software changes usually costs money? [L3]

    a. Patch

    b. Upgrade

    c. Update

    d. Service release

5. Which of the following is most likely to be a benefit of an upgrade? [L3]

    a. New features

    b. Less training time

    c. Lower cost

    d. Lower hardware requirements

6. Which of the following types of software would be appropriate for keeping monthly customer bill payment records at a credit card company? [L7]

    a. Word processing

    b. Spreadsheet

    c. Presentation

    d. Database

7. Which of the following types of software would be appropriate for writing a memo? [L4]

    a. Word processing

    b. Spreadsheet

    c. Presentation

    d. Database

8. Which of the following types of software would be appropriate for accounting? [L5]

    a. Word processing

    b. Spreadsheet

    c. Presentation

    d. Database

9. Which of the following types of software would be appropriate for communicating ideas at a meeting? [L6]

    a. Word processing

    b. Spreadsheet

    c. Presentation

    d. Database

10. Which of the following is a common mistake in matching the correct software to a task? [L10]

    a. Using an e-mail program to communicate with other people

    b. Using a table in a word processing program to analyze financial information with calculations

    c. Using a database to prepare reports

    d. Using JPEG file compression on large image files

MATCHING

Match each term in the second column with its correct definition in the first column by writing the letter of the term on the blank line in front of the definition.

_____ **1.** A group of different programs bundled together [L9]

_____ **2.** A minor change to software that is usually free [L3]

_____ **3.** A type of uncompressed sound file [L8]

_____ **4.** A Web log [L4]

_____ **5.** The end version of beta testing that gets sent to the manufacturer [L2]

_____ **6.** In a presentation, the place where default fonts, colors, and backgrounds are identified [L6]

_____ **7.** The process of identifying and fixing errors in program code [L2]

_____ **8.** To display only the information that meets your criteria [L5]

_____ **9.** In a spreadsheet, a built-in formula [L5]

_____ **10.** In a database, the field with unique values [L7]

A. Blog

B. Debugging

C. Filter

D. Function

E. Primary key field

F. RTM

G. Slide master

H. Suite

I. Update

J. WAV

Skill Drill

Skill Drill exercises reinforce chapter skills. Each skill reinforced is the same, or nearly the same, as a skill presented in the chapter. Detailed instructions are provided in a step-by-step format.

Each exercise is independent of the others, so you can do the exercises in any order.

1. Finding Versions of Windows

Information about the version of software may flash on the screen briefly while a program is starting, but if you want to find it again, you have to know where to look. The version of Windows 7 and the build number are not in an obvious place.

To find the version and build number of your copy of Windows 7, follow these steps:

1. Click the **Start** button, and then click **Control Panel**.

2. In the **Control Panel**, be sure **Small icons** view is selected, and then click **Administrative Tools**.

3. In the **Administrative Tools** window, double-click **System Configuration**.

4. In the **System Configuration** dialog box, click the **Tools** tab. Click the **About Windows** option, if necessary, and then click the **Launch** button. Notice that the operating system name, version number, and Service Pack number appear in a new window.

5. Use the skills you practiced previously to start the **Snipping Tool** and create a **Window** snip of the **About Windows** window. Save a copy of this snip to the folder where you store your files. Name the file U1Ch04WindowsStudentName substituting your name as indicated.

6. Close all windows.

7. Submit the snip as directed.

2. Copying a Formula in Excel

Formulas in Excel use references to other cells that are stored in terms of relative position to the currently selected cell. If you copy a formula and paste it into another cell, the specific cell references change, but the relative positions of the new cell references remain the same. This is a software feature of Excel that neither Word nor Access can match and is one of the reasons Excel is so useful when working with numbers.

To copy a formula into another cell and observe how it changes cell references, follow these steps:

1. Click the **Start** button. Point to **All Programs**. Locate and click the **Microsoft Office** folder, and then locate and click **Microsoft Office Excel**. A blank worksheet opens. Cell A1 is selected by default.

2. Type 15 and press ⏎Enter. The selection moves down to cell A2.

3. Type 7 and press ⏎Enter. The selection moves down to cell A3.

4. Type =A1-A2 and press ⏎Enter. Cell A3 should display **8**, which is 15 minus 7. This formula is stored as an instruction to work with the two cells immediately above the currently selected cell. If you do not get this result, click cell A3 and type the formula again. Be sure to use the dash as a minus sign.

5. Click cell **B1**, type 23, and press ⏎Enter. The selection moves to B2.

6. Type 10 and press ⏎Enter.

7. Click cell **A3**. On the Ribbon, on the left end of the **Home** tab, in the **Clipboard** group, click the **Copy** button. The formula is copied.

8. Click cell **B3**. On the Ribbon, on the left end of the **Home** tab, in the **Clipboard** group, click the **Paste** button. The formula is pasted into cell **B3**. The new formula works with the two cells immediately above cell B3.

9. Double-click cell **B3**. The formula displays. It should be **=B1-B2**.

10. Use the skills you practiced previously to start the **Snipping Tool** and create a **Window** snip of the **Excel** window. Save a copy of this snip to the folder where you store your files. Name the file U1Ch04ExcelStudentName substituting your name as indicated.

11. In the upper-right corner of the Excel window, click the **Close** button. Click **Don't Save** when prompted to save changes. Close the Snipping Tool.

12. Submit the snip as directed.

3. Looking for Updates in Windows 7

Writing software is a continuous process that does not end when the product is released. Changes and improvements are made that may be added to your existing copy of the software.

To look for free updates that may be downloaded from Microsoft's website, follow these steps:

1. Click the **Start** button, click **All Programs**, and then locate and click **Windows Update**.

2. In the left pane of the **Windows Update** window, click **Check for updates**. The program will take a while to analyze your Windows installation and determine what updates are necessary for your computer.

3. Use the skills you practiced previously to start the **Snipping Tool** and create a **Window** snip of the **Windows Update** window. Save a copy of this snip to the folder where you store your files. Name the file U1Ch04UpdateStudentName substituting your name as indicated.

4. If you are using your own computer and you wish to install updates, click the **Install updates** button. This may take several minutes and may require you to reboot your computer.

5. Use the **Close** button to close all open windows.

6. Submit the snip as directed.

Explore and Share

Explore and Share questions are intended for discussion in class or online. Look for information that is related to the learning outcomes for this chapter as directed. Submit your answers as directed by your instructor.

1. Microsoft provides guidelines for creating an effective PowerPoint presentation. Open PowerPoint, click the Help button on the right side of the Ribbon, and then in the Search box, type presentation tips. Read through these tips. Have you been in a meeting where the speaker used presentation software? Did the use of the presentation software help or distract from the speaker's presentation? Give examples, using the presentation tips you found in Help. [L6]

2. If you had to use a typewriter instead of a computer, what would the biggest differences be? If you have never used a typewriter, find one and try to type a paragraph to see what it is like, and then tell the group about it. [L4]

3. Use your Web browser to find further information on *beta testing* or *software testing*. If you were offered a chance to be a beta tester on a new version of Microsoft Office, would you participate? Why or why not? If you were offered a chance to be a beta tester for a new version of the Microsoft operating system, would you participate? Why or why not? If your answer is different from the one you gave for Microsoft Office, why would you participate in one and not the other? [L2]

In Your Life

In Your Life questions are intended for discussion in class or online where you can share your personal experience. Restrict your answers to the topics described in each exercise. Submit your answers as directed by your instructor.

1. In this chapter, you learned how to apply a software rule in Word. If you wanted to create a rule for your e-mail software to use that would block unwanted mail, what would you tell the software to look for? Would you want the blocker to simply not allow the unwanted e-mail at all, or would you want it to put the e-mail all together in a special "blocked e-mail" folder? [L1]

2. An engineer once said, "I use my spreadsheet program for everything. If I need a word processor, I set the width of column A to the width of the page and format the first cell to wrap text and away I go." What do you think of this attitude? [L10]

3. Describe other types of software you have used that are not mentioned in this project. [L9]

Related Skills

Related Skills exercises expand on or are somewhat related to skills presented in the lessons. The exercises provide a brief narrative introduction, followed by instructions in a numbered-step format that are not as detailed as those in the Skill Drill section.

1. Learning About Microsoft Office Live

Microsoft has recently decided to offer Microsoft Office in a different format, through a product called Microsoft Office Live Workspace. Using this program, you can access your files from anywhere, using a Web browser.

To learn about the reasons you might want to use Microsoft Office Live Workspace, follow these steps:

1. Start Internet Explorer or your favorite Web browser. In the address line, type http://office.live.com and press ⏎Enter.

2. Explore the Products menu and other links to learn about the options for accessing files online from a variety of devices. Click the **OneDrive** link to read about Microsoft's Web applications.

3. Use the skills you practiced previously to start the **Snipping Tool** and create a **Window** snip of the On**OneDrive** window. Save a copy of this snip to the folder where you store your files. Name the file U1Ch04OneDriveStudentName substituting your name as indicated. These Web pages change frequently. If you do not see a page titled Office Web Apps, search for links that take you to pages related to the use of Word or Excel as online programs.

4. In the upper-right corner of the browser window, click the **Close** button, and then submit your snip as directed.

2. Checking Your Installation Discs for Readme Files

Software programmers usually include *readme* files on most installation discs because they make changes after the manuals go to the printer. Place the Office installation disc or the installation disc from another program in your CD drive. (Note: If the program attempts to automatically install itself, cancel the installation.) Click the **Start** button, and then click **Computer**. Click the disc drive that has your installation CD in it. If necessary, right-click the drive and then click Open. In the upper-right corner of the Computer window, click in the **Search box**, and then type readme (If no readme files display, in the **Content** pane, click **Advanced Search**, and then select the hard drive **C:** and search again.)

A list of files with *readme* as part of the file name are displayed. Double-click one of the files to read it. Read a few of them, and then write a description of the kinds of things that are included in these files. Use the skills you practiced previously to start the **Snipping Tool** and create a **Window** snip of one of the **Readme** windows. Save a copy of this snip to the folder where you store your files. Name the file U1Ch04ReadmeStudentName substituting your name as indicated. Submit your snip as directed.

3. Installing Optional Programs from Windows Essentials

In addition to Windows Live Movie Maker, several other programs are available for free download. To review the free programs for Windows at Windows Essentials, follow these steps:

1. Start Internet Explorer or your favorite Web browser. In the address line, type http://windows.microsoft.com/en-US/windows-live/essential and press ⏎Enter. The **Windows Essentials** page opens.

2. Read the information on the page, and when you are finished, if necessary click **Other Programs**, and then click **Learn More**. Optional programs related to e-mail, family safety, and synchronizing files on several computers are available.

3. Click the **Overview** tab and read about each free program. Use the skills you practiced previously to start the **Snipping Tool** and create a **Window** snip of the **Overview** window. Save a copy of this snip to the folder where you store your files. Name the file U1Ch04EssentialsStudentName substituting your name as indicated.

4. **Close** all windows, and then submit the snip as directed.

Discover

Discover exercises give you general directions for exploring and discovering more advanced skills and information. Each exercise is independent of the others, so you may complete the exercises in any order.

1. Learning About the Speech Recognition and Voice Synthesis Features in Windows 7

Computers can recognize speech and convert text into speech. This feature is available as part of Windows 7, but it is often not installed.

From the **Start** menu, open the **Control Panel**. Be sure **Small icons** view is selected. Click **Speech Recognition**. Examine the steps involved in setting up speech recognition.

Locate and click the *Open the Speech Reference Card* link. Read how you would give verbal commands to the computer that would do the same thing as clicking with the mouse.

Write a one- to two-page essay on how you would set up speech recognition on your computer and how you might use it. Submit it as directed.

2. Learning About Audio Compression

Audio compression methods have made it possible to exchange audio files conveniently over the Internet, which has had a dramatic effect on the sale of music CDs. Video compression techniques may have a similar effect on video sales in the future.

To learn more about audio compression, use your Web browser and go to the following sites to read about this topic.

- Wikipedia, the Free Encyclopedia: **en.wikipedia.org/wiki/Audio_data_compression**

- HowStuffWorks.com: **computer.howstuffworks.com/mp3.htm**

- The Beginner's Guide to Compression: **audio.tutsplus.com/tutorials/mixing-mastering/the-beginners-guide-to-compression**

Write three paragraphs that describe what you learn about audio compression from each of these sites. Submit them as directed.

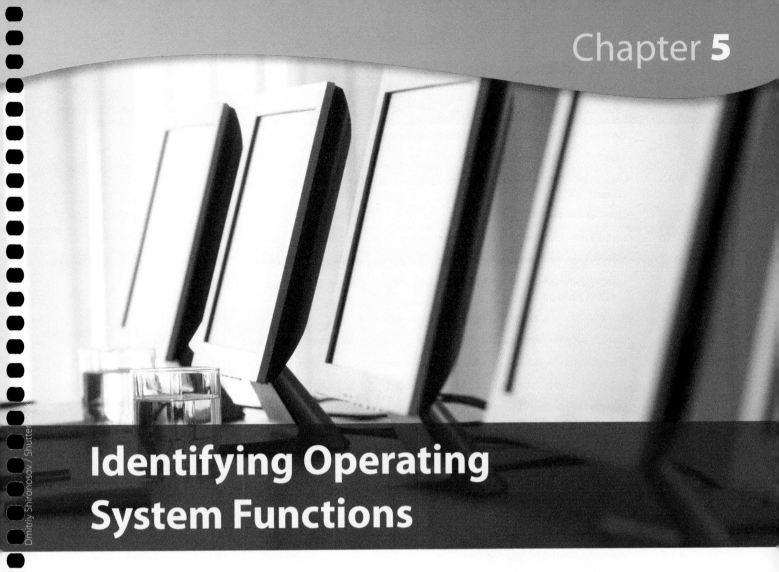

Chapter 5

Dmitriy Shironosov / Shutter...

Identifying Operating System Functions

Why Would I Do This?

The operating system controls the computing environment in which you work. It enables you to change display settings such as the screen resolution, desktop image, or screen saver. It also enables you to install or delete programs and hardware. You need to know the benefits and limitations of the operating system to make the best use of your computer.

Chapter at a Glance

Lesson	Learning Outcomes	Page Number	Related IC3 Objectives
1	Identify the difference between operating system and application software	155	1.1.1
1	Identify types of operating systems	155	1.1.2, 4.1.2
1	Identify the difference between character-based, GUI, and natural user operating systems	157	1.1.2
1	Use multiple operating systems	157	1.1.0, 4.3.1
2	Identify limitations imposed by the operating system—file names	158	1.2.0
2	Identify limitations imposed by the operating system—application software	159	1.1.4
2	Identify common operating system problems—corrupted files and restore previous condition	159	4.4.0
2	Identify common operating system problems—security	159	1.3.6
2	Identify common operating system problems—unusual hardware combinations	160	4.2.0
2	Identify common operating system problems—improper logon procedures	160	4.0.0
3	Open the Control Panel and change visual options	161	1.3.1
3	Identify the purposes and consequences of changing system settings including date, time, and language	162	1.3.1
3	Identify how centrally managed computer networks restrict setting changes using groups with access and editing rights	163	1.3.6
3	Identify commonly used Control Panel categories	163	1.3.1
3	View Control Panel categories: Programs, Network and Internet, System and Security, and Ease of Access	163	1.3.1
4	Use the Control Panel to change the time and date	166	1.3.1
4	Identify examples of date and time	168	1.3.1
4	Change display settings—monitors	169	1.3.1
4	Change display settings—appearance	169	1.3.1
4	Change display settings—power options	170	1.3.1
4	Change display settings—desktop and themes	171	1.3.1
4	Use the Control Panel to change the desktop background image	171	1.3.1
4	Change audio volume, mouse, and keyboard settings	171	1.3.1
4	Use the Control Panel to mute or unmute the speakers	171	1.3.1
4	Use the Control Panel to display and install printers	172	4.3.3
5	Use the Control Panel to manage user accounts and rights	172	1.3.6
5	Identify default installation options	173	1.3.6
5	Use the Control Panel to install, update, uninstall, or add features to software	173	3.1.1
5	Start installed programs	174	3.1.1
5	Subscribe to an online application	176	3.0.0
6	Identify installation problems—lack of permission and security settings	176	4.1.0
6	Identify installation problems—partially uninstalled programs	177	4.1.0
6	Identify installation problems—damaged or lost installation discs	177	4.1.0
6	Identify installation problems—reinstalling registered software	177	3.1.3

Chapter at a Glance

Lesson	Learning Outcomes	Page Number	Related IC3 Objectives
6	Identify installation problems—installation program does not start automatically	177	4.1.0
6	Identify installation problems—installation stops	178	4.1.0
6	Identify installation problems—conflicts with other programs	178	4.1.0
6	Identify software and firmware problems	178	4.1.0, 4.2.1, 4.3.2
6	Use Safe Mode to access the Control Panel to restore the system	179	4.1.4
6	Identify methods of backing up software and files and managing versions	180	4.4.1. 4.4.2, 4.4.3, 4.4.4

Visual Summary

In this chapter, you will learn about the features and limitations of operating systems. Some of the features can be accessed through the Control Panel, as shown in Figure 5.1. The operating system used in this project is Windows 7.

FIGURE 5.1
Windows 7 Control Panel has options for customizing the operating system.

List of Student Files

In most cases, you will create files using the Windows snipping tool. You will add your name to the file names and save them on your computer or portable memory device. Table 5.1 lists the files you start with and the names you give them when you save the files.

TABLE 5.1	ASSIGNMENT:	STUDENT SOURCE FILE:	SAVE AS:
	Lessons 1–6	none	U1Ch05DOSStudentName
			U1Ch05UpdateStudentName
			U1Ch05IconsStudentName
			U1Ch05ControlStudentName
			U1Ch05TimeStudentName
			U1Ch05BackgroundStudentName
			U1Ch05MuteStudentName
			U1Ch05AnalysisStudentName
	Skill Drill	none	U1Ch05BackupStudentName
			U1Ch05RestoreStudentName
			U1Ch05DetailsStudentName
	Explore and Share	none	none
	In Your Life	none	none
	Related Skills	none	U1Ch05NISTStudentName
			U1Ch05ResolutionStudentName
			U1Ch05StartStudentName
	Discover	none	none

Identifying the Purpose and Functions of an Operating System

The *operating system*, often referred to as the *OS*, is a type of software program that determines how the processor interacts with the user and system components, including the way information is displayed on the screen, how it is printed, and how the mouse works. It also controls how data is written on disks and provides a group of common functions that other programs can use. Manufacturers of peripherals such as printers provide small programs called *drivers* that are used by the operating system to manage communications between the computer and the components.

Identifying the Difference Between Operating System Software and Application Software

The operating system provides the computing environment in which the application software functions. For example, it provides the program used to display a window on the screen. The Minimize, Maximize, Restore Down, and Close buttons, as well as scroll bars, activate programs that exist in the operating system. An *application program*—such as a word processor, a spreadsheet, or a photo-editing program—makes use of the programs in the operating system every time it uses a window, stores a document in RAM, or saves a file. An operating system, combined with a particular family of processors, makes up a *platform*. This provides an environment in which application programs function. Intel has become the dominant designer of processors for personal computers; other manufacturers, such as AMD, make Intel-compatible processors. Windows/Intel, Apple/Intel, and Linux/Intel are examples of common platforms on desktop and portable computers.

Identifying Types of Operating Systems

Operating systems are optimized to help application software use the computer hardware. Hardware limitations of size, capacity, and computing power require different types of operating systems.

Mainframe Operating Systems

Companies that make computers for use by large organizations often supply operating system software along with the computer to provide a complete platform. Consequently, there are many different operating systems available for organizational computers, such as OS/390 or Z/OS from *International Business Machines (IBM)*. An early effort to provide a common operating system that would run on a variety of organizational computers resulted in *UNIX*, which originated in Bell Labs in 1969. UNIX is still popular because of its simplicity, stability, and security.

Personal Computer Operating Systems

When personal computers became available in the 1970s, they did not have enough memory or processor power to use UNIX. A smaller and simpler operating system was needed.

DOS

When IBM decided to make a PC, it recognized the need to bring a machine to market in less time than it would need to develop an entire system. It chose to design a personal computer that could be assembled from parts made by other manufacturers and to hire a small company named Microsoft to develop the operating system. Because the operating system could be stored on a disk and loaded into RAM when the computer started, the operating system was called the **Disk Operating System (DOS)**. Microsoft agreed to the project, but retained the option of selling the operating system to other PC manufacturers. The operating system was known as *PC-DOS* on IBM personal computers and *MS-DOS* on other brands of personal computers.

To run a command from the DOS prompt

1 **Click the Start button 🕮, and then click All Programs.**

2 **From the Start menu, click Accessories, and then click Command Prompt.** The Command window displays, showing the DOS prompt.

3 **At the blinking cursor, type** Dir C:\ **and then press** ⏎Enter. A directory of folders on your main hard drive displays, as shown in Figure 5.2.

FIGURE 5.2
The Command window.

4 **Use the skills you practiced previously to start the Snipping Tool and create a Window snip of the Command window. Save a copy of this snip to the folder where you store your files. Name the file** U1Ch05DOSStudentName **substituting your name as indicated.**

5 **In the Command window, click the Close button 🗙. Submit the snip as directed.**

Graphical User Interface

Apple computers popularized the **graphical user interface (GUI)** in its operating system in 1984, and Microsoft followed with Windows in 1990. Since the release of Windows 3.1, nearly all desktop and portable computers have used a GUI environment, which includes dialog boxes, windows, toolbars, icons, menus, and other graphical elements that the user controls with a mouse or keyboard. A graphical user interface displays a document on-screen the same way it will look when printed. The use of familiar icons that perform the same function in a variety of application programs makes the GUI easy to use. The three popular operating systems that were described in Chapter 3—Windows, Apple, and Linux—are all examples of operating systems that use GUIs.

Programming an operating system that uses a graphical user interface is far more complex than programming an operating system that uses a text-based interface. The first version of DOS used about 4,000 lines of programming code, whereas early versions of Windows used around 4 million lines of code. Red Hat Linux now uses about 30 million lines of code, Windows 7 uses about 50 million lines of code, and the current Mac OS uses an estimated 80 million lines of code.

Touch Screen Tablet Computers

Most portable computers use the same operating systems as desktop computers. Some portable computers have screens that pivot and fold flat for use as tablets. The user can write on the screen with a stylus or a fingertip. Newer versions of traditional operating systems such as Windows 8 have the ability to work with this type of hardware. Apple popularized the tablet format with the iPad. The iPad and iPhone have a natural user interface that interprets finger motions on the screen along with voice commands and tilting of the device.

Smartphones and Cell Phones

Smartphones and some cell phones are becoming multifunction computers that can take pictures, surf the Internet, exchange e-mail, manage address books, update calendars, and open some application files, such as word processing documents and spreadsheets. Smartphones and tablets need different operating systems to handle the natural user interface, digital video, satellite connections, and cell phone connections. Examples of smartphone operating systems are *iOS* from Apple, *Android* from Google, and *Windows Phone* from Microsoft. These operating systems are combined with processors from several different manufacturers that are compatible with each OS to make platforms.

Embedded Operating Systems

An *embedded operating system* is an operating system that is used in computer appliances and special-purpose applications, such as a car, an ATM, a portable media player, a computer router, or another piece of machinery that contains a microprocessor. Embedded operating systems tend to be compact, efficient, and often single-purpose. If you are driving an automobile and using an MP3 player plugged into an MP3 jack in your car, you are using two different embedded operating systems that are working together.

Identifying the Difference Between Command-Line Interface and GUI Operating Systems

A *command-line interface (CLI)* is a way of interacting with the operating system using the keyboard. The best known of these are DOS and UNIX. The Windows operating system is compatible with DOS and, as you saw earlier, still contains the DOS Command prompt as an option. A character-based OS does not use a mouse but instead relies on the keyboard for input. The GUI interface has become the standard for computing, yet some knowledge of DOS is still useful for troubleshooting problems with Windows. DOS is small enough to fit on a flash drive; you can boot a computer from the CD/DVD drive or a flash drive if Windows is damaged and the hard drive is disabled.

Using Multiple Operating Systems

In some cases, you may be using two or more operating systems and not even be aware of it. If you connect your iPhone to a Macintosh or an Android smartphone to a personal computer running Windows 7, you are using two operating systems at the same time. The operating systems contain instructions that enable the two operating systems to work with each other. If you are working on a network, you may be working with a third operating system on the server.

Lesson 2

Identifying Capabilities, Limitations, and Common Problems

Recall that the operating system, combined with a particular family of processors, makes up a platform. Some platforms are optimized for certain tasks at the expense of other features. Platforms from Apple are well known for the strength of their graphics and audio features, but they have not maintained backward compatibility with older platforms. Apple maintains close control of the software and hardware components. Although this provides the opportunity for better consistency, it also limits the number of options for third-party hardware and software vendors.

The Windows platforms are backwardly compatible and will even run some programs written for DOS. They are open to a variety of competitive makers of hardware and software, but due to the dominant market position of Windows and Microsoft Office software, many third-party vendors find it hard to compete. Linux—an open-source operating system—is relatively new to the desktop computer, and there are fewer fellow users upon whose experience you can rely for help with problems. Because it can be used for free on desktops and inexpensively for businesses, Linux is a favorite operating system for Web page servers.

Identifying Limitations Imposed by the Operating System

Some limitations of the operating system are due to the limitations of the hardware it works with. Other limitations are due to the differences between operating systems.

File Names

The operating system controls the process of writing files to storage. The early DOS naming convention required a file name of eight characters or fewer, followed by a period, plus a *file extension* of up to three characters. This is known as the *8.3 convention*. In this file name convention, differences in capitalization are ignored and no spaces are allowed in the name. Underscore characters are commonly used in file names to provide the appearance of spaces. Most special characters like *&* and # are not allowed.

Mainframe operating systems like UNIX allow longer file names, and capitalization matters, which is also true for its offspring, Linux. Underscore characters are also used in file names to provide the appearance of spaces.

Windows allows long file names with up to 255 characters that include spaces, but it still typically uses three- or four-letter file extensions to identify types of files. Mixes of capital and lowercase letters are allowed, and the program can often find the correct file if you do not capitalize the file name correctly. Most Web servers use software like UNIX or Linux that consider capitalized file names as completely different from the same names in lowercase, so it is common practice to avoid the use of spaces and capital letters in file names that will be used on the Web, even if you are working in Windows.

Mac OS allows long file names, but its application files do not always use file extensions. Files created on a Mac may be in the correct format for use on another platform, but the user may need to add the correct file extension so that the type of file is recognized on a Windows platform.

Application Software

Application software is written to work with a particular platform. This compatibility issue was discussed in the previous chapter on choosing a computer because it is a significant limitation. To overcome this limitation, leading software makers are using a new method of saving files that uses *Extensible Markup Language (XML)*. Like HTML, which made it easy for different platforms to display the same Web page, XML is a language used to store files as simple text along with information on how the application software should interpret the text. Competing application software like Microsoft Office, WordPerfect Office, and OpenOffice write separate versions for major operating systems like Windows, Apple, and Linux. Some of them read each other's proprietary file formats, but all of the newer versions can save their files as XML files for easier file exchange.

Identifying Common Operating System Problems

An operating system is complex software that enables a wide variety of hardware and software to work together. However, unusual combinations of tasks, software, and hardware may occur that programmers did not anticipate that can cause malfunctions. Bugs in the operating system can be minor annoyances or they can halt production. Fortunately, some of the most common problems are becoming easier to fix.

Corrupted Files

The operating system is a set of files that reside on the hard drive. If some of the code in these files is erased or damaged, the OS, or one of its functions, may not work properly. Symptoms of OS problems include freezing, error messages, and extremely slow operation. Some virus programs intentionally erase or damage the OS files. Recent versions of operating systems like Windows 7 make periodic copies of themselves to serve as backups.

If the system starts working erratically, and a simple restart does not solve the problem, you can choose a feature called *system restore*, which enables you to undo changes to the operating system and switch it back to one of the previous states. Many computers come with discs that have OS files on them, which may be copied onto the hard drive if necessary to repair or replace damaged files.

Security

The operating system manages the computer's interaction with other computers, and it has certain security features built in to prevent unauthorized users or automated programs from gaining access to the files. If a way is discovered to circumvent the security features of the OS, the manufacturer will change the design to prevent further intrusions and will publish an update. You can set your computer to check for new updates and install them automatically or to notify you when they become available.

To set the Windows Update

① **Click the Start button** 📀. The Start menu displays.

② **On the Start menu, click All Programs, and then locate and click Windows Update.** The Windows Update window opens.

③ **In the left pane of the Windows Update window, click Change settings.** The Change settings dialog box displays. You can download updates automatically on a daily or weekly basis, and you can set the time of the download, as shown in Figure 5.3.

FIGURE 5.3
Windows Updates.

④ **Use the skills you practiced previously to start the Snipping Tool and create a window snip of the Control Panel window. Save a copy of this snip to the folder where you store your files. Name the file** U1Ch05UpdateStudentName **substituting your name as indicated.**

⑤ **Close** ❌ **the Change settings window. Close the Snipping Tool. Submit the snip as directed.**

Unusual Hardware Combinations

Systems such as Windows that are intended for use with a wide variety of hardware and software from independent manufacturers cannot require that all of them write their programs and drivers to work well with each other. Because there are innumerable combinations of hardware and software, it is inevitable that some of them may not work together. If the operation of a device or software causes a malfunction, Windows will request permission to report this problem over the Internet to the home office, where the report will be compared with those collected from other users to look for patterns. An update will be issued that may not be listed as critical but is important for those who use certain devices or combinations of devices.

Improper Logon Procedures

If the computer is used by more than one person, the operating system can be set to require each person to identify him- or herself. Normally, this involves providing a user name and a password. Some operating systems require that you change your password regularly and, if you forget, you may not be able to gain access. Most operating systems require that the password match the one it has on record exactly, including capitalization and spaces. Mainframe computer operating systems have used passwords and logon procedures from the beginning, and they are required when you use your PC to access a network or the Internet.

Windows gives you the option of setting up several users on a PC who may not have access to all possible privileges. If you choose this option, someone is required to take on the role of **administrator**. When you log in as administrator, you can add or delete other users and make significant changes, such as adding and deleting software. However, if you forget the administrator's password, you may not be able to perform these functions. Unfortunately, this problem is not easy to fix if the administrator's password is completely forgotten or lost. If you choose to use this feature of Windows, be sure to record the administrator's user name and password in a safe location or to designate more than one person as administrator.

Lesson 3 ▸ # Identifying Functions of the Control Panel

Operating systems can be customized to work with a variety of hardware and software components. They can also be customized to meet the preferences of individual users. The Windows operating system uses a program called the **Control Panel** to organize these choices. The Control Panel provides a group of options that sets default values for the Windows operating system. Windows 7 is used for these lessons. If you have a different version of Windows, your screens may differ in some respects from those shown.

To open the Control Panel and change views

① **Click the Start button** **.** The Start menu displays.

② **On the right side of the Start menu, click Control Panel.** The Control Panel window opens. The section at the top of the window is the *title bar*.

③ **Double-click the Title bar, if necessary, to maximize the window. At the top-right of the window, click the View by arrow, and then select Category from the menu.** The Control Panel window is maximized. In this view, Windows groups the options into categories, as shown in Figure 5.4.

FIGURE 5.4
Control Panel: Categories.

④ **Click the View by arrow, and then click Small icons.** A more detailed list of options is displayed, as shown in Figure 5.5.

FIGURE 5.5
Control Panel: Small Icons.

⑤ **Use the skills you practiced previously to start the Snipping Tool and create a full-screen snip of the Control Panel window. Save a copy of this snip to the folder where you store your files. Name the file** U1Ch05IconsStudentName **substituting your name as indicated.**

⑥ **On the title bar, click the Close button** ⊠ **. Close the Snipping Tool. Submit the snip as directed.**

Identifying the Purposes and Consequences of Changing System Settings

Some settings are used to customize the appearance of the screen or the behavior of input devices to suit individual preferences. Other settings affect important functions of the computer, such as printing or Internet connections. If you change system settings on any computer, it is always good practice to record the original settings—either write them down and store them in a safe place, or capture a screen with the settings before and after you change them.

In some laboratories, the settings are restored to standard defaults each time the computer is restarted. If you make changes to a computer that you do not own, be sure to return the settings to their original values. You should not assume that the next user will know how to do this or that they should take the time to return the computer to its original settings. Some changes are hard to reverse. For example, you may find it interesting to change the default setting on the language used by the operating system. However, if you do not read the language you choose, it may be difficult to understand the instructions for changing the language of the system back to English. There can also be unexpected consequences when you change even the simplest setting. For example, if you change the system date to another year, your yearly subscriptions to application and antivirus software may end prematurely because subscription software always checks the system date to see if the software has expired. It may be difficult or impossible to reactivate the software without paying a fee. Other changes are simple and recommended. For example, if you move the computer to a location in a different time zone, it is appropriate to change the time zone setting so the system records the proper times when you create new files.

Identifying How Centrally Managed Computer Networks Restrict Setting Changes

If a system is designed to share resources, the right to change system settings is usually restricted to a few people who fully understand the effects of making changes. Some of the settings discussed in the following lesson may not be viewable or changeable in a network environment unless you have been authorized to make such changes. The people with the most control of system settings are the administrators. An administrator may add or delete the names of other users on the system and assign to them the resources they need while restricting the types of changes they can make. Normal practice is to create groups with certain privileges and then assign people to one or more groups. The privileges would include access to certain folders and the ability to read, edit, or delete files in those folders. If an administrator has not granted the appropriate group approval, you might not be able to find the folders or files that you seek or you might be able to read the file but not make changes.

Identifying Commonly Used Control Panel Categories

The Control Panel can display individual icons for each operation or it can display icons in groups of similar operations. The groups are named and organized according to function by the Windows operating system and cannot be changed or rearranged. Each category has subcategories into which the individual tasks are placed. It is sometimes easier to find a function using the Categories view if you are not certain what the function might be called but have a general idea of what you want to control.

To view Control Panel categories

① Click the Start button 🔵, and then click Control Panel. If necessary, change the view to Category.

② In the Control Panel Content pane, click Appearance and Personalization. You can change display characteristics, taskbar and Start menu options, and folder options such as the display of file extensions. See Figure 5.6.

FIGURE 5.6
Control Panel: Appearance and Personalization.

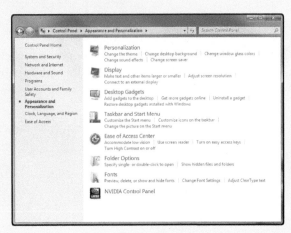

③ **Click the Back button** ⬅. **In the Control Panel Content pane, click Programs.** Using these options, you can *uninstall* or remove a program, set up default programs to run certain types of files, and add gadgets to the Windows sidebar. See Figure 5.7.

FIGURE 5.7
Control Panel: Programs.

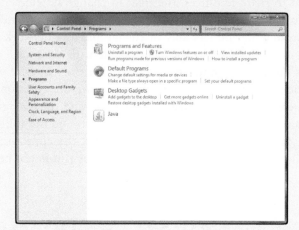

④ **Click the Back button** ⬅. **In the Control Panel Content pane, click Network and Internet.** Using these programs, you can adjust your network and Internet settings, and you can also synchronize your computer with other computers or mobile devices, as shown in Figure 5.8.

FIGURE 5.8
Control Panel:
Network and Internet.

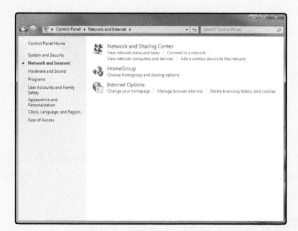

⑤ **Click the Back button** ⬅. **In the Control Panel Content pane, click System and Security.** These programs enable you to change your system and security settings and options. See Figure 5.9.

FIGURE 5.9
Control Panel: System and Security.

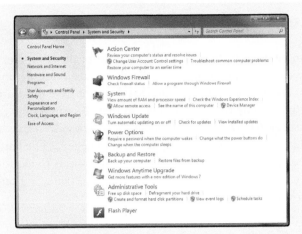

6 **Click the Back button** ⊙**. In the Control Panel Content pane, click Ease of Access.** These programs allow users to customize the interface for their own physical preferences for interacting with the operating system. See Figure 5.10.

FIGURE 5.10
Control Panel: Ease of Access.

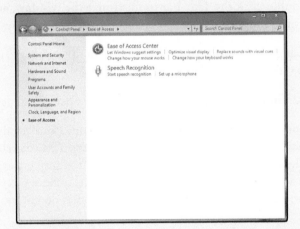

7 **Use the skills you practiced previously to start the Snipping Tool and create a window snip of the Control Panel window showing the Ease of Access features. Save a copy of this snip to the folder where you store your files. Name the file** U1Ch05ControlStudentName **substituting your name as indicated.**

8 **On the title bar, click the Close button** ✕ **.**

9 **Close** ✕ **the Control Panel window. Close the Snipping Tool and submit the snip as directed.**

Lesson 4 ▶ Using the Control Panel

The Control Panel can be used to change basic operations of the computer. Some operating systems, such as Windows 7, record system settings periodically to create restore points. If you have an older version of Windows or another operating system that does not have this feature, care must be taken to record the original settings before you change them so that you can restore them manually.

The computer has a *system clock* that works like a wristwatch. It uses a battery mounted on the motherboard to provide power when the computer is unplugged. (The battery that keeps the system clock running may need to be replaced if the system clock appears to lose time, which happens infrequently.) If you move a computer to a location in another time zone, you can use the Control Panel to change the system clock setting.

To use the Control Panel to change the time and date

1 **Click the Start button ⊙, and then click Control Panel.** The Control Panel window opens.

2 **If necessary, double-click the Title bar to maximize the window, and then change the view to Category.** The Control Panel window is maximized and categories of options are displayed.

3 **Click Clock, Language, and Region.** The options in this category are displayed, along with a list of common tasks for which they could be used.

4 **Click Date and Time.** The Date and Time dialog box opens.

5 **Under Time Zone, click the Change time zone button. Confirm that the check box next to *Automatically adjust clock for Daylight Saving Time* is selected, as shown in Figure 5.11.** The time will be set forward one hour in the spring and back one hour in the fall. Some time zones do not use daylight saving time; the check box does not display if one of those zones is selected. Some time zones contain areas that do not use daylight saving time.

FIGURE 5.11
Changing the time zone and adjusting for Daylight Saving Time.

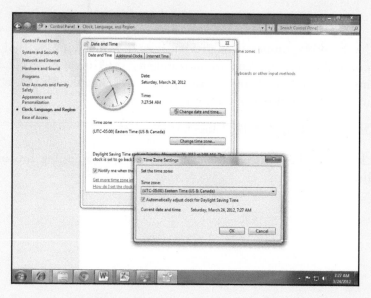

6 **Use the skills you practiced previously to start the Snipping Tool and create a Window snip of the Time Zone Settings dialog box. Save a copy of this snip to the folder where you store your files. Name the file** U1Ch05TimeStudentName **substituting your name as indicated.**

7 In the Time Zone Settings dialog box, in the box under *Time zone*, click the arrow. Time zones are measured by their difference from the time zone centered on Greenwich, England. For example, the eastern time zone in the United States is five hours behind England during daylight saving time, and it would be represented as GMT-05:00, as shown in Figure 5.12.

FIGURE 5.12
Time zones are identified by the number of hours before (West) or after (East) zero longitude.

8 Click in an open area of the Time Zone Settings box to close the list of time zones.

9 Close all open windows and dialog boxes.

Identifying Examples of Date and Time

The time kept by the system clock is usually displayed at the right end of the taskbar. If you click on the time display, the Date and Time Properties dialog box opens, as shown in Figure 5.13. The date and time can also be changed in this dialog box.

FIGURE 5.13
The date and time can be changed from the taskbar clock.

Changing Display Settings

The display settings are often changed to create a custom screen appearance.

Theme and Background

You can use the Appearance and Personalization options to change the style and color scheme of the windows. You can choose from a set of background images or choose an image of your own to display in the background.

Screen Resolution

How information is displayed on the screen also can be modified from the Control Panel by selecting the Appearance and Personalization category. Some video cards come with two plugs for separate monitors that can be set to different resolutions, as shown in Figure 5.14. If you pick a high screen resolution, the text used in the windows may be too small to read. If that is the case, you can click *Make text and other items larger or smaller* and change to a larger font size, as shown in Figure 5.15.

FIGURE 5.14
Microsoft Windows 7 can support simultaneous use of two monitors.

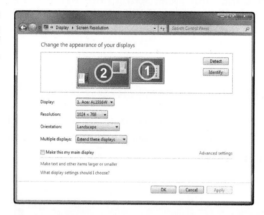

FIGURE 5.15
Larger fonts are useful at high resolutions.

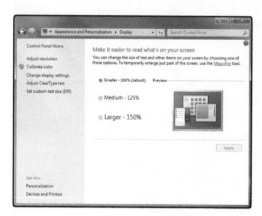

Power Options

When the computer is not in use, it consumes energy for tasks such as illuminating the screens and spinning the hard drive. The System and Security category contains Power Options, which can be used to shut off the screen and stop the hard drive when the computer isn't in use, to save energy. This feature is also useful for security purposes, because work will not display within a few minutes after a user has left the room and a password can be required to resume operation. Because it takes time to resume full function, there are tradeoffs among convenience, energy savings, and security. Windows recommends a balanced approach of turning off the screen after 10 minutes and shutting down the hard drive after 30 minutes, as shown in Figure 5.16.

FIGURE 5.16
Shutting down displays saves energy.

To use the Control Panel to change the desktop background image

1. **Click the Start button ⊛, and then click Control Panel.** The Control Panel displays.

2. **Click Appearance and Personalization. In the Content pane, under Personalization, click Change desktop background.** The Desktop Background window opens, as shown in Figure 5.17. If you have changed the desktop background with pictures from one of your own folders, the pictures in that folder will display; otherwise, the sample pictures provided by Microsoft display. If you want to look for your own photos, click the Browse button.

FIGURE 5.17
Desktop Background
options.

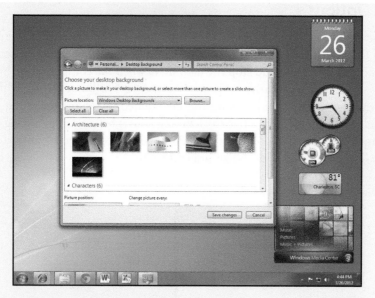

3 **Locate a picture you want to use as a desktop background, click it, and then click Save
Changes. Close the Control Panel.** The new picture replaces the previous picture as the
screen background, as shown in Figure 5.18. If the shape of the picture is not roughly the same
shape as the monitor, or if the picture is of low resolution, you may not be satisfied with the
results, and should either crop the picture to the right dimensions or choose another picture.

FIGURE 5.18
A new background
applied to the desktop.

4 **Close** ❌ **all open windows. Use the skills you practiced previously to start the Snipping
Tool and create a full-screen snip of the new desktop background. Save a copy of this snip
to the folder where you store your files. Name the file** U1Ch05BackgroundStudentName
substituting your name as indicated.

5 **Submit your snip as directed.**

Changing Mouse, Keyboard, and Audio Volume Settings

The Control Panel can be used to change mouse settings. You can switch the function of the right and left buttons, change screen pointers, and control how quickly the mouse reacts. Mouse settings can be changed from the Control Panel under the Hardware and Sound category, as can keyboard settings such as the repeat rate.

Desktop computers often come with an external microphone and speakers, but portable computers and many tablets have the microphone and speakers built into the case. If the microphone and speakers are too close to each other, the microphone will pick up the sounds from the speakers and produce a loud howling noise. To prevent this, some laptops are shipped with the speakers turned off by setting the mute option. Muting the speakers on a portable computer will also prevent the sound effects from being heard when you start Windows. You can use the Control Panel to unmute (or mute) the speakers.

To use the Control Panel to mute or unmute the speakers

1. Click the Start button 🏁, and then click Control Panel. In the Category view of the Control Panel, click Hardware and Sound.

2. Under Sound, click Adjust system volume.

3. In the Volume Mixer dialog box, below Speakers, click the Mute button. The Mute button works as an on/off switch to turn the speakers on and off. If the Mute button has a red circle with a line through it, like the one shown in Figure 5.19, it means the speaker is muted.

FIGURE 5.19
Speakers muted.

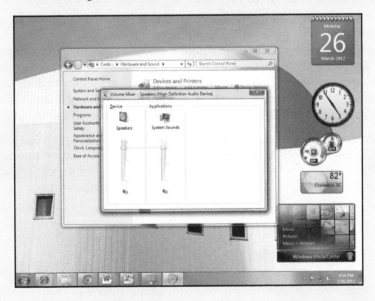

4. Use the skills you practiced previously to start the Snipping Tool and create a Window snip of the Speakers Properties dialog box. Save a copy of this snip to the folder where you store your files. Name the file U1Ch05MuteStudentName substituting your name as indicated.

⑤ **Return the Mute setting to its original value.** If you are using a portable computer, use the mute setting so you do not inadvertently distract others in public places.

⑥ **Click OK, and Close** **all open windows and dialog boxes. Submit your snip as directed.**

Using the Control Panel to Display Installed Printers

You can use several different printers from your computer if you have multiple printers connected directly to the computer or are connected to a network. Recall from Chapter 1 that to see which printers are already installed on your computer, open the Control Panel, and in the Category view, under Hardware and Sound, click View Devices and Printers. A list of installed printers is displayed.

To delete a printer from this list, right-click on its icon, and then choose Delete from the shortcut menu.

Using the Control Panel to Aid Users with Special Needs

The display settings and the mouse settings on the Control Panel can be used to help those with special needs to access the computer more easily. The Ease of Access Center can also be used to turn on a narrator—which reads all text on the screen out loud—and a Magnifier—which enables the user to magnify portions of the screen.

Extend Your Knowledge

USING THE CONTROL PANEL TO CHECK OR SET SECURITY LEVELS

If you have administrative privileges on a computer—which is almost never true in a computer lab—you can set security levels for other users and create accounts for new users. You can also open the Windows Security Center to determine how well your computer is protected. The Windows Security Center determines whether you have a firewall installed and whether the firewall is turned on, enables you to set the level of updates from manual to fully automatic, determines whether your computer is protected from adware and spyware, and checks your Internet security settings and User Account Control settings. To check your security levels do the following:

1. Open the Control Panel. In the Category view, click System and Security.
2. In the System and Security Window, click Action Center. Click the arrow to the right of Security to display the status of protection programs. A list of protection programs is displayed including the status of the firewall, virus, and spyware protection.

Lesson 5 ▶ Installing Software

If you are logged into the operating system with administrative privileges, you can install new software. If you are using a computer at work or in some laboratories, you may not be able to install software, and the options demonstrated in this lesson may be disabled or not displayed. Software can be obtained on an optical disc or downloaded from an Internet site. If you have a disc, a program typically named Setup or Startup will run automatically when you insert the disc, or you can begin the installation process from the Control Panel and provide the disc when asked.

When you buy software, you buy a license to use it called an end-user license agreement (EULA). The terms of the license are provided when you install the software, and most programs require that you acknowledge acceptance of the terms of the license before you continue. If a license is for a single user, you may not install the same software on multiple computers that would be used by different people at the same time. You may copy the installation disc to protect the original from damage, but you may not distribute the software or you will be in violation of the license agreement. Recent versions of software from Microsoft and Adobe require users to register the software over the Internet or by telephone to activate it. This deters unlicensed use.

Identifying Default Installation Options

Many programs offer an option between Normal and Custom installation. Choosing the Normal option might allow the installation program to add a toolbar to your browser or make the program the default choice for handling files with certain file extensions like music or video files. If you choose the custom installation option, you can opt out of these choices. Some software, such as Microsoft Office, has many options that are not installed by default. For example, when you install Office, some of the Microsoft Office Excel tools are not installed or are set to be installed on first use. One of these is the Analysis ToolPak, which is a group of advanced statistical programs. The process of installing additional options to existing software is similar to installing a new program and can be done using the Control Panel or in the Options dialog box within the program.

To use the Control Panel to install, update, uninstall, or add features to software

1. **Click the Start button** **, and then click Control Panel. In the Category view, click Programs.**

2. **Under Programs and Features, click** Uninstall a program. It may seem odd to click Uninstall a program, but that is also where you make changes to programs.

3. **Scroll down the list of programs and click Microsoft Office 2010.** Your program may be called Microsoft Office Professional or Microsoft Office Business or some other name. Compare your screen with Figure 5.20. Notice that at this point you can uninstall the software or make changes to it.

FIGURE 5.20
Microsoft Office program selected.

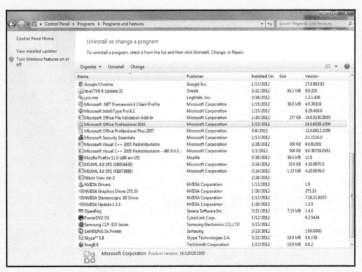

④ In the Command bar, click the Change button. In the displayed dialog box, be sure the **Add or Remove Features** option button is selected, and then click **Continue.** The Add or Remove Programs dialog box opens.

⑤ Under **Installation Options,** click the plus sign to the left of **Microsoft Excel,** and then click the plus sign to the left of **Add-ins.**

⑥ To the left of **Analysis ToolPak,** click the arrow, and then compare your screen with **Figure 5.21.** Click the arrow again to hide the list.

FIGURE 5.21
The Installation options for Microsoft Excel.

⑦ Use the skills you practiced previously to start the Snipping Tool and create a Window snip of the Installation Options dialog box. Save a copy of this snip to the folder where you store your files. Name the file U1Ch05AnalysisStudentName **substituting your name as indicated.**

⑧ If you want to install the Analysis ToolPak on your computer, click *Run from My Computer* and then click **Continue.** If not, Close [✕] the dialog box; when asked if you want to cancel setup, click **Yes.**

⑨ Close all open windows and dialog boxes. Submit the snip as directed.

Installing Programs from the Internet

As mentioned earlier, many software programs can be installed directly from the Internet. You pay for the program license online, and then click a Download button. You are usually given the option of installing directly from the website, or downloading the installation file to your computer. It is generally best to download the file. This enables you to install the program from your hard drive, and you can install it again if something goes wrong with the installation. By downloading the file, you also avoid the possibility that your installation will be ruined by an interruption in your Internet connection.

Starting Installed Programs

Once programs are installed, they are added to the list of programs that are shown in the All Programs menu. To start a program, click the Start button on the toolbar. The programs at the top of the left column are permanently added to the Start menu; recently used programs that haven't been added to the top of the Start menu are listed at the bottom of the Start menu. Your list of programs will differ from the example shown in Figure 5.22.

FIGURE 5.22
Varieties of programs are listed on the Start menu.

If the program you want is not listed in the Start window, point to All Programs. A complete list of installed programs or groups of programs displays. If you click a program group, the next level of menus displays more programs. To start a program, click on the listed program. To add the program to the Start menu, right-click the program name, and then click Pin to Start Menu, as shown in Figure 5.23. When you *pin* a program to the Start menu, it displays in the upper part of the left column.

FIGURE 5.23
You can pin programs you use frequently to the Start menu.

Subscribing to an Online Application

Some applications are available on the Internet, where you can use all or part of the programs and save your files on the Web so that they are available to you anywhere. One of these applications is Google Docs. To sign up to use Google Docs, go to docs.google.com. If you do not have a Google e-mail account, you need to create one—it is free. The Google Docs home page is shown in Figure 5.24.

FIGURE 5.24
Google Docs is an example of an online application.

Troubleshooting Common Installation and Operating System Problems

Most software installations proceed without a problem. However, some problems occur due to security settings that prevent the installation or from incompatibility with other software that is already installed. In this lesson, you learn about some of the common problems you might encounter and some solutions.

Lack of Permission

You must have the authority to install software. This authority is usually reserved for administrators. If you try to install software and you find the necessary windows are missing or the options are gray, see the network administrator. Many companies have a policy that prohibits installation of software that is not approved or purchased by the company, and this is a way of enforcing that policy.

Extend Your Knowledge

RUNNING AN INSTALLATION PROGRAM AS ADMINISTRATOR

If you are trying to install a program on your own computer but get a message stating that you need to have administrative privileges to install the program, you can sometimes continue the installation by right-clicking the installation program icon and then clicking Run as Administrator.

Security Settings

If you try to download and install a program from the Internet, the process may be blocked by security software that must be disabled before you can proceed. This is done to prevent unauthorized programs from taking over your computer, and it is also a reason why companies do not allow you to install your own software. Look at the right end of the taskbar for antivirus or firewall programs that are running and may block the download or operation of executable files.

Partially Uninstalled Programs

Some programs are updates of previous versions, and the first step they take during installation is to delete the old version. In some cases, some of the old files are not removed successfully, causing the new version to not install until they are removed. If this occurs, go to the program's website and search for help. The manufacturers are often aware of this problem and provide instructions or special programs to complete the uninstall process.

Damaged or Lost Installation Discs

If you install the program and later decide to make changes such as activating features, you may need to insert the installation disc. If the disc is not available at your location or if it is scratched or damaged, you will not be able to proceed. Protect your installation discs by storing them in a labeled location for convenient retrieval or by making a copy. You may be able to obtain a replacement disc from the manufacturer if you have proof of purchase of the original.

Reinstalling Registered Software

Some manufacturers, such as Microsoft, require that you activate your software. During the activation process, they record information about your computer. If you make significant changes to the computer hardware, it may no longer match the registered machine and the software may not function. Another common scenario occurs when a computer breaks down and you buy a replacement. You can install the registered software on another computer or on a modified computer by contacting the manufacturer and obtaining a special code.

Installation Program Does Not Start Automatically

Most installation discs will run the Setup program automatically when the disc is inserted. If this does not happen, you can open the files on the disc via Computer and search for a program named *Setup.exe* or *Startup.exe*. If you double-click this program, it will start the installation process. Alternatively, you can use the Control Panel to add the new program.

Installation Stops

Some programs take a long time to install. If there is no indicator on the screen to track the progress, look at the indicator lights for the hard drive or optical disc drive. If either of them is flickering on and off, something is not loading correctly and you should give the process more time. If there is no activity after about 10 minutes, cancel the installation and try again. If the installation program is stalled, press and hold Ctrl + Alt, and then press Delete and select Start Task Manager. Choose the Applications tab, select the stalled program, and then click End Task.

Conflicts with Other Programs

If a program works with a common file type—like Web pages, pictures, or music—it may attempt to make itself the default program for that type of file. If this happens, the default program will start automatically when you double-click on the name of an appropriate file type in the Computer window. Some software manufacturers try to capture this feature from competing software without asking your permission, or they do not explain it clearly when you are installing the software. If this happens, you can change the default setting for each type of file in the Computer window. To do this, in the Content pane of the Computer window, select a file of the desired file type. In the Command bar, click Organize, and then click Properties. In the Properties dialog box, on the General tab, click the Change button to the right of *Opens with*, and select the desired program to open the file.

Problems with Newly Installed Programs

If the software doesn't work after installation, you may have a conflict with other software, as mentioned earlier. You may need to uninstall and reinstall the software, or update your operating system software. Check the software company's website for possible solutions, or contact company support personnel. Once the program is successfully installed, you may still encounter problems. If you have files created using an old version of the software, these files may not open using the new software. Most software manufacturers will provide solutions to this problem if you check their website.

If the newly installed software has a Web component, your computer security may prohibit you from using the software, or your subscription may not be current. See your network administrator for help. If you can access the online software, but it quits working, it is possible that the problem lies with the online application or the server. Wait a while and see if the software starts working again; otherwise, contact the company's support department.

Using the Control Panel to Restore the System

Sometimes things happen to your system that cause the computer to work erratically or not work at all. This can happen when you install a new utility program, update an existing program, catch a computer virus, or for any number of other reasons. Windows 7 automatically sets a ***restore point***, which is a representation of the state of your computer's system files at a particular point in time.

To restore a computer to settings from a previous time, in the Control Panel, display the Category view, and then click System and Security. Under Action Center, click *Restore your computer to an earlier time*. Click the Open System Restore button to open the System Restore dialog box. In the System Restore dialog box, click Next. If no restore points display, at the bottom of the System Restore dialog box, select the *Show more restore points* check box, which is shown in Figure 5.25. Select a restore point, and then follow the rest of the steps in the wizard to restore your system settings.

FIGURE 5.25

Restore points are copies of the installation of the operating system and programs at a given time.

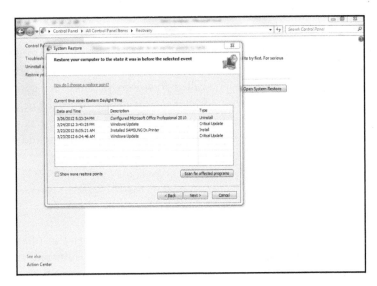

Starting in Safe Mode

Some problems with devices or their driver programs can interfere with the startup procedure, but it might not be apparent which program is causing the problem. Instead of starting Windows normally, you can start it in *Safe Mode*. In Safe Mode, the operating system loads the fewest drivers and utility programs possible and displays their names as they load to help identify which device or program is causing a problem. If it stops loading at a particular program, you can focus your efforts on that program. For example, a program might be trying to communicate with a device that has been removed and will not proceed without that device. You could use the Device Manager to disable or remove the device.

If the computer was shut down using the power button or because of loss of power, it may display a menu of startup choices that includes starting Windows normally, starting in Safe Mode, and starting in Safe Mode with network support, as shown in Figure 5.26. If this menu does not appear when you restart the computer, you can force it to appear by pressing the F8 key repeatedly while the computer is starting. Choose Safe Mode with network support because this mode will allow you to use the Internet to get advice regarding the problem online or to download programs that can fix the problem. To resume normal operation, shut down from the Safe Mode, and restart normally.

FIGURE 5.26

Options for starting in Safe Mode.

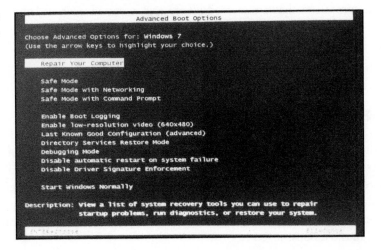

Updating Firmware

Devices such as printers, cell phones, routers, televisions, and monitors have programs that control their operation. Unlike device driver software that resides in the computer, these programs are stored in memory within the device; they are called *firmware* because they control a piece of hardware. If a device is not working properly with another, newer device, it might be that it was not programmed to do so because the newer device did not exist when the firmware was written. To update firmware, go to the manufacturer's website and search for firmware downloads and advice on how to update the firmware for your device.

Backing Up Software and Files

If the hard disk fails, it can take hours to reinstall all of the operating system and application software and then customize them. An alternative to reinstalling the software is to make a *ghost image* or *clone*, which is a compressed file that contains a copy of the installed software. Network administrators often use this method to duplicate an installation among several computers. Individual data files such as documents, spreadsheets, or presentations can be copied and the copies can be stored in other locations. Care must be taken to keep track of the differences between *versions* of the same file that are slightly different. It is not wise to rely on the date associated with the file to determine which is the most recent. Moving a file or changing its name can reset the date. Some organizations use a consistent naming system to distinguish copies of the same file from each other. For example, a contract named Thomas01 is an earlier version than Thomas02. If the name of the file includes a date or version number, use zeros as needed to make all the numbers the same length. Because the number is part of a name, the file name will be sorted as if it is all text. For example, Thomas02 would come before Thomas10, but Thomas2 would come after Thomas10. Choosing the best location in which to store duplicate files is an important decision and should be based on considerations such as security, risk, and cost. The easiest and cheapest method is to make a copy and place it in another folder on the same storage device, but if the device fails or if the computer is stolen, the copies are also lost. If the copies are saved to an external device such as a plug-in hard disk or an optical disc that is stored in the same location, a fire could destroy both. Copies of important records are usually kept *offsite*. Offsite storage is less convenient, but limits the risk of loss of both copies. Older offsite storage solutions were simply storage lockers where physical copies of the files were stored. Now there are options for storing files offsite on other computers and using an Internet connection to access them. Files stored on computers that are located offsite and accessed over an Internet connection are said to be stored in the *cloud*.

Summary

You learned about the capability of operating systems and how to perform common operations in Windows 7, such as installing software and printers and using the Control Panel. You learned about the differences between character-based and graphics-based operating systems and how to solve problems related to operating systems and software installation.

You can extend your learning by reviewing concepts and terms and by practicing variations of skills presented in the lessons.

Key Terms

8.3 convention *(p. 158)*

administrator *(p. 161)*

Android *(p. 157)*

application program *(p. 155)*

clone *(p. 180)*

cloud *(p. 180)*

command-line interface (CLI) *(p. 157)*

Control Panel *(p. 161)*

Disk Operating System (DOS) *(p. 156)*

embedded operating system *(p. 157)*

Extensible Markup Language (XML) *(p. 159)*

file extension *(p. 158)*

firmware *(p. 180)*

ghost image *(p. 180)*

graphical user interface (GUI) *(p. 156)*

International Business Machines (IBM) *(p. 155)*

iOS *(p. 157)*

offsite *(p. 180)*

operating system (OS) *(p. 155)*

pin *(p. 175)*

platform *(p. 155)*

restore point *(p. 178)*

Safe Mode *(p. 179)*

system clock *(p. 166)*

system restore *(p. 159)*

uninstall *(p. 164)*

version *(p. 180)*

Windows Phone *(p. 157)*

Checking Concepts and Terms

MULTIPLE CHOICE

Circle the letter of the correct answer for each of the following.

1. Which of the following is *not* an operating system? [L1]
   a. GUI
   b. UNIX
   c. DOS
   d. Windows

2. Which of the following operating systems has a text-based user interface? [L1]
   a. GUI
   b. Mac OS
   c. DOS
   d. Windows

3. Which of the following is *not* a limitation imposed by an operating system on file names? [L2]
   a. 8.3 file name (DOS)
   b. Eight-character maximum length (UNIX)
   c. Spaces not allowed in file names (Windows)
   d. Long file names (Mac OS)

4. Which of the following is a method of returning the operating system to an earlier state of software installation? [L2]
   a. Undo
   b. Uninstall
   c. Delete
   d. System restore

5. Which category of user has the most control of the operating system? [L3]
   a. Power user
   b. Guest
   c. Administrator
   d. Programmer

6. Which category in the Control Panel contains the options for changing the screen resolution? [L3]
   a. Appearance and Personalization
   b. Hardware and Sound
   c. Programs
   d. Ease of Access

7. The system clock will probably need to be reset when which of the following occurs? [L4]

a. The computer is restarted.

b. The computer is unplugged.

c. Daylight saving time changes.

d. You move to a different time zone.

8. Which of the following is typically turned off first to save power when the computer is not in use? [L4]

a. Keyboard

b. Screen

c. Mouse

d. Hard drive

9. Which of the following is **not** a method for installing or uninstalling software? [L5]

a. Use the Programs option in the Control Panel.

b. Insert the installation CD.

c. Double-click the *Startup.exe* program.

d. Copy and paste the installed program files from another computer.

10. If you cannot download a program from the Internet that you want to install, what is the most likely source of the problem? [L6]

a. Security software is blocking the download of an executable file.

b. The file is too large to download before your connection times out.

c. A previously installed version of the software is preventing the download.

d. You have not paid for a previous software download and your credit with the company is revoked.

MATCHING

Match each term in the second column with its correct definition in the first column by writing the letter of the term on the blank line in front of the correct definition.

_____ **1.** A representation of the state of your computer's system files at a particular point in time [L4]

_____ **2.** The letters following the period in a file name [L2]

_____ **3.** A group of programs that manages system settings in the Windows operating system [L3]

_____ **4.** A language used to store files as simple text along with information on how the application software would interpret that text [L2]

_____ **5.** Includes screen elements such as dialog boxes, windows, toolbars, icons, and menus, and displays a document on-screen the same way it will look when printed [L1]

_____ **6.** A time-of-day device included with the operating system, which can be set for different time zones [L4]

_____ **7.** An operating system with a text-based user interface [L1]

_____ **8.** A way of naming files that includes a file name and a file extension [L2]

_____ **9.** A person who has the right to change computer settings and install and remove software [L2]

_____ **10.** A feature that enables you to undo changes to the operating system back to one of the previous states [L2]

A. 8.3 convention

B. Administrator

C. Control Panel

D. DOS

E. File extension

F. GUI

G. Restore point

H. System clock

I. System restore

J. XML

Skill Drill

Skill Drill exercises reinforce chapter skills. Each skill reinforced is the same, or nearly the same, as a skill presented in the chapter. Detailed instructions are provided in a step-by-step format.

Each exercise is independent of the others, so you can do the exercises in any order.

1. Backing Up Your Computer

The Backup and Restore Center in the Windows Control Panel enables you to set restore points and restore a computer. If you happen to lose data from your hard drive that you can't recover by restoring your computer, you will need to have backup files available. You can back up your computer one time or set it to back up automatically on a regular schedule.

To back up the files on your computer:

1. Click the **Start** button, and then click **Control Panel**. If necessary, click the View by button, and then click Category.

2. Under **System and Security**, click **Back up your computer**.

3. Under Backup, click **Set up backup**. (Note: If you are doing this on a notebook computer, the computer must be plugged into an electrical outlet. The backup procedure will not work on battery power.)

4. Choose a place to back up your files—it can be an external hard drive, a network drive, or an optical disc drive with write capability—and then click **Next**. You cannot back up your files to the drive they are currently on. If you do not have a suitable external backup device attached, skip to Step 6.

5. Click the *Let me choose* option, and then click **Next**. Select the type of files you want to backup—such as pictures, videos, documents, some combination of file types, or all file types.

6. Use the skills you practiced previously to start the Snipping Tool and create a **Window** snip of the **Backup Files** dialog box. Save a copy of this snip to the folder where you store your files. Name the file U1Ch05BackupStudentName substituting your name as indicated.

7. If you wish, click **Change schedule** to set up your backup for a regular schedule: daily, weekly, or monthly.

8. If you wish to continue the backup process, click **Save Settings and run backup**. Otherwise, close the window.

9. Close all windows and dialog boxes, and then submit the snip as directed.

2. Creating a System Restore Point

Restore points can be set automatically or manually. When you are going to install a program or upgrade an existing program, or when you are making changes to the computer's operating system, it is a good idea to set a restore point manually.

To create a system restore point:

1. Click the **Start** button, and then click **Control Panel**. If necessary, click the View by arrow, and then click **Small icons**.

2. Click **System**. In the left panel, click **Advanced system settings**.

3. In the System Properties dialog box, click the **System Protection** tab, and then click the **Create** button.

4. In the **System Protection** dialog box, in the **Create a restore point** box, type a short description of why you are creating the restore point.

5. Use the skills you practiced previously to start the Snipping Tool and create a **full-screen** snip that includes the **System Protection** dialog box. Save a copy of this snip to the folder where you store your files. Name the file U1Ch05RestoreStudentName substituting your name as indicated.

6. Click the **Create** button to create a restore point.

7. Close all windows and dialog boxes, and then submit the snip as directed. Note that you may not be able to create a Restore Point if you are doing this activity on a computer that has a high level of security.

3. Viewing File Dates and Times in Detail View

Each time a file is opened and then saved, the operating system updates the date and time. This is useful for finding or sorting files. To see the date and time, you must choose to display it.

To view dates and times associated with file names do the following:

1. Click the **Start** button, and then in the right pane click **Computer**. The Computer window opens.

2. If necessary, click the expand arrow next to Libraries. Under **Libraries**, click the expand arrow next to **Documents** and then click **My Documents**.

3. At the top-right of the window in the Command bar, move the pointer to the arrow on the third icon from the right and click to display **More Options**. Click **Details**. File names display in list form followed by columns of other information such as the date modified and the file type.

4. At the top of the **Documents library** pane, in the **Name** column heading, right-click. If necessary, from the list of possible information, click **Date Modified** to select it, and then following the same procedure, click **Size**. The folders and files are sorted in the order the folder was last sorted. Folders and file names are sorted separately. A small arrow on the top of the column heading indicates by the direction of an arrow whether the sort is ascending or descending. If necessary, drag the right edge of the panel to the right to display the Date Modified, Type, and Size columns.

5. Click the **Size** column heading. Notice that the folders and the files are both sorted but shown in groups. Click the **Size** column heading again and notice that the sort order is reversed.

6. Use the skills you practiced previously to start the Snipping Tool and create a **window** snip of the **Computer** window. Save a copy of this snip to the folder where you store your files. Name the file U1Ch05DetailsStudentName substituting your name as indicated.

7. Close all windows, and then submit the snip as directed.

Explore and Share

Explore and Share questions are intended for discussion in class or online. Look for information that is related to the learning outcomes for this chapter as directed. Submit your answers as directed by your instructor.

1. On your computer at home or at work, check to find out what kind of security software you have installed, such as Microsoft Security Essentials, Norton AntiVirus, MacAfee AntiVirus, Ad-Aware, Spyware Doctor, or other similar programs. Open each program and check to see how updates are performed on the software. Is it automatic? Is the software set up to prompt you when updates are available? Or do you have to remember to perform the updates with no prompting? Prepare to discuss the advantages and drawbacks to each method of update. [L2]

2. If you have access to a smartphone that uses an operating system different from Windows 7—such as iOS, Android, or another—take a look at the instruction manual for that device or go online to find the manual. What kinds of limitations do you find in the device operating system that are not present in a full operating system? Prepare to discuss the differences in the operating systems. [L2]

3. The Windows Control Panel displays its functions in two ways. The default method groups functions into categories and provides direct links for common processes. The icon views show the functions in an alphabetical list. Take a few moments and use both formats to try to find Control Panel functions you used in this chapter. Do you find that it is easier for you to locate programs if they are grouped in categories or in an alphabetized list? If you used the list view earlier in your computing, do you think that influences which way you prefer to use the Control Panel? Prepare to discuss which you prefer and why. [L3]

4. What type of desktop image do you prefer? Do you change yours frequently? Have you tried a picture of your own? Take a look at some of the photos that you have on your computer that are not the same shape as your computer screen. Try one of these photos as a desktop image, and then prepare to discuss what happened and what you might want to do to fix the problem. [L3 & L4]

5. In your workplace or college lab, use the Control Panel to determine how many printers are available to the computer on which you are working. Have you ever seen a document in the output tray of a printer that was sent there by mistake from a coworker? Prepare to discuss the advantages and drawbacks of having multiple printers installed on any one computer or a network of computers. [L3 & L4]

In Your Life

In Your Life questions are intended for discussion in class or online where you can share your personal experience. Restrict your answers to the topics described in each exercise. Submit your answers as directed by your instructor.

1. Have you ever used a natural user operating system on a phone or tablet computer? How does it compare to a GUI-based operating system? What are the advantages of each type of operating system compared to the other? [L1]

2. Have you ever been annoyed by hearing the "ta-da" sound of a laptop computer starting up in a public place such as a library or a meeting room, or the ringing sound of someone's cell phone? Do you have the speaker muted on your own portable computer or cell phone? [L3 & L4]

3. Have you ever had trouble installing software? Was the problem you had mentioned in this chapter, or was it something else? [L5]

4. Have you ever had trouble installing security software where an earlier version would not uninstall? How did you resolve the problem? [L6]

5. If you have moved since you installed your software, do you know where your installation discs are? What process would you recommend to keep track of installation discs? If you couldn't find your installation discs and the software would not activate, what would you do? [L6]

Related Skills

Related Skills exercises expand on or are somewhat related to skills presented in the lessons. The exercises provide a brief narrative introduction, followed by instructions in a numbered-step format that are not as detailed as those in the Skill Drill section.

1. Synchronizing System Clock with Internet Server

The system clock in a computer can run fast or slow and may require resetting. You can use the Internet to keep your computer's system clock set correctly. You can choose to synchronize your system clock to a Microsoft server or to the National Institute of Standards and Technology (NIST). In this exercise, you synchronize your system clock to the NIST clock. You must have your computer connected to the Internet.

To synchronize your computer's system clock with the NIST server, follow these steps:

1. Click the **Start** button, and then click **Control Panel**.

2. In the Small Icons view, click **Date and Time**. The Date and Time dialog box opens.

3. Click the **Internet Time** tab, and then click the **Change settings** button.

4. In the **Internet Time Settings** dialog box, be sure the *Synchronize with an Internet time server check box* is selected.

5. Click the **Server** list box arrow, and then click **time.nist.gov**.

6. Click the **Update Now** button. Your computer connects to the server used by the National Institute of Standards and Technology and synchronizes your system clock. The time shown at the end of the taskbar is the correct time.

7. Use the skills you practiced previously to start the **Snipping Tool** and create a **Window** snip of the dialog box. Save a copy of this dialog box to the folder where you store your files. Name the file U1Ch05NISTStudentName substituting your name as indicated.

8. Close the dialog box, the window, and the Snipping Tool.

9. Start **Internet Explorer**. In the Address box type http://www.nist.gov and then press ⏎Enter. The website for the National Institute of Standards and Technology opens.

10. In the upper-left part of the screen, click the **NIST Time** tab. If this link or its position has changed, look for a link to the current time. A map of the world displays.

11. Use the time zone arrows to select your time zone. The current date and time displays and shows the time to the second. If your time does not display, you may see a yellow Information Bar under the Address bar. In order to see the time, you will need to click this bar and install a special control on your computer.

12. Compare the time on the website with your system clock time on the taskbar. They should be the same.

13. Watch the time on the website as it counts the seconds to the next minute. Confirm that your system clock time changes minutes when the NIST time site changes minutes.

14. Click the **Close** button in the upper-right corner to close Internet Explorer. Submit your snip as directed.

2. Adjusting the Screen Resolution

By using one of the Control Panel programs, you can change the resolution of your monitor to make the items on the screen larger or to display more on the screen by reducing the size of screen elements and text. This can be very helpful when using a large screen monitor. Different screens can have a different ratio of length to height. To get the best display, it is important to pick a screen resolution that matches the shape of your screen. You can always test various settings and then go back to the original setting if desired.

To change the screen resolution:

1. Click the **Start** button, and then click **Control Panel**. If necessary, click the Restore Down button.

2. If necessary, change to Category view and then click **Appearance and Personalization**.

3. Under **Display**, click **Adjust screen resolution**. You can also go to the Display Settings dialog box by right-clicking on an open area of the desktop, and then clicking Screen Resolution from the shortcut menu.

4. Make a note of your original screen resolution, and then click the list arrow next to **Resolution**. Drag the slider (the pointing triangle on the line) to change the resolution of your screen.

5. Use the skills you practiced previously to start the **Snipping Tool** and create a **Fullscreen** snip of the **Display Settings** dialog box. Save a copy of this snip to the folder where you store your files. Name the file U1Ch05ResolutionStudentName substituting your name as indicated.

6. Use the slider to select a different resolution. If you would like, click **OK**, and then follow instructions to see the new screen resolution. Change the resolution to its original setting when you are finished.

7. Close the **Control Panel** window and the Snipping Tool. Submit your snip as directed.

3. Customizing the Start Menu

If you use a particular program frequently, you can start it more quickly if you place a shortcut icon on the desktop, Start menu, or taskbar. Placing Startup icons on the desktop may result in a cluttered desktop, where it takes as long to find the icon you want as it would to start it from the All Programs menu. If you limit your choices to a few of the most commonly used programs, you can place icons on the Start menu.

To pin an icon to the Start menu do the following:

1. Click the **Start** button. Notice that there are programs listed on the left side of the menu. The programs listed at the bottom of the Start menu change as your program use changes; the programs listed at the top are there permanently unless you delete them.

2. Click the **Start** button again to close the Start menu.

3. Right-click the **Start** button, and then from the displayed shortcut menu, click **Properties**.

4. In the **Taskbar and Start Menu Properties** dialog box, click the **Start Menu** tab, and then click the **Customize** button.

5. In the **Customize Start Menu** dialog box, near the bottom of the box, under **Start menu size**, click the **Number of recent programs to display** up spin arrow to display **12** items.

6. Use the skills you practiced previously to start the **Snipping Tool** and create a **Window** snip of the **Customize Start Menu** dialog box. Save a copy of this snip to the folder where you store your files. Name the file U1Ch05StartStudentName substituting your name as indicated.

7. **Close** the **Customize Start Menu** dialog box. In the **Taskbar and Start Menu Properties** dialog box, under **Privacy**, be sure both check boxes are selected. The first check box enables the program to display a list of the files that you have opened recently; the second check box enables a list of programs that you have used recently to display at the bottom of the left half of the Start menu. If you are working on a computer that other people use, you might want to clear these check boxes for privacy reasons.

8. Close the **Taskbar and Start Menu Properties** dialog box and any other open windows. Submit your snip as directed.

Discover

Discover exercises give students general directions for exploring and discovering more advanced skills and information. Each exercise is independent of the others, so you can complete the exercises in any order.

1. Learning About the Microsoft/Apple and Linux/UNIX Lawsuits

Because operating systems are an important part of any decision about what computer or software to buy, the manufacturers of operating systems want to preserve and protect the uniqueness of their products from unlicensed copying. Bitterly contested lawsuits have affected the development of personal computers in the past and are likely to do so again in the future.

To learn about the history of two major lawsuits that have affected personal computers in the past and present, follow these steps:

1. Use your Web browser to read about the history of the graphical user interface at **en.wikipedia. org/wiki/History_of_the_GUI**. Concentrate on the sections related to Xerox Parc, Apple, and Microsoft.

2. Read the transcript of a PBS interview with the people involved to get an appreciation of the people and their passion for creating GUI. Use your Web browser to go to **www.pbs.org/ nerds/part3.html** and read what they have to say about the development of the GUI and how they feel about each other.

3. The GUI was introduced to the world by one of the most famous advertisements in history during the 1984 Super Bowl football game. To understand the significance of this advertisement, go to **http://en.wikipedia.org/wiki/1984)(advertisement** and read about the significance of the year 1984.

4. Use your Web browser to search for "Apple commercial 1984," which at times is available on the **www.apple.com** website. You may need to download and install the QuickTime player from Apple. If the ad does not play, use the button on the website to download the player. If you are asked to switch your default video player to Apple's QuickTime player, you do not need to do so. (Alternatively, you can look at the commercial using YouTube: **www.youtube.com/ watch?v=OYecfV3ubP8**.) This is an example of how a company tries to make its software the default for a type of file.

5. The newest major competitor in the operating system area is Linux, an open-source operating system that is free and maintained by volunteers worldwide. Linux is already commonly used on Web servers, and its advocates hope it will challenge the dominance of Microsoft Windows on the PC. However, a company named SCO bought the rights to UNIX, and claims that

large portions of UNIX code were copied and used in Linux. It filed a major lawsuit against IBM for billions of dollars in damages. Use your Web browser to go to **en.wikipedia.org/ wiki/SCO_v._IBM_Linux_lawsuit** and read about this lawsuit and how it turned out.

6. Write a short paper that answers these questions: (a) If you were a corporate personal computer user, how would you feel if you saw the Apple ad in 1984, and would you be favorably inclined to buy its product? (b) What are some of the similarities and differences between the Apple/ Microsoft and SCO/IBM lawsuits? Submit the paper as directed.

2. Controlling Programs That Run Automatically at Startup

After your operating system loads and starts, it starts a list of other programs. This feature is useful because it assures that certain programs such as your antivirus software are always started. Some software manufacturers write their installation programs to add their program to this list without asking. As a result, some programs are loaded into RAM and run continuously even if they are seldom used. This can slow down the start process and the operation of your computer if too many programs start automatically.

To discover which programs are running on your computer and how to prevent them from starting automatically, follow these steps:

1. Look at the icons at the right end of the taskbar. Click the expand arrow if necessary to show all the programs. Point at each icon to see its name. Write down the names of any programs you did not start and you think you could do without.

2. Click the **Start button**. In the **Search** box, type msconfig and press **Enter**. Notice that the **System Configuration** dialog box opens. This is another example of a DOS command still in use by Windows 7.

3. In the **System Configuration** dialog box, click the **Startup** tab. A list of programs is displayed. If there are programs running that you do not need, you can deselect them and they will not start automatically. This does not remove the program, it just does not start it automatically when you start the computer.

4. Remove check marks from programs you do not need to start automatically. Be sure you know what the programs you deselect are. This choice is easily reversible, so a mistake is not hard to fix.

5. Create a Window snip of the **System Configuration** dialog box and name it U1Ch05ConfigStudentName. Submit the file as directed.

6. Click **OK**. Restart your computer. Observe how fast it loads and is ready for use. Check the list of icons at the right end of the taskbar to see if the programs you deselected did not start automatically.

7. Repeat Steps 2 through 4 and select the original list of programs if you want to return the computer to its original state.

3. Using Windows Task Manager to Stop Stalled Programs

If a program uses resources in an unauthorized way that causes conflicts with other programs, or if there is a dip in the electrical voltage provided to the computer, a program may cease to function. You can use the Task Manager to end the program without having to restart the computer and the rest of the programs.

To use the Task Manager to view running programs, do the following:

1. Press and hold down Ctrl + Alt, and then press Delete. Click **Start Task Manager**. The Windows Task Manager opens.

2. Click the **Applications** tab, if necessary. Observe the status of the programs that are running. If one of these programs is stalled, you could select it and end it by clicking the **End Task** button. Do not use this method on a running program because it may not close its open files correctly.

3. Create a Window snip of the **Windows Task Manager Applications** dialog box. Name the file U1Ch05ApplicationsStudentName and submit the file as directed.

4. Click the **Processes** tab. Click the **CPU** column heading once or twice to sort the processes and bring the Windows Task Manager (named *taskmgr.exe*) to the top of the list. These are processes that are currently running, and you can see what percentage of the computer's time is devoted to each process in the CPU column.

5. Create a Window snip of the **Windows Task Manager Processes** dialog box. Name the file U1Ch05ProcessesStudentName and submit the file as directed.

6. Click the **Close** button on the menu bar to close the window.

Dmitry Shironosov / istockphoto.com

Chapter 6

Using Windows 7

Why Would I Do This?

The Windows operating system is the most common operating system used on desktop personal computers. Almost all the retail software products that are intended for use on a desktop PC have a version written for Windows. One of the benefits of this situation is that once you learn how to manipulate files and window elements, you can use these skills with almost all common applications.

Chapter at a Glance

Lesson	Learning Outcomes	Page Number	Related IC3 Objectives
1	Identify the taskbar and its uses	195	1.3.1
1	Identify desktop icons and their uses	196	1.3.1
1	Identify windows and their uses and versions of the Windows operating system	196	1.3.1, 4.1.2
1	Identify dialog and warning boxes and their uses	197	1.3.1
1	Add a gadget to the Windows desktop	198	1.3.1
2	Identify how to minimize, maximize, and restore down windows	200	2.1.1
2	Identify how to use a mouse or trackball	200	1.1.2
2	Identify how to navigate, resize, move, and scroll windows	201	1.1.2
3	Identify how to shut down and restart the computer	204	1.1.2, 1.3.2, 1.3.3, 1.3.4
3	Identify how to log off and switch users	205	1.1.2
3	Identify how to put the computer in sleep mode	205	1.1.2, 1.3.5
3	Identify how to put the computer in lock mode	206	1.1.2
3	Identify how to shut down nonresponsive programs	206	4.1.6
4	Identify how to use the Start menu	206	1.1.2
4	Identify how to use online help	207	4.1.5
4	Pin a shortcut to the Start menu	208	1.1.2
4	Move between programs	210	1.1.3
5	Understand folders	212	1.2.1
5	Use folders on the desktop	213	1.2.2
5	Display properties	216	1.2.0
5	Rename and delete desktop shortcut icons	216	1.2.2
6	Identify file types and file extensions	217	3.4.1
6	Create folders and change views	217	1.2.2
6	Sort files	218	1.2.2
6	Create, copy, move, rename, and delete folders	219	1.2.2
6	Select, copy, move, and delete files using keyboard shortcuts	220	1.2.2
7	Search for files and folders	223	1.2.2
7	Restore files from the Recycle Bin	225	1.2.2
8	Name folders and files with standard conventions	225	1.2.2
8	Manage files and folders	226	1.2.2
8	Open problem files	227	4.1.0

Visual Summary

In this chapter, you identify the elements of a Windows desktop, like the one shown in Figure 6.1. You learn to identify the elements of a window and how to change its shape, size, and location. You learn how to create folders in which to store files on different types of storage media, and you learn about problems you may encounter and precautions to take to prevent some common problems.

FIGURE 6.1
The Windows desktop.

List of Student Files

In this chapter, you will capture windows or screens. You will add your name to the file names and save them on your computer or portable memory device. Table 6.1 lists the files you start with and the names you give them when you save the files.

TABLE 6.1

ASSIGNMENT:	STUDENT SOURCE FILE:	SAVE AS:
Lessons 1–8	22 sample files	U1Ch06GadgetStudentName
		U1Ch06WindowsStudentName
		U1Ch06SplitStudentName
		U1Ch06SearchStudentName
		U1Ch06PaintStudentName
		U1Ch06ShortcutsStudentName
		U1Ch06TypeStudentName
		U1Ch06CopyStudentName
		U1Ch06FindStudentName
Skill Drill	none	U1Ch06RestoreStudentName
		U1Ch06AltStudentName
		U1Ch06DateStudentName
Explore and Share	none	none
In Your Life	none	none
Related Skills	none	U1Ch06TaskbarStudentName
		U1Ch06CoopStudentName
		U1Ch06DetachStudentName
Discover	none	none

Lesson 1 ▶ Identifying Elements of the Desktop and Windows

When reading through this chapter, it is important to understand the difference between *Windows* with a capital *W* and *windows* with a lowercase *w*. When you see the word ***Windows*** with a capital letter, it usually refers to the operating system that runs the computer. A ***window*** (lowercase *w*), on the other hand, refers to a rectangular area on the screen, sometimes expanded to fill the whole screen, which is used by an application program to work with files or interact with the user. When you see the word *Windows,* it is often accompanied by the version, such as Windows XP, Windows Vista, or Windows 7 (the version used in this chapter). These operating systems are similar, and all use a graphical user interface (GUI). The version of Windows can be determined by clicking the Start button, and then entering Winver in the Start Search box. A dialog box appears that describes the version of Windows.

In the background, behind any open windows, is the ***desktop***, which represents a work area from which you begin to use the applications. The desktop has ***icons*** that may be located on the taskbar or arranged on the desktop. You can start programs by double-clicking desktop icons or clicking taskbar buttons. The desktop may also have icons that represent folders and individual files. Desktop components are shown in Figure 6.2 and described in Table 6.2.

FIGURE 6.2
The desktop organizes the work area in Windows.

Shortcut icons

Gadgets

Desktop with picture used as background

Taskbar

TABLE 6.2

PARTS OF WINDOWS DESKTOP	FUNCTION
Computer icon	Shortcut to the Computer window; gives you access to the drives, files, and folders on your computer.
Desktop	The basic screen from which Windows and applications are run. The desktop consists of program icons, a taskbar, a Start button, an optional Windows Sidebar, and a mouse pointer.
Icon	Graphic representation; often a small image on a button that enables you to run a program or program function.
Recycle Bin	Shortcut to the Recycle Bin, which is a storage area for files that have been deleted from the hard drive. Files can be recovered from the Recycle Bin or permanently removed from the computer.
Taskbar	A bar, usually at the bottom of the screen, that contains the Start button, buttons representing open programs, and other buttons that activate programs.
Taskbar program icons	Icons placed on the taskbar for quick access to commonly used programs.
Windows Sidebar	An area on the right edge of the desktop where you can place gadgets.

Taskbar

The *taskbar* is typically located at the bottom of the screen, but it may be relocated to the sides or top, and it may be hidden if it is not in use. If the taskbar is hidden, you can display it by moving the pointer to the edge of the screen where it is located and it will display again. The taskbar has the Start button at its left end. Files in use are represented by buttons in the middle of the taskbar. If one application, such as Microsoft Office Word, has several files open, they may be represented by a stack of Word icons that represents the open files. When you point to the application icon, a *thumbnail*— an icon that displays a small representation of a file—displays for each open file. You can click on the thumbnail to display the document that you want.

At the right end of the taskbar is the ***notification area***, where icons indicate programs that are running—such as antivirus software programs—but are not necessarily displayed in a window. The system clock also typically displays in this area. If more than a few programs have icons in this area, an arrow displays that you can click to show all the icons. To the right of the Start button you may see icons that represent commonly used applications in the taskbar, as shown in Figure 6.3.

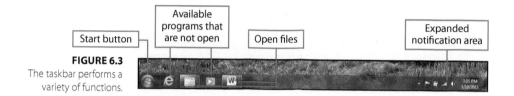

FIGURE 6.3
The taskbar performs a variety of functions.

Desktop Icons

Icons on the desktop, like the ones shown in Figure 6.4, may be used to start programs or open commonly used folders and files. See Table 6.2. Some common program icons that are often placed on the desktop are the ***Recycle Bin***, Internet Explorer, and ***Computer***. Icons are typically added to the desktop when a new program is installed, or are added by previous users. Your desktop will display different icons than those shown in the figure.

FIGURE 6.4
Icons are shortcuts to programs, websites, files, and folders.

Computer manufacturers place shortcut icons on the desktop for programs they hope you will use. These icons have a blue arrow on them and can be deleted. When you delete a shortcut icon from the desktop, the program itself is not deleted and may be started using other means. Icons that represent folders or individual files start programs that locate the folder or file where it resides in storage. These shortcut icons are not the files themselves, which is an important distinction that will be discussed later in the lesson on file management. If a file is in use, you may see another icon on the desktop that represents a temporary file that will close when the file is closed. However, it is important to note that if you delete files and folders that are actually stored on the desktop, the files and folders are deleted.

Windows

A window can be opened and closed. It can also be resized and moved around the screen. You can have more than one window open at a time on the screen. They can overlap each other, or one window can take up the entire screen, with other windows hidden behind it. You can also minimize a window, in which case the window is represented by a button on the taskbar. Windows are used extensively, and it is important to become familiar with how each part works. See Figure 6.5 and Table 6.3.

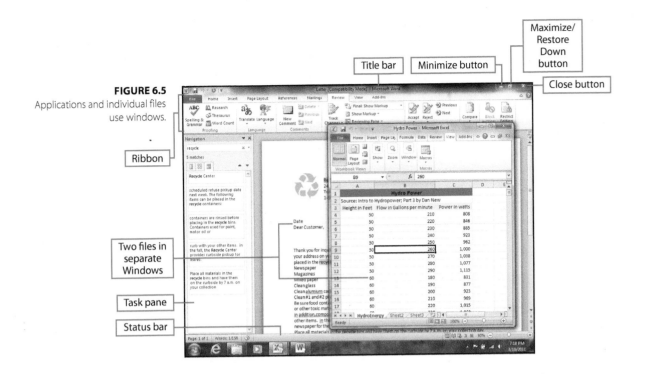

FIGURE 6.5
Applications and individual files use windows.

Title bar · Minimize button · Maximize/Restore Down button · Close button

Ribbon

Two files in separate Windows

Task pane

Status bar

TABLE 6.3	PARTS OF A WINDOW	FUNCTION
	Ribbon	In Microsoft Office 2007 and 2010, the area containing groups of commands and command buttons. In other programs, a menu bar displays in this area.
	Status bar	The bar at the bottom of a window that gives additional information about the window.
	Task pane	A pane that opens on the side of a window and is used to display commonly used tools or navigation commands.
	Title bar	The bar at the top of a window that often contains the name of the application and document, along with the Minimize, Maximize/Restore Down, and Close buttons.
	Toolbar	A bar, usually just under a menu bar, that contains command options. These commands are buttons with icons or words. More than one bar may be displayed at once and they may share the same row.

Dialog Boxes

A *dialog box* is similar to a window, but it is used for a specific purpose and requires an action by the user. If you choose to save a file to a new location, use the Save As dialog box, as shown in Figure 6.6. Notice that your options to resize the dialog box with buttons are missing; it does not have buttons to minimize, maximize, or restore. A dialog box has a combination of buttons or check boxes for user input—boxes in which you can type information and buttons for accepting or rejecting the input.

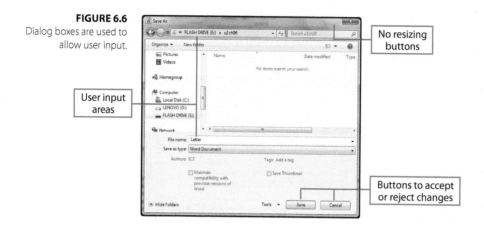

FIGURE 6.6
Dialog boxes are used to allow user input.

No resizing buttons

User input areas

Buttons to accept or reject changes

Warning Boxes

A warning box alerts you to a potential problem and gives you the options of continuing or stopping the process, as shown in Figure 6.7.

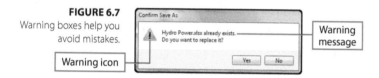

FIGURE 6.7
Warning boxes help you avoid mistakes.

Warning message

Warning icon

Gadgets

Dynamic programs—also known as *gadgets*—such as a currency converter, a calendar, or a clock can be placed anywhere on the desktop. Your screen gadgets may be different than the ones shown in this chapter.

To add a gadget to the desktop

1. **In an open area of the desktop, right-click. From the shortcut menu, click Gadgets.** A list of available gadgets displays; your list may vary.

2. **Click the Currency gadget, hold down the left mouse button, and then drag the Currency gadget to an open area of the Windows Sidebar. Release the mouse button.** The Currency gadget is added to your desktop. Using the mouse to move an object to a new location is called *dragging* the object.

3. **In the Currency gadget, click the bottom arrow, and then scroll and select British Pound.** The currency equivalent between the U.S. dollar and the British Pound displays in the gadget, as shown in Figure 6.8.

FIGURE 6.8
Gadgets can be added to the Windows Sidebar.

Add Gadget dialog box

Currency gadget has been added

④ Use the skills you practiced previously to start the Snipping Tool and create a Full-screen snip of the screen. Save a copy of this snip to the folder where you store your files. Name the file U1Ch06GadgetStudentName substituting your name as indicated.

⑤ In the Gadget dialog box, click the Close button ▣ , and then submit your snip as directed.

⑥ Close the Snipping Tool. Right-click the Currency gadget, and then from the shortcut menu, click Close Gadget. The gadget is removed from the Windows Sidebar.

How Do You Feel About It?

ADDING GADGETS TO THE DESKTOP

Do you like to have gadgets that keep you informed about weather or news displayed on your desktop? If so, which ones and why? If not, why not?

Lesson 2 ▶ Changing the Size and Position of Windows

If all your windows are using the full screen, you can switch between them by clicking the corresponding button on the taskbar. If you want to see two or more windows on the screen at the same time, you can use the Restore Down button to reduce the size of each window, and then arrange the windows next to each other or allow them to overlap.

Minimize, Maximize, or Restore Down

To use the entire screen to display a window, use the *Maximize* option. If you want to remove the window from the screen but not close the application or file, use the *Minimize* option. You can bring the window back to the screen by clicking its button on the taskbar. The window can occupy less than the full screen if you click the *Restore Down* option when the window is maximized.

To minimize, maximize, and restore a window

1 **Click the Start button ⊛, and then on the right side of the Start menu, click Computer. On the title bar, if necessary, click the Maximize ▭ button.** Windows Explorer opens the Computer window and it is maximized. The window may or may not be maximized when you opened it, depending on its condition the last time the window was closed. ***Windows Explorer*** is the program within Windows that displays the files and folders on your computer. After it has been used, Windows Explorer displays as an option on the left side of the Start menu, and it can also be opened from that side of the menu. The title bar always displays Computer.

2 **On the title bar, click the Minimize button ▭.** The window is removed from the screen, but its button remains on the taskbar.

3 **Click the Windows Explorer button ▭ on the taskbar.** The Computer window displays again.

4 **On the title bar, click the Restore Down button ▭.** The Computer window shrinks to a size that does not fill the screen.

5 **Click the Minimize button ▭ again.** The window is removed from the screen, but its button remains on the taskbar.

6 **Right-click the Windows Explorer button ▭ on the taskbar, and then on the shortcut menu click Windows Explorer.** Leave this window open for use in the following exercise.

Using a Mouse or Trackball

A graphical user interface like Windows 7 or Macintosh OS makes extensive use of the mouse to activate buttons and menu items. A mouse that is intended for use with Windows has at least two buttons. A mouse or trackball that is intended for exclusive use on a Macintosh computer may have only one button. The mouse can be used to select text or objects on the screen and to move or resize the text and objects. A trackball uses different methods of controlling the pointer on the screen, but it also has buttons. A touchpad on a portable computer may have buttons, but you may also be able to simulate a button click by tapping the touchpad. See Table 6.4 for a summary of common instructions that apply to using a mouse or trackball.

TABLE 6.4

INSTRUCTION	ACTION
Click	Move the mouse or roll the trackball to position the tip of the mouse pointer on the screen at the desired location, and then click the left button.
Double-click	Similar to a single-click, but you press the mouse button twice in rapid succession. It is important to avoid moving the mouse between clicks.
Triple-click	Similar to double-clicking except that you click three times.
Right-click	Similar to a click, but you click the button on the right side of the mouse or trackball.
Drag	Move the screen pointer to the desired location on the screen. Hold down the left mouse button and use the mouse to move the pointer to another location on the screen and then release the mouse button. Commonly used to resize windows, move objects, or move selected text.

Resize, Move, and Scroll Windows

When a window opens on your screen, it generally opens in the same size and shape as when it was last used. If the window is not maximized, you can drag a corner or side of a window to change its size, and you can drag the title bar to move the entire window. If the window is too small to display all the information, you can use *scroll bars* to move the view within the window to display different parts of the file or other content. If multiple windows are visible on the screen, the title bars of the inactive windows are dimmed.

To resize, move, and scroll a window

1 **In the pane at the left, navigate to a folder that has a long list of files in it. Move the pointer to the lower-right corner of the Computer window to display the ⬉ pointer.** When the mouse pointer takes the shape of a two-headed arrow—vertical, horizontal, or diagonal—you can drag the item you are pointing at to change its size and shape. Notice in Figure 6.9 that there are different kinds of drives available in the *Navigation pane*, including the main hard drive (C:), an optical disc drive, a flash drive, and media device drives. Network drives would also display here. At the top of the Navigation pane is the *Favorites list*, with links to the most commonly used folders for the current user, including the Desktop, Downloads, and Recent Places. There are also personal folders—called *Libraries*—for the current user that contain Documents, Music, Pictures, and Videos. Your Navigation pane will differ from what is shown in the figure.

FIGURE 6.9
Areas of the Computer window.

- Navigation pane
- Favorites list
- Libraries
- Main hard drive
- Optical drive
- Flash drive
- Selected folder
- Horizontal scroll bar
- Files in selected folder
- Vertical scroll bar

2 **Hold down the left mouse button, and drag diagonally up and to the left until the window is too small to display an entire list of files and a vertical scroll bar appears.** The window is now smaller. If it is too small to display all the information, scroll bars will appear at the side and bottom as needed. Windows may be resized by dragging corners or sides.

3 **Release the mouse button. Point to a blank area on the Computer window title bar. Click and hold down the left mouse button, drag down and to the right, and then release the mouse button.** The entire window moves down and to the right.

④ **Click the arrow at the bottom of the vertical scroll bar at the right side of the window.** The items at the bottom of the window scroll up so that you can see the folders and icons that were not visible before. You can click and hold down the left mouse button on the down arrow to scroll rapidly through many items. The arrow at the other end of the scroll bar will work in the opposite direction. This method works in a similar manner for the horizontal scroll bar.

⑤ **Click the scroll box in the vertical scroll bar and drag up.** The *scroll box* enables you to move quickly up or down a window. The relative location of the scroll box indicates your relative location in the window. The relative size of the scroll box and the scroll bar indicates the relative size of the information displayed and the total information that can be displayed by scrolling.

⑥ **Click the gray area of the scroll bar below the scroll box.** The window scrolls by one complete display each time you click the scroll bar above or below the scroll box.

⑦ **Click the Start button** ⊕**, and then click All Programs. Click the Accessories folder, and then click Calculator.** The Calculator program opens in its own window. This application does not use all the features of a window because it does not need to scroll or change size. Consequently, the Maximize button is dimmed and you cannot drag its corners or sides to change its size.

⑧ **Drag the title bars to move the Calculator and Computer windows to appear side by side, as shown in Figure 6.10. Resize the Computer window if necessary.** Use the skills from previous steps to drag and resize the windows.

FIGURE 6.10
Windows can be rearranged
on the desktop.

Title bar of inactive
window is dimmed

Computer window
is resized

Calculator window

⑨ **Click the title bar of the Computer window.** Notice that the title bar of the Calculator window, which is no longer the active window, is dimmed.

⑩ **Use the skills you practiced previously to start the Snipping Tool and create a Full-screen snip of the screen. Save a copy of this snip to the folder where you store your files. Name the file** U1Ch06WindowsStudentName **substituting your name as indicated. The specific files in your figure will be different, but it should display scroll bars in the window on the right and the calculator should be on the left.**

⑪ **Click the Close button** 🗙 **on the title bar of the Calculator window to close the window. Close the Snipping Tool, or leave it open for the next steps. Submit the snip as directed. Leave the Computer window open.**

Other Ways to Resize Windows

Maximizing, minimizing, and restoring windows works well, but there are also ways to resize and position windows by dragging the title bar. When the screen is filled with one or more windows, you can also view the underlying desktop and desktop gadgets without closing or minimizing the windows.

To resize windows by using the title bar

1 **Point to the Computer window title bar, and then drag the window to the top edge of the screen.** Notice that the window is maximized.

2 **Drag the window title bar down from the top of the screen until the window is centered on the screen, and then release the mouse button.** The size and shape of the window returns to the size and shape from before the window was maximized.

3 **Click the Start button , and then click All Programs. Click the Accessories folder, and then click Paint. If the window fills the screen, click the Restore Down button .**

4 **Drag the Paint window to the left until the pointer touches the left edge of the screen.** The Paint window maximizes vertically, but takes up exactly half of the screen horizontally.

5 **Drag the Computer window to the right until the pointer touches the right edge of the screen.** The Computer window maximizes vertically, but takes up exactly half of the screen horizontally. Each window occupies one-half of the screen, as shown in Figure 6.11. When you are writing papers or working with spreadsheets, you can open two windows side by side and drag information from one document to the other.

FIGURE 6.11
Windows can be arranged side-by-side.

Paint window occupies half the screen

Computer window occupies half the screen

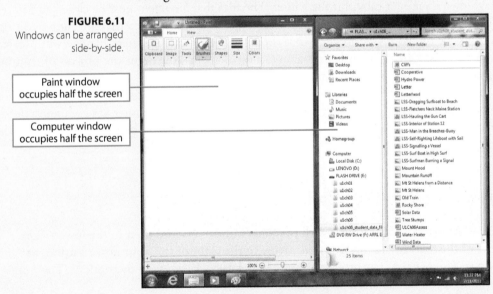

6 **Use the skills you practiced previously to start the Snipping Tool and create a Full-screen snip of the screen. Save a copy of this snip to the folder where you store your files. Name the file** U1Ch06SplitStudentName **substituting your name as indicated.**

7 **Move the pointer to the lower-right corner of the screen. On the right edge of the taskbar, point to the Show desktop button .** The desktop displays, and the outlines of the open windows also display, as shown in Figure 6.12. You can also click the Show desktop button, move the pointer around the screen and perform actions on the desktop, and then click the Show Desktop button again to reopen all the windows that were closed.

FIGURE 6.12
Use the Show Desktop button to display the desktop.

Open windows are transparent but not minimized

Show desktop button

8 Click the Close button ⊠ to close both open windows. Close the Snipping Tool.

Lesson 3 — Shutting Down and Restarting the Computer

Shutting down the computer is a process that is more complicated than simply turning off a switch. It is like closing down a summer cabin for the winter. The files that are open must be closed and stored properly. Services like network connections must be stopped, and programs that are running in the background must be turned off. A program that is part of the operating system handles this process. This program must be started like other programs, which is why you begin the process of shutting down by—paradoxically—clicking the Start button.

When the computer starts, it loads the operating system and then loads other programs that are on its startup list. If a program is not working properly, restarting the computer is a common remedy because settings that have been changed, which may be causing the problem, are reset when the program restarts.

To shut down and restart the computer

1 Close all files and applications. Click the Start button 🕐, and then in the lower-right corner of the Start menu, point to the arrow to the right of the Shut down button, as shown in Figure 6.13. The program starts and displays a menu with five options. There are six options if you are using a laptop (see Figure 6.13).

Shut Down arrow   Shut Down options

FIGURE 6.13
The Start menu is used to restart the computer.

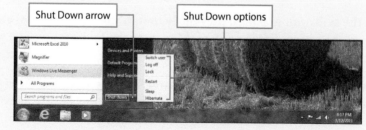

② **From the Shut down menu, click Restart.** The program starts closing files. It also checks to see if any of your open files have not been saved since the last time you made a change. If so, a dialog box will open for each unsaved file, asking if you want to save your work. This process takes a minute or two. Eventually, the screen goes dark.

③ **Wait while the computer shuts down and restarts. Observe the hard drive indicator light on your system unit and notice that it is in use while the program closes files and then reloads the operating system.**

④ **If your system requires a logon name and password, type those in the appropriate dialog box and click OK.** The operating system loads your personal settings and the desktop appears.

⑤ **Notice the icons appearing in the notification area on the taskbar as the operating system starts each program.** The mouse pointer may appear as a rotating circle during this time to indicate that you must wait until the computer is ready to use.

Log Off and Switch Users

If your computer is set up to accommodate multiple users, you have the option to log off or to switch between users. If you *log off*, your personal settings are closed, and you must supply the user name and password to log on again before using the computer. If you choose to *switch users*, you must supply the password for the second user. The settings for the first user remain loaded. The system may be set to log off any user who is not active for a set period of time, which will require a password to log back in.

Extend Your Knowledge

SHUTTING DOWN THE COMPUTER BY USING THE KEYBOARD

If a problem causes your computer to lose the connection to your mouse, you can use the keyboard to start the shutdown procedure. To shut down the computer from the keyboard, press the Start button—a button to the right of Ctrl on the bottom left edge of your desktop keyboard that displays the flag-type emblem similar to the one on the screen. If your keyboard does not have a Start button, hold down Ctrl + Esc to display the Start menu. Press → one time to select the *Shut down* button, and then press ↵Enter.

Sleep and Hibernate Modes

When you click Sleep from the Shut down menu, the computer makes a record of the status of the files and programs that are in use and stores that information in RAM. In *Sleep mode* some devices are turned off but power is still provided to the RAM memory to keep it active. When the computer is revived from Sleep mode it returns to full operation quickly with the same files and programs open as when it was put to sleep. Another option that saves more energy is the *Hibernate* option. When Hibernate is selected, a record of the status of files and programs is written to the hard drive and power to the RAM memory is turned off. When the computer is revived, it must load the operating system into RAM, and then the computer refers to the information stored on the hard drive to open the same files and programs that were open when it was placed into hibernation. This process saves more energy than the Sleep mode, but takes longer to return to full operation. It is useful for extending battery life on portable computers.

Lock Mode

If more than one user has an account on a computer, each user has a set of personal settings, and each uses a password to log on to the computer. The *Lock mode* enables a person who wants to leave the computer for a little while without logging off to come back to his or her own personal settings. When you use Lock mode, you still have to type in your user ID and password when you return. When you choose Lock from the Shut down menu, the operating system displays the logon screen and keeps the user's personal settings loaded and all programs and files open that were open when the computer was locked.

Shut Down Nonresponsive Programs

Sometimes a program will hang up and *not responding* displays to the right of the title in the title bar. If the program does not resume after several minutes, you may have to stop the program manually. To do this, press and hold Ctrl + Alt, and then press Delete. From the displayed menu, click Start Task Manager to open the Windows Task Manager. Click the Applications tab, select the nonresponsive program, and then click End Task and follow instructions to close the program.

Lesson 4 ▶ Using the Start Menu, Taskbar, and Help

A common method of starting programs begins with the Start button at the left end of the taskbar. After a program starts, it is represented by a button on the taskbar, where you can switch between programs by clicking the corresponding button, or switch between multiple open documents in the same program by pointing at the button, and then clicking one of the displayed thumbnails.

Using the Start Menu

When you click the Start button, the Start menu displays, as shown in Figure 6.14. It is divided into areas. The name of the current user is shown in the top-right corner. At the left is a list of programs that is divided into two parts. The top part shows names of programs that are always displayed on the Start menu—they are *pinned* to the Start menu. Below those program names is a list of recently used programs. You can start any of these programs by clicking on the name.

Near the bottom of the Start menu is a command named *All Programs* that you can click to display menus of installed programs. Below the All Programs command is a search box, which enables you to search the computer from the Start menu without opening the Computer window first. The right side of the Start menu is divided into two sections. The top section contains personal folders for the current user, and the bottom section contains links to common functions and commands available in Windows.

FIGURE 6.14

The Start menu can be used to start programs, including the program that turns the computer off.

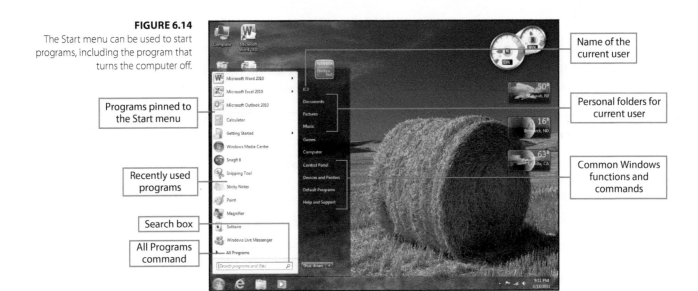

Programs pinned to the Start menu

Recently used programs

Search box

All Programs command

Name of the current user

Personal folders for current user

Common Windows functions and commands

Using Online Help

User manuals in book form are being replaced by electronic versions. Most programs like Windows come with a file that contains the instructions and support information that used to be included in a paper manual. Due to the rapid development of software, the version you buy may require updates, and so will the accompanying manuals. The manuals are stored on the company's website where they can be changed and updated as needed.

In most programs, you can search the manual through the Help feature. If you are connected to the Internet, you can search the most up-to-date version of the manual from the manufacturer's website, where you can also ask others for assistance. The Help feature for Windows, shown in Figure 6.15, is called Windows Help and Support and is available from the Start menu. In some cases, this window may be modified by the manufacturer of the computer to offer hardware support as well as support for Windows.

FIGURE 6.15

Windows Help and Support enables you to get help from a variety of sources.

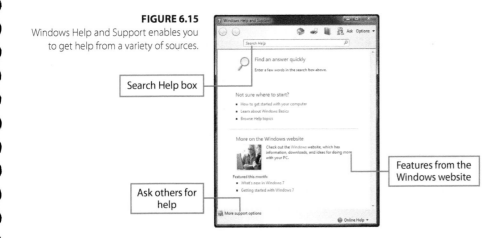

Search Help box

Ask others for help

Features from the Windows website

To use Windows 7 Help

① **Click the Start button ⊕, and then from the Start menu, click Help and Support.** Your computer will need to be online to complete this exercise.

② **In the Search Help box, type** Pin a program to the Start menu **and then press** ⏎Enter. A list of search results displays.

③ **From the list of search results, locate and click** *Customize the Start menu.* **Under Customize the Start menu, scroll down and click** *To pin a program icon to the Start menu.* Instructions on how to pin a program icon to the Start menu display, as shown in Figure 6.16. You may have to scroll up to see the instructions.

FIGURE 6.16
Help instructions to pin a program to the Start menu.

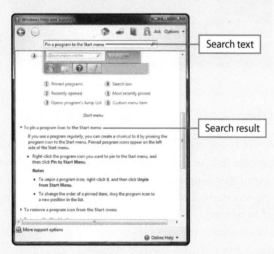

④ **Use the skills you practiced previously to start the Snipping Tool and create a Full-screen snip of the screen. Save a copy of this snip to the folder where you store your files. Name the file** U1Ch06SearchStudentName **substituting your name as indicated.**

⑤ **Take a moment to scroll down and read the instructions for pinning an icon to the Start menu.**

⑥ **When you are finished, Close** ⬛ **the Windows Help and Support Window. Submit your snip as directed. Close the Snipping Tool.**

Starting Programs

Programs may be started in a variety of ways. You can use the Start button to open the Start menu, and then point to All Programs to reveal a menu of programs that can be started by clicking their names. If a program you use often is several levels down in the menu, it may take a while to find and start it. To save time starting a commonly used program, you can add a shortcut icon to the desktop, the Start menu, or the taskbar.

To pin a shortcut to the Start menu and add programs to the Quick Launch toolbar

1 **Click the Start button 🏵, and then click All Programs.** The menu of installed programs opens.

2 **From the Start menu, click the Accessories folder, and then right-click Paint.** A shortcut menu appears, as shown in Figure 6.17. Be sure to use the right mouse button.

FIGURE 6.17
The shortcut menu can be used to pin a program to the Start menu.

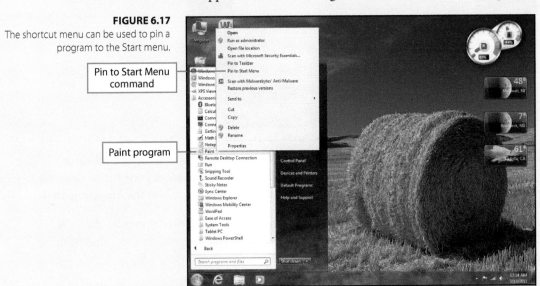

Pin to Start Menu command

Paint program

3 **From the shortcut menu, click Pin to Start menu.** A shortcut to start the Paint program is added to the Start menu, but you will not immediately see it.

4 **Click the Start button 🏵 to close the menu. Click the Start button 🏵 again to open the Start menu.** The Paint program has been added to the list of programs that will display every time you open the Start menu.

5 **From the Start menu, click Paint.** The Paint program starts and displays a Paint window.

6 **Click the Start button 🏵, and then right-click Paint. From the shortcut menu, click Pin to Taskbar.** The Paint program icon is added to the taskbar.

7 **With the Start menu still displayed, click All Programs, click the Accessories folder, and then right-click Paint. From the shortcut menu, click Send To, and then click Desktop (create shortcut). Click anywhere in an open area of the desktop, and then move the Paint window so that you can see the desktop icon for the Paint program.** A desktop icon and a taskbar icon have been added, as shown in Figure 6.18.

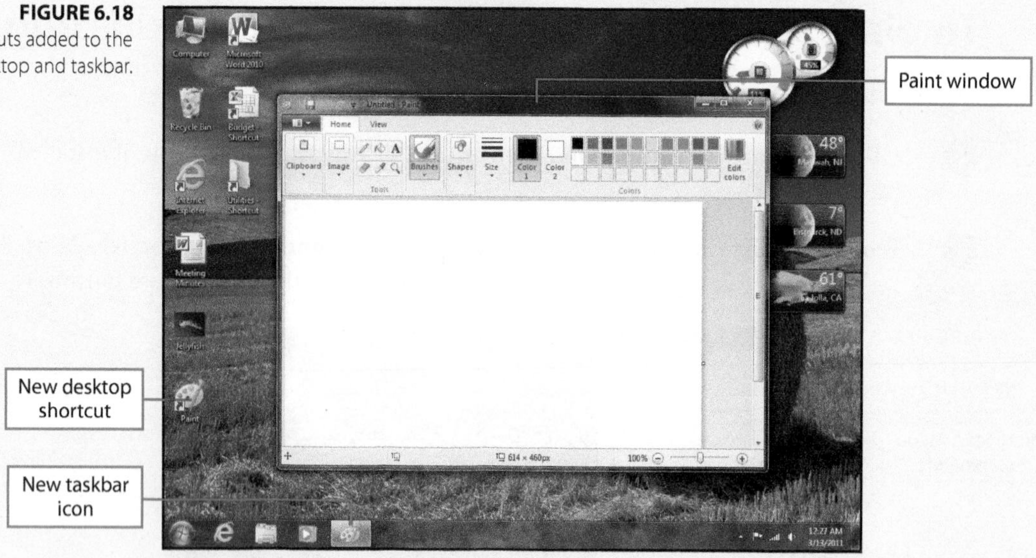

FIGURE 6.18
Paint shortcuts added to the desktop and taskbar.

Paint window

New desktop shortcut

New taskbar icon

8 Use the skills you practiced previously to start the Snipping Tool and create a Full-screen snip of the screen. Save a copy of this snip to the folder where you store your files. Name the file U1Ch06PaintStudentName **substituting your name as indicated. Close the Snipping Tool.**

9 **On the desktop, right-click the Paint icon, and then from the shortcut menu, click Delete. When asked if you want to remove the file, click Yes.** The shortcut icon has been removed, but the program remains on the computer.

10 **On the taskbar, right-click the Paint icon, and then from the shortcut menu, click Unpin this program from the taskbar. If you are asked if you want to remove the file, click Yes.** The shortcut is removed from the taskbar, but the program remains on the computer and the icon remains on the taskbar until the program is closed.

11 **Click the Start button ⊛, right-click Paint, and then from the shortcut menu, click Unpin from Start Menu.** The shortcut is removed from the Start menu, but the program remains on the computer.

12 **Leave the Paint program open, and submit the snip as directed.**

Moving Between Programs and Displaying Programs

When you have several programs open at the same time, there are several ways to move from one program to another. You can also hide all the open windows with a single click.

To move between programs

1 **Click the Start button ⊛, click All Programs, click the Accessories folder, and then click Notepad.** The Notepad program opens—this is a text-editing program.

2 **Use the technique you used in Step 1 to open the Getting Started and the Calculator programs.**

③ **Click the Start button** **, and then from the Start menu, click Control Panel to open the Control Panel window. If the Control Panel is maximized, click the Restore Down button** 🔲**.** You should now have five windows open, including the Paint window.

④ **In the taskbar, click the Paint button.** Notice that the Paint window moves in front of the other windows.

⑤ **Click several of the other taskbar buttons to switch between windows.**

⑥ **Click the Paint button to make the Paint window the active window.**

⑦ **On the right end of the taskbar, click the Show desktop button** ▮**.** Notice that all windows are minimized.

❓ If You Have Problems

The Show Desktop button is only available if Aero is enabled on your computer. **Aero** is the advanced graphical user interface introduced in Windows 7 and is used throughout this chapter. It is not available on some of the basic versions of Windows 7.

⑧ **Move the pointer to any of the open program buttons on the taskbar.** Notice that a thumbnail of each open window displays. If two or more files are open in the same program, two or more thumbnails will display side by side.

⑨ **Move the pointer to the Getting Started button, and then point to the thumbnail.** The full window displays temporarily—it will close when you move the pointer away from the thumbnail.

⑩ **Move the pointer back to the Getting Started button and right-click.** A *jump list* displays, as shown in Figure 6.19. A jump list displays that functions as a mini start menu for a program.

FIGURE 6.19
Jump list.

Jump list

Getting Started button

Locations associated with selected program

Tasks associated with selected program

⑪ **On the taskbar, right-click each open window, and then click Close window.**

⑫ **Close** 🔳 **all windows.**

A computer's storage media can hold hundreds of thousands of files. If the files on your computer are not well-organized, you will spend too much of your time searching for the files you need.

Understanding Folders and the Computer Window

Microsoft Windows uses the desktop metaphor to describe the screen. It uses a file cabinet metaphor to describe how files are stored. In a real file cabinet, you store papers in labeled folders. In Windows, you create folders in which to store electronic files. In Windows, you can create folders within folders to further subdivide the files when they become numerous. The Computer window has a Navigation pane that shows the folders and their relationships to each other, as shown in the expanded folder in Figure 6.20. If a folder is a subfolder, it is indented to the right. When you point 👆 to the storage device, if a ▷ triangle displays, this means that a folder contains subfolders that are not shown. A ◢ triangle indicates an open folder. The parts of the Computer window are described in Table 6.5.

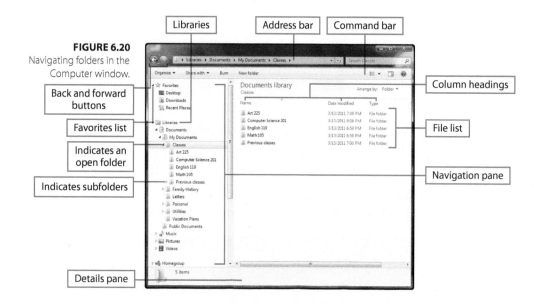

FIGURE 6.20
Navigating folders in the Computer window.

Labels: Libraries, Address bar, Command bar, Column headings, Back and forward buttons, Favorites list, File list, Indicates an open folder, Indicates subfolders, Navigation pane, Details pane

TABLE 6.5

PARTS OF THE COMPUTER WINDOW	FUNCTION
Address bar	Displays your current location in the folder structure as a series of links separated by arrows.
Back and Forward buttons	Enable you to navigate back and forth between folders you have already opened. These identify the columns; click the headings to sort the file list.
Details pane	Displays the most common properties associated with the selected file.
Favorites list	A list of commonly used folders.
File list	Displays the contents of the folder selected in the Navigation pane—the active folder.
Library	A collection of items, such as files and folders, assembled from various locations.
Navigation pane	The area on the left side of a folder window that enables you to view the folder structure in a vertical list. The Computer window, for example, displays the Favorites list, a list of folders and storage devices, and all libraries.
Title bar	The bar at the top of a window; often displays the name of the program and the name of the open document.
Toolbar	Provides buttons to perform common tasks.

Using Folders on the Desktop

Some folders are used more frequently than others. To facilitate access to these folders, you can place shortcut icons on the desktop that enable you to open the folders by double-clicking. You can move the shortcut icons to different places on the desktop. You can also place one shortcut icon into the folder represented by another shortcut icon by dragging one icon onto the other. These icons are not the file or folder themselves but are pointers to their actual location. *Because a lot of files and folders can clutter the desktop, use these shortcuts sparingly.*

To create, move, and nest desktop folder icons

1 **Click the Start button ☺, and then click Computer.** A list of folders on your computer displays, as shown in Figure 6.21. Your folders will vary, but be sure the Libraries display in the Navigation pane.

FIGURE 6.21
Libraries displayed by
Windows Explorer in the
Computer window.

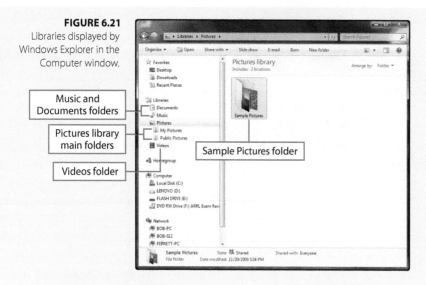

Music and
Documents folders

Pictures library
main folders

Videos folder

Sample Pictures folder

2 **Expand** ▷ **the Pictures library, and then click the Public Pictures folder.** The Sample Pictures folder displays in the file list, as shown in Figure 6.21. These pictures are installed with Windows 7. Notice that the Pictures library has two subfolders—My Pictures and Public Pictures. You can use the Public Pictures folder to share files with others on your network. All four libraries have similar folders.

3 **Right-click the Sample Pictures folder. From the shortcut menu, click Send to, and then from the menu click Desktop (create shortcut).** A shortcut icon is placed on the desktop. It may be behind an open window.

4 **Use the procedure you practiced in Step 3 to create desktop shortcuts to the Sample Music folder and Sample Videos folder—both of these folders are in the Public folders under Music and Videos.**

5 **Close** ✕ **the Computer window and Minimize** — **any other program windows that are open.** The three shortcut icons are added to the desktop as shown in Figure 6.22. Your desktop may display several other icons, so you may need to search for the new icons.

FIGURE 6.22
Folders can be added to
the desktop.

New desktop
folder icons

6 **Double-click the shortcut icon to the Sample Pictures folder on the desktop.** The Sample Pictures folder opens. This folder contains sample pictures and may also contain folders and other pictures.

7 **Close** ✕ **the Sample Pictures folder. Double-click the shortcut icon to the Sample Music folder on the desktop.** The Sample Music folder opens. This folder contains sample music and may contain other folders and music files.

8 **Close the Music window. In an open area of the desktop, right-click one time. From the shortcut menu, point to New, and then click Folder.** A folder is created on the desktop, and the file name is in edit mode. If you accidentally leave edit mode, right-click the file name, and then click Rename.

9 **For the new folder name, type** Favorite Folders **and then press** ⏎Enter.

10 **Point to the shortcut icon for the Sample Music folder. Drag the icon onto the Favorite Folders folder, and then release the mouse button.** The shortcut to the Sample Music folder is not shown on the desktop but has been placed in the Favorite Folders folder.

11 **Use the technique you practiced in Step 10 to drag the icons for the Sample Videos and Sample Pictures folders onto the Favorite Folders folder.**

12 **Double-click the Favorite Folders icon.** The Favorite Folders window displays, with the three shortcuts visible in the file list, as shown in Figure 6.23. Notice that the folder icons have a small arrow, which indicates a shortcut.

FIGURE 6.23
Folders can be moved into other folders on the desktop.

Favorite Folders window

New shortcuts with shortcut arrows

13 **Close** ⊠ **the Favorite Folders window. Open Internet Explorer or another browser, and in the Address box, type** www.archives.gov **and then press** ⏎Enter. **If necessary, right-click the browser toolbar and click Menu Bar to display the menus. From the menu bar, click File, point to Send, and then click Shortcut to Desktop. Click Yes if prompted. Close** ⊠ **the browser window.** A shortcut to the U.S. National Archives site is sent to the desktop, as shown in Figure 6.24.

FIGURE 6.24
Shortcuts to favorite websites can be added to the desktop.

National Archives website icon

14 **Use the skills you practiced previously to start the Snipping Tool and create a Full-screen snip of the screen. Save a copy of this snip to the folder where you store your files. Name the file** U1Ch06ShortcutsStudentName **substituting your name as indicated.**

15 **Close the Snipping Tool and turn in your snip as directed.**

Displaying Properties and Renaming and Deleting Desktop Shortcut Icons

If you right-click a desktop shortcut icon, you can view its properties, rename it, or delete it. When you delete the shortcut icon, you do not delete the folder or its contents, just the shortcut.

To rename, view properties of, and delete desktop icons

1 **Right-click the shortcut to the National Archives website. On the shortcut menu, click Rename. Type** NARA **and then press** ⏎Enter**).** NARA is an acronym for the National Archives and Records Administration and makes an easier icon name to read.

2 **Double-click the Favorite Folders icon to open the folder. Right-click the Music shortcut, and then from the shortcut menu, click Properties. Be sure the General tab is selected.** The properties of the shortcut display, including the location on the hard drive that the shortcut takes you to when you double-click it, as shown in Figure 6.25.

FIGURE 6.25
The Properties dialog box shows the location of a folder shortcut on the hard drive.

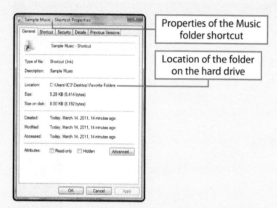

Properties of the Music folder shortcut

Location of the folder on the hard drive

3 **Close** ⌧ **the Properties dialog box, and then Close** ⌧ **the Favorite Folders window. Point to the Favorite Folders folder, and then right-click. From the shortcut menu, click Delete.** The Delete Folder dialog box displays, asking if you want to move the folder to the Recycle Bin. Recall that removing shortcuts does not affect the folders themselves in any way.

4 **In the Delete Folder dialog box, click Yes.** The Favorite Folders folder and all three of the shortcuts it contains are sent to the Recycle Bin.

5 **Double-click the NARA shortcut to confirm that the shortcut works, and then Close** ⌧ **the browser window. Click the NARA shortcut icon one time to select it, and then press** Delete**).** Pressing Delete is the same as selecting Delete from a shortcut menu.

6 **In the Delete File dialog box, click Yes to confirm the deletion.** The shortcut is removed from the desktop.

Lesson 6 ▶ Managing Files with Windows Explorer

Windows provides a file management program named Windows Explorer that can be started from the Start menu or by double-clicking the Computer icon that is typically displayed on the desktop or as a Windows Explorer icon on the taskbar.

Identifying File Types

Files can be grouped into three main categories. The first type of file is one you will use virtually all the time—data files. Data files are the files you create when you work with a word processing program or a spreadsheet program, or files that you download from a digital camera or scan into the computer using a scanner. These files are stored in your User area, in folders called Documents, Pictures, Music, and Videos. The other two types of files are application files—which are the programs themselves—and system files—which are files necessary to support the operating system and the application files. Some of the system files are hidden, even if you have access to the area in which they are stored.

If you are using a computer in a lab environment or at work, you will probably not have access to the application and system files, which are generally found in the main hard drive folder on your computer. It is generally a good idea to leave these files alone anyway; if you accidentally delete one of them, one or more programs may not work any longer.

Files that you create by using application programs are automatically associated with that program. Sometimes you will have a choice of programs to associate with a particular file type. This is especially true of graphics files. Many computers have several programs, for example, that can manipulate JPEG files. To check a file association, right-click the file, click Properties, and then under Opens with, click Change.

Using Windows Explorer to Manage Files

Files are stored in folders. You can use Windows Explorer to open the Computer window, in which you can create folders and move files between them. In this lesson, you will need to have a storage area in which to create and manipulate files and folders. The following examples assume the use of a flash drive, sometimes called a thumb drive or a USB drive.

To create folders, change the view, and sort files

① **Click the Start button ⊕, and then click Computer. In the title bar, click the Maximize button ⧉.**

② **Plug your flash drive into a USB port.** If you are using another type of storage device, locate and open your storage device.

③ **In the Navigation pane, click the flash drive icon—your flash drive will have a different name from the one shown in the figures. Point to the flash drive, and then to the left of the flash drive name, click the triangle ▷.** The folders on the flash drive display—yours may have no folders or it will show different folders.

④ **On the toolbar, click the New Folder button. Type** Chapter 6 **and then press** ⏎Enter. The folder is named.

⑤ **In the Navigation pane, navigate to the location of your student files for this chapter.** The files may be on a CD-ROM, they may be on a network drive, or they may be located on your computer or USB drive.

⑥ **Click on any of the student data files, and then on the toolbar, click the Organize button. From the menu, click Select All to select all the files. Press** Ctrl + C **to copy all the files to your Clipboard.**

⑦ **In the Navigation pane, navigate to and click the Chapter 6 folder you just created. In the empty file list, right-click, and then click Paste.** The files are copied from your student folder into your Chapter 6 folder.

⑧ **On the toolbar, click the Change your view button arrow** ⊞ ▾**, and then from the menu, click Large icons.** Notice in the file list that a list of files displays as icons with the file names underneath. These icons are called *thumbnails*—they show a small version of the actual file.

⑨ **On the toolbar, click the Change your view button arrow** ⊞ ▾ **again, and then from the menu, click Extra Large icons.** Notice that you can see many of the details of the file, but fewer of the icons display on the screen at any one time. Scroll down and notice that some files display icons, whereas other files—typically graphic files—display the contents of the file.

⑩ **On the toolbar, click the Change your view button arrow** ⊞ ▾ **again, and then from the menu, click Details.** Notice in the file list that a list of files displays. Your file list may only show the file name but no further details.

⑪ **In the file list, right-click the Name heading at the top of the column of files. If there is not a check mark next to Size, click Size. Use the same procedure to add Date modified and Type columns.** Compare your screen with Figure 6.26.

FIGURE 6.26
In Details view, files can display several characteristics including name, date, size, and type.

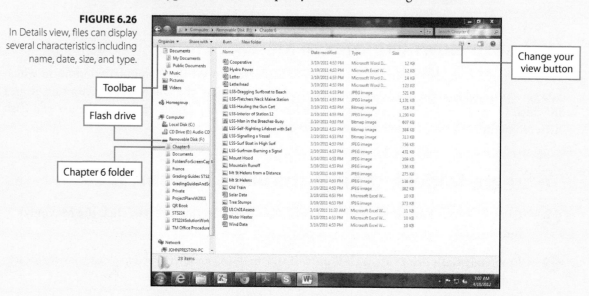

⑫ **In the file list, click the Size column heading, and notice that the files are sorted from largest to smallest.**

⑬ **In the file list, click the Size column heading again, and notice that the files are sorted from smallest to largest.** When you click a column heading, the column is sorted on that category. When you click the same heading again, it sorts in the opposite direction.

⑭ **In the file list, click the Type column heading, and notice that the files now are sorted by file type.**

⑮ **Use the skills you practiced previously to start the Snipping Tool and create a Full-screen snip of the screen. Save a copy of this snip to the folder where you store your files. Name the file** U1Ch06TypeStudentName **substituting your name as indicated. Close the Snipping Tool.**

⑯ **In the file list, click the Name column heading to sort the files by name. Leave the Computer window open for the next exercise.**

Creating, Copying, Moving, and Deleting a Folder Using Shortcuts

To copy or delete a folder, right-click the folder name and choose the Copy or Delete command from the shortcut menu. You can also use the Organize button from the toolbar, but the ***keyboard shortcuts*** are quicker. A keyboard shortcut is a combination of keys that perform a command as an alternative to using the ribbon or menu. A folder can be moved by dragging it to another location or by using the Cut and Paste options from the shortcut menu. Copying a file leaves the original in its original location and places a copy in the new location; moving a file removes the file from the original location.

To create, copy, rename, move, and delete a folder

1 **In the Navigation pane, locate and right-click your Chapter 6 folder. From the shortcut menu, point to New, and then click Folder. Type** LSS Pictures **and then press** ⏎Enter**.** The new folder displays below the Chapter 6 folder but is indented, indicating that it is a subfolder located in the Chapter 6 folder.

2 **Use the same procedure to create three more folders called Energy, Movies, and Letters in the Chapter 6 folder.**

3 **In the file list, click the Name column header as necessary to move the folders to the top of the list.**

4 **If the Details pane does not display at the bottom of the screen, on the toolbar, click the Organize button, point to Layout, and then click Details pane.** The Details pane displays at the bottom of the Computer window.

5 **In the file list, click the Movies folder. Press and hold** Ctrl **and then press** C **to copy the folder. In the file list, click anywhere. Press and hold** Ctrl **and then press** V **to paste the folder to create a copy of the folder. Click the Name header as necessary to move the new folder to the top of the list with the other folders.** The new folder has the same name as the copied folder, with the word *Copy* added, as shown in Figure 6.27. The most commonly used keyboard shortcuts combine Ctrl with X for cut, C for copy, and V for paste.

FIGURE 6.27
Copies of folders can be made.

Organize button

Copied folder

Details Pane

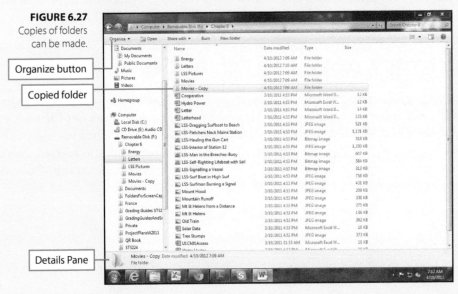

6) In the file list, right-click the Movies - Copy folder, and then from the shortcut menu, click Rename. Type Vacation and then press ↵Enter. The folder name is changed.

7) In the file list, move the pointer to the Vacation folder. Drag the Vacation folder over the Movies folder and notice the ScreenTip, as shown in Figure 6.28. You can drag a folder to another folder, and when you release the mouse button, the folder is moved as a subfolder to the highlighted folder.

FIGURE 6.28
Folders can be dragged into another folder.

Folder dragged to another folder

ScreenTip

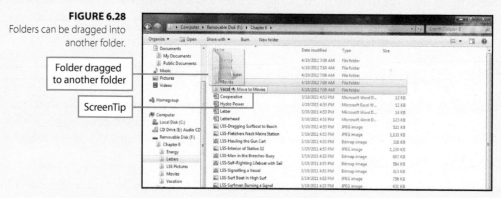

8) Release the mouse button to finalize the folder move. Move the pointer to the Navigation pane, and then point to the Movies folder. Click the ▷ triangle. The new subfolder is displayed in the Navigation pane and in the file list.

9) In either the Navigation pane or the file list, click the Chapter 6 folder, and then right-click the Letters folder. From the shortcut menu, click Delete. When asked to confirm the Delete, click Yes. The folder is deleted. You can copy, move, create, or delete folders from either the file list or the Navigation pane.

10) Leave the Computer window open for the next exercise.

Selecting, Copying, Moving, and Deleting Files

Individual files can be copied, moved, and deleted using the same methods as those used on folders. You can select more than one file at a time using Ctrl or ↑Shift.

To select, copy, move, and delete files

1) In the Navigation pane, be sure the Chapter 6 folder is selected. In the file list, click the first file with a name beginning LSS. Move the pointer down to the last file with a name beginning with LSS, hold down ↑Shift, and then click the file. When you click a file, hold down ↑Shift, and then click another file, all the files in between are also selected. Notice that the Details pane displays the number of items selected and the combined size of all the files, as shown in Figure 6.29.

FIGURE 6.29
Use Shift to select several contiguous files.

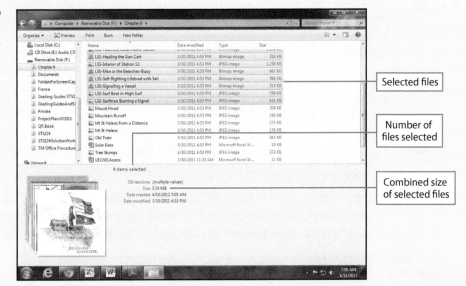

Selected files

Number of files selected

Combined size of selected files

② **Move the pointer anywhere over the selected files, and then drag them to the left to the LSS Pictures folder in the Navigation pane.** All nine files are moved from the Chapter 6 folder to the LSS Pictures subfolder, and they no longer display in the file list for the Chapter 6 folder.

③ **In the file list, click the Hydro Power Excel file. Hold down** Ctrl**, and then click the Solar Data, Water Heater, and Wind Data Excel files.** Notice that four files are selected. If you want to select two or more files that are not next to each other, use Ctrl instead of ⬆Shift.

④ **Drag the selected files to the Energy folder.** You can drag them to the Energy folder in either the Navigation pane or the file list.

⑤ **In the file list, right-click the Letterhead file, and then from the shortcut menu, click Copy. Right-click the Energy folder, and then from the shortcut menu, click Paste.** Notice that the Letterhead file is still displayed in the Chapter 6 folder.

⑥ **In the file list, double-click the Energy folder.** Notice that the folder contains the four Excel files and the Word file that you just copied, as shown in Figure 6.30.

FIGURE 6.30
Files can be copied or moved to a new folder.

Five files copied or moved to the folder

Energy folder

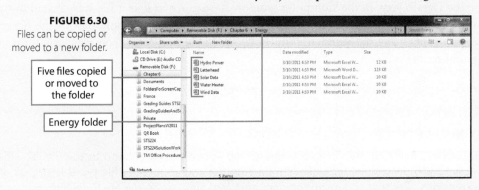

⑦ **Use the skills you practiced previously to start the Snipping Tool and create a Full-screen snip of the screen. Save a copy of this snip to the folder where you store your files. Name the file** U1Ch06CopyStudentName **substituting your name as indicated. Close the Snipping Tool.**

⑧ **Right-click the selected Letterhead file, and then from the shortcut menu, click Properties.** Notice under Attributes that one of the options is *Read-only*. A **read-only** file can be opened and read but cannot be edited. To edit a read-only file, you need to either clear the read-only check box or save the file with another name. The latter is usually the best idea.

⑨ **Close ▣ the Properties dialog box. Click on your flash drive or other storage device, and notice the path that is displayed in your address bar.** Each of the arrows acts as a link to the folder displayed to the left.

⑩ **In the address bar, click the arrow to the right of your Chapter 6 folder.** Notice that all the folders on in this folder are displayed in a menu, as shown in Figure 6.31. This enables you to quickly click any of the folders to open them. The computer assigns letters to storage devices. The main storage device is usually the hard drive and it is given the letter C. Other drives are assigned letters as they are detected, and they might change if they are removable like a flash drive. The drive letter assigned to your flash drive might differ from the letter in the figure.

FIGURE 6.31
Files in a folder or on a drive can be displayed from the address bar.

Flash drive arrow

Folders located on the flash drive (yours will vary)

⑪ **Click anywhere in the window to close the menu. Submit your snip as directed, and leave the Computer window open for the next lesson.**

Lesson 7 ▶ Finding Files and Using the Recycle Bin

Organizing your files into logically named folders and subfolders will help you find the files you need. You can use the Details view in the Computer window to sort by the date a file was created or by the file type to help find files. If you are unsure of the location or you know only part of the file name, you can search for files using the Search option. If the file has been deleted, you may look for it in the Recycle Bin and restore it if you wish.

Extend Your Knowledge

IDENTIFYING FILE TYPES

When you copied the files to the Chapter 6 folder, you added a Type column to the file list. This makes it easy to identify the file type of each file. Another way to identify file types is to look at their file extensions. Files that end in *.doc* or *.docx* are Word files, *.xls* or *.xlsx* are Excel files, and *.ppt* and *.pptx* are PowerPoint files. In these examples, the four-letter extensions are from Office 2007 and Office 2010 and the three-letter extensions are from earlier versions of Office. Some file extensions indicate program files. For example, an *.exe* file is an executable file; it will start a program. See Table 6.6 for a list of common file extensions and the programs that are often associated with them.

TABLE 6.6	COMMON FILE EXTENSIONS	ASSOCIATED PROGRAM
	.avi	Audio/video file; audio and video programs like Windows Media Player
	.doc	Microsoft Word versions 2003 and earlier
	.docx	Microsoft Word versions 2007 and later
	.xls	Microsoft Excel versions 2003 and earlier
	.xlsx	Microsoft Excel versions 2007 and later
	.exe	Executable files that run a program
	.jpg	Compressible image; graphics programs such as Paint
	.M4V	Audio and video file; Apple iPod
	.mp3	Compressible audio file; audio programs like Windows Media Player
	.mpeg	Audio and video file; video programs like Windows Media Player
	.pdf	Acrobat reader or Adobe Acrobat
	.eps	Uncompressed image file; graphics programs like Paint
	.zip	Compressed file, Windows XP or later or WinZip

Searching for Files

Windows Explorer has a search option in which you can provide partial information about the file and it will search for all files that include the information you provide. You can limit the scope of your search to a particular storage device or to a folder within it.

To search for files and folders

① **In the Navigation pane, click the Chapter 6 folder. In the upper-right corner of the window, click the Restore Down button 🔲. Near the upper-right corner of the Computer window, in the Search box, type** LSS **and then watch the file list.** All the files containing the letters *LSS* (in that order) display, as shown in Figure 6.32. Notice that both files and folders are included in the search results. If you want to save this search, you can click the Save search button on the toolbar.

FIGURE 6.32
Locate files using the Search box.

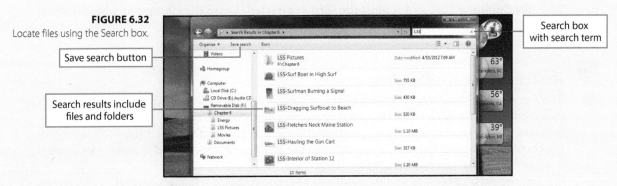

Save search button

Search results include files and folders

Search box with search term

② **On the right side of the Search box, click the Close 🔳 button.** The search is removed, and all files and folders in the Chapter 6 folder are displayed.

③ **In the Search box, type** st **and watch the file list.** All files that contain the letters *st* in that order are displayed.

④ **At the bottom of the search results, under** *Search again in* **click the File Contents button.** The files that contain the letter *st* in either the file name or in the file contents are displayed.

⑤ **In the Search box, type** jpg **and watch the file list.** Notice that all the JPEG files display, even though the letters *jpg* do not display in the file name; this is an example of a file extension, which are typically hidden. Notice also that some of the file information in the file list is hidden or cut off, as shown in Figure 6.33.

FIGURE 6.33
Search for file types using the file extension.

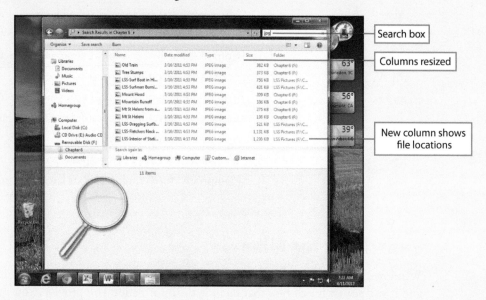

- Search box
- Columns resized
- New column shows file locations

⑥ **Maximize** ▭ **the Computer window. Move the pointer to the line between the Name column heading and the Date modified column heading until the** ⬌ **pointer displays. Double-click the line and notice that the column width is expanded to display the longest file name.** You can also drag the line to expand or narrow the column width.

⑦ **Widen the Folder column, and then use the skills you practiced previously to start the Snipping Tool and create a Full-screen snip of the screen. Save a copy of this snip to the folder where you store your files. Name the file** U1Ch06FindStudentName **substituting your name as indicated.**

⑧ **In the Navigation pane, locate and click the Chapter 6 folder to close the search. Close the Snipping Tool and submit the snip as directed. Leave the Computer window open.**

If You Have Problems

If you have problems finding a file, there are a couple of possible reasons. First—and most likely—is that the file name you gave the file is not descriptive, and the search term you are using will not help find the file. The first solution is to name the file by using words that are closely associated with the contents of the file. The second solution is to use an advanced search and search for an unusual word or phrase that you know is contained in the file.

The second possible reason you cannot find a file is that the file is hidden. To locate a hidden file, in the Computer window, click Organize, and then click Folder and Search Options. Click the View button, and then click the Show hidden files, folders, and drives option button. Repeat the search.

Restoring Files from the Recycle Bin and Emptying the Recycle Bin

If you do not find a file, it may have been deleted. If the file was deleted from the hard drive, it can usually be recovered from the Recycle Bin. Once you are confident that the Recycle Bin has no files that you may later want to recover, you can empty the Recycle Bin to make more space available on your hard disk.

To open the Recycle Bin, you either double-click the Recycle Bin icon on the desktop or click the arrow to the right of the Folder icon on the address bar, and then click Recycle Bin. To restore a file from the Recycle Bin, in the file list, click the file, and then in the toolbar, click the Restore this item button. If, for example, you accidentally deleted the Hydro Power file from the hard drive, it could be found in the Recycle Bin, as shown in Figure 6.34. The file is restored to the folder from which it was deleted. You can restore several files at the same time. You can also restore a folder, which restores not only the folder, but also all the files that were contained in that folder when it was deleted.

FIGURE 6.34
Using the Recycle Bin.

Empty the Recycle Bin button

Restore this item button

Extend Your Knowledge

IDENTIFYING WHICH FILES CAN BE FOUND IN THE RECYCLE BIN

In this book, it is assumed that you are using a flash drive to store your files. When you delete files from the flash drive, other removable media, or network drives, the files are not sent to the Recycle Bin. The only way to recover deleted files from removable media is through the use of third-party software; you cannot restore these files from the Recycle Bin.

Lesson 8

Identifying Precautions and Problems When Working with Files

If you follow some basic guidelines, you can avoid some common file management problems.

Naming Folders and Files Using Standard Conventions

Create folders with relatively short names, and organize them in a logical manner with some folders inside others. Use a standard naming convention that will work well when you sort the files or folders. File names are sorted alphabetically even if they have numbers in them. If you have sequential numbers in file names, use zeros to make all the numbers the same length. For example, use Chapter 02 instead of Chapter 2; otherwise, Chapter 10 would come before Chapter 2 in a sorted list of file names.

Windows recognizes file names with spaces, but it does so by scanning the file name and inserting a special code for each space in the name. This may pose a problem if you use the file on some other operating systems. If it is likely that you may save the file as a Web page or on another operating system such as Linux or UNIX, do not use spaces. Many people use an underscore character to simulate a space in a file or folder name, as in *My_House*. This does not work well if the file name may be converted to a hyperlink in a Web page, which is typically represented with an underline that overlaps the underscore character.

Managing Files and File Folders

Windows 7 gets you started organizing your files. For each user added to the computer, four libraries are created by default. These folders are shown in Figure 6.35. The name of each folder defines its purpose. Typically, the most commonly used library is Documents, which is where you store your spreadsheets, presentations, word processing documents, database files, and other files you create. Media files are stored in the Music, Pictures, and Videos libraries. The Navigation pane displays your libraries, as well as your storage devices and network links.

FIGURE 6.35
Default libraries in Windows 7.

Default folders

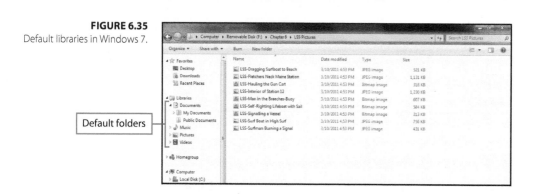

Extend Your Knowledge

DISPLAYING FILE EXTENSIONS

By default, Windows hides the three- or four-letter file extensions for known file types and assigns them automatically when you save files from within an application. To change the default setting to display file extensions for all files, click Start, and then click Computer. On the toolbar, click the Organize button, click Folder and search options, and then click the View tab. Under Advanced Settings, clear the *Hide extensions for known file types* check box, and then click OK.

Choose short, descriptive names for your folders and nest them in a logical manner. The highest level folders should be your most important topics. For example, you might have a folder for school, one for home, one for activities, and one for family. The school folder might have subfolders for each semester, and each semester folder could have folders for each class you take. The school folder might also have a subfolder for correspondence—one for clubs and organizations—and so on. This type of structure enables you to quickly find files.

It is also a good idea to delete unnecessary files regularly, although with the size of hard drives getting larger, it is often a good idea to keep older files if there is any possibility that you might need to refer to them in the future. The files that really need to be deleted are duplicates of music and video files, which take up a lot of space on your hard drive. You can minimize the number of duplicate files by using a logical file structure.

Backing Up Files

You should ask yourself what would happen if your hard disk suddenly stopped working. If there are files on your hard disk that you must have, you should make copies of those files at regular intervals to removable storage media. If you are working on important documents and have an Internet connection, you can use the program's Send command to send a copy of your file to your e-mail account every half hour or so to help avoid losing work if something should happen to your computer. Free storage space is provided on the Internet, including SkyDrive from Microsoft. This type of storage has the benefit of being accessible from anywhere there is an Internet connection.

Opening Problem Files

A file may become damaged and, as a result, it may not open in its application program. This problem may be partially solved if the file is a text document. You can open the file using a simple text editor program, like WordPad, which is available from the Start menu. You may be able to read some of the plain text amid other meaningless code symbols. If the file is not yours, it may be protected by a password that prevents people from opening it without the owner's permission. You may need to obtain the password from the owner to open such a file.

If you are trying to open a file on a network drive and are denied access, it may mean that the file is in use by another person and the program's settings restrict use to one person at a time. It may also mean that the network is temporarily down.

Summary

In this chapter, you identified the Windows 7 desktop elements and learned how to manipulate windows. You learned various ways to shut down a computer and how to start and run programs. You used the Computer window to create, move, copy, rename, and delete files and folders. Finally, you used the Search box to find files.

Key Terms

address bar *(p. 213)*	Favorites list *(p. 201)*	maximize *(p. 199)*
Aero *(p. 211)*	file list *(p. 213)*	minimize *(p. 199)*
All Programs *(p. 206)*	Forward button *(p. 213)*	Navigation pane *(p. 201)*
Back button *(p. 213)*	gadget *(p. 198)*	notification area *(p. 196)*
click *(p. 200)*	Hibernate *(p. 205)*	pin *(p. 206)*
Computer icon *(p. 196)*	icon *(p. 194)*	read-only *(p. 222)*
desktop *(p. 194)*	jump list *(p. 211)*	Recycle Bin *(p. 196)*
details pane *(p. 213)*	keyboard shortcut *(p. 219)*	Restore Down *(p. 199)*
dialog box *(p. 197)*	Library *(p. 201)*	ribbon *(p. 197)*
double-click *(p. 200)*	Lock mode *(p. 206)*	right-click *(p. 200)*
drag *(p. 198)*	log off *(p. 205)*	scroll bar *(p. 201)*

scroll box *(p. 202)*

Sleep mode *(p. 205)*

Status bar *(p. 197)*

switch users *(p. 205)*

taskbar *(p. 195)*

task pane *(p. 197)*

thumbnails *(p. 195)*

title bar *(p. 197)*

toolbar *(p. 197)*

triple-click *(p. 200)*

window *(p. 194)*

Windows *(p. 194)*

Windows Explorer *(p. 200)*

Windows Sidebar *(p. 195)*

Checking Concepts and Terms

MULTIPLE CHOICE

Circle the letter of the correct answer for each of the following.

1. Which of the following is the part of the Windows screen that displays icons for programs that are running in the background? [L1]
   a. Sidebar
   b. Operations
   c. Desktop
   d. Notification area

2. The title bar button that changes names depending on the present size of the window can have which of the following pairs of names? [L2]
   a. Minimize/Maximize
   b. Maximize/Restore Down
   c. Open/Close
   d. Minimize/Restore

3. Which of the following commands from the Shut down menu will often solve problems by closing and opening programs? [L3]
   a. Sleep
   b. Log off
   c. Restart
   d. Turn off

4. If two files are open at the same time, you can switch between the windows for each file by doing which of the following? (Choose the method that will work regardless of the size of the window.) [L4]
   a. Click the title bar.
   b. Click in the notification area.
   c. Click the program's button on the taskbar.
   d. Press Ctrl and Home to switch between open files.

5. Which of the following is *not* a good use of a desktop icon? [L5]
   a. To open a commonly used file
   b. To store copies of all word processing files
   c. To open a commonly used folder
   d. To start a program

6. Which of the following is the view in the Computer window that displays a list view and can show the size of the file and the date it was last changed? [L6]
   a. Details
   b. Thumbnails
   c. Slideshow
   d. Icons

7. When you display the files in the file list as Large Icons, which type of icons display? [L6]
   a. Thumbnails
   b. Details
   c. GUI
   d. Program

8. When you restore a folder from the Recycle Bin, [L7]
   a. the files that were in the folder are restored, but the folder is not.
   b. the folder and all its contents are restored to the original location.
   c. the folder is restored, but any files that were in the folder when it was deleted remain in the Recycle Bin.
   d. nothing happens; you cannot restore a folder from the Recycle Bin.

9. You can recover deleted files from the Recycle Bin from which type of device? [L7]

a. Flash drive

b. Network drive

c. Removable DVD-RW

d. Hard drive

10. To reduce the potential for problems if you expect a file to be used on Linux or UNIX operating systems, it is a good idea to avoid use of which character(s) in file names? [L8]

a. Space

b. Period

c. Numbers

d. Lowercase letters

MATCHING

Match each term in the second column with its correct definition in the first column by writing the letter of the term on the blank line in front of the correct definition.

_____ **1.** In the file list, icons that show small versions of the files [L6]

_____ **2.** Command from the Shut down menu that enables a person to leave the computer and close all personal settings [L3]

_____ **3.** Small program—such as a currency converter, a calendar, or a clock—that displays on the desktop [L1]

_____ **4.** Process or button that reduces the size of a maximized window [L2]

_____ **5.** Command used to add a program to the Start menu [L4]

_____ **6.** Located in the scroll bar, it can be used to drag a work area up and down or left and right [L2]

_____ **7.** An area on the right side of the taskbar that keeps you informed about processes that are running in the background [L1]

_____ **8.** Command from the Shut down menu that enables a person who wants to leave the computer for a little while without logging off to come back to his or her own personal settings [L3]

_____ **9.** Command from the Shut down menu that shuts down nearly all the power to the computer but keeps power to the CPU and to RAM, while greatly reducing energy consumption [L3]

_____ **10.** A file that can be opened and read but not edited [L6]

A. Gadget

B. Lock

C. Log off

D. Notification area

E. Pin

F. Read-only

G. Restore down

H. Scroll box

I. Sleep

J. Thumbnail

Skill Drill

Skill Drill exercises reinforce chapter skills. Each skill reinforced is the same, or nearly the same, as a skill presented in the chapter. Detailed instructions are provided in a step-by-step format.

Each exercise is independent of the others, so you can do the exercises in any order.

1. Restoring Files from the Recycle Bin

In this chapter, you used a flash drive to store your files. When you delete a file from a flash drive, it is not sent to the Recycle Bin; however, when you delete a file from the main hard drive, it is sent to the Recycle Bin and can be restored. To complete this exercise, you will need to be able to copy files to the hard drive.

To restore a file from the Recycle Bin, follow these steps:

1. Click the **Start** button, and then click **Computer**. Click the **Change your view** button arrow and then click **Details**. Under **Libraries**, expand the Documents library, and then click **My Documents**.

2. On the toolbar, click the **New folder** button. Type Chapter 6 and then press ⏎Enter.

3. Navigate to the location of your student files for this chapter. Select the first four files that begin with *LSS*, copy the files, move to your new **Chapter 6** folder, and then paste the files in the folder.

4. In the **Chapter 6** folder, select the first two files that begin with *LSS*, and then press Delete. When prompted, click **Yes**.

5. On the left edge of the address bar, click the arrow to the right of the icon to display a menu, and then click **Recycle Bin**. Recall that you can also open the Recycle Bin by double-clicking the icon on the desktop. Select the two files you just deleted.

6. Use the skills you practiced previously to start the **Snipping Tool** and create a **Full-screen snip** of the **Recycle Bin**. Save a copy of this snip to the folder where you store your files. Name the file U1Ch06RestoreStudentName substituting your name as indicated.

7. On the toolbar, click the **Restore the selected items** button. Navigate back to your **Chapter 6** folder to confirm that the files have been restored.

8. **Close** the Computer window. Submit your snip as directed. Delete the Chapter 6 folder.

2. Using the Keyboard to Switch Between Windows

If you need to switch between windows quickly and repeatedly, it is often faster to use the keyboard shortcuts instead of reaching for the mouse.

To switch between open windows using the keyboard, follow these steps:

1. Click the **Start** button, click **All Programs**, click the **Accessories** folder, and then click **Calculator**.

2. Use the same procedure to open **WordPad** and **Paint**.

3. Press and hold Alt. Keep this key down during the following steps.

4. Press and release Tab⇆. A window displays with a thumbnail of each open window and one for the desktop. One of the windows is selected and you can see the full window in front of the other windows. Press and release Tab⇆ (keep Alt depressed). The selection moves to another icon.

5. Press and release Tab⇆. The selection rotates among the icons that represent the open windows. Continue this process until the **Calculator** window displays.

6. Release Alt. The Calculator window displays on top of the other windows, even if it was minimized.

7. Use the skills you practiced previously to start the **Snipping Tool** and create a **Full-screen snip** of the screen. Save a copy of this snip to the folder where you store your files. Name the file U1Ch06AltStudentName substituting your name as indicated.

8. **Close** all windows. Submit your snip as directed.

3. Searching Files by Date

Windows records the date and time along with the file when you edit a file. If you forget the name of a file, you may be able to find it if you know when it was last edited.

To search for a file by the date it was last edited, follow these steps:

1. If you are using a flash drive, be sure it is inserted into a USB port. Click the **Start** button, and then click **Computer**.

2. In the Navigation pane, click the flash drive on which you are storing your files. (Note: If you are using another storage location, select that instead.) In the upper-right corner of the screen, in the **Search** box, type jpg and press ⏎Enter. All the *.jpg* files on the flash drive display in the file list.

3. Click in the search box, and then at the bottom of the displayed menu, click **Date modified**. If you worked on documents yesterday, click **Yesterday**. If you worked on documents for this chapter several days ago, click **Earlier this week**. If you know the day you worked on a document, you can click the date in the calendar at the top of the menu.

4. When you find files you worked on previously—they match the Date modified search term that you used, and the files display in the file list—use the skills you practiced previously to start the **Snipping Tool** and create a **Full-screen snip** of the **Computer** window. Save a copy of this snip to the folder where you store your files. Name the file U1Ch06DateStudentName substituting your name as indicated. Your list of files and the date range will depend on the files stored on your flash drive and when you worked on them, but it should show a list of files that end with .jpg.

5. **Close** the Computer window. Submit your snip as directed.

Explore and Share

Explore and Share questions are intended for discussion in class or online. Look for information that is related to the learning outcomes for this chapter as directed. Submit your answers as directed by your instructor.

1. If you use Microsoft Office frequently, you will likely run into corrupted files at some point. Use your browser to go to **www.microsoft.com/windows**. In the **Search** box, type corrupted files and then press ⏎Enter. Read about corrupted files and how to solve them. Prepare some tips on how to fix or recover these files. [L8]

2. In this chapter, you learned that you cannot use the Recycle Bin to restore files that you have deleted from a flash drive. Use your browser to search for ways to restore deleted files on these devices. Can they ever be restored, or is the delete final? Are there programs that claim to be able to recover the files? [L7]

3. You can create a new user account using the Control Panel. Open Windows Help and Support center, and in the Search box, type add a new user and press ⏎Enter. Read about creating new user accounts. If you buy a computer and are the only one who will use it, is there a reason why you might want to create a second account with fewer privileges to use on a daily basis? Why else might you add new accounts to a computer? [L7]

In Your Life

In Your Life questions are intended for discussion in class or online where you can share your personal experience. Restrict your answers to the topics described in each exercise. Submit your answers as directed by your instructor.

1. If you expect to be away from your computer for more than 10 minutes, do you use Sleep or Hibernate mode to save energy? Now that you know about these options, do you think you will use them? If so, when would you use Sleep and when would you use Hibernate? [L1]

2. Do you prefer to maximize all the windows and switch between them, or do you like to use them at less than full size so you can open several of them at once and click an exposed part to bring a window to the foreground? You practiced switching windows by using Alt + Tab⇄ in the Skill Drill exercises. Do you think you might use that method of switching windows? [L2]

3. Have you ever used the Recycle Bin to restore a deleted file? If so, did it save you much time? Have you ever tried to recover a file that you deleted from a flash drive? [L7]

4. What problems have you experienced opening files? Do you have some tips to prevent or solve the problem you had? [L8]

5. On your personal computer, do you have a lot of icons on your desktop? After going through this chapter, do you think you will continue to keep the shortcuts there, or will you try to reduce the clutter on your desktop? If you have a number of icons on the desktop, do you think it would be good idea to organize them in a desktop folder? [L1, L8]

Related Skills

Related Skills exercises expand on or are somewhat related to skills presented in the lessons. The exercises provide a brief narrative introduction, followed by instructions in a numbered-step format that are not as detailed as those in the Skill Drill section.

1. Hiding, Moving, and Resizing the Taskbar

The taskbar may be set to stay on the screen continuously or only when you point to it. The taskbar is usually located at the bottom of the screen, but it may be placed at either side or at the top. You can also widen it to provide more room to display button names.

To change the location of the taskbar and hide its settings, follow these steps:

1. Display the **Start** menu, open the **Control Panel**, and change the view to **Category**. Open the **Appearance and Personalization** window.

2. Under **Taskbar and Start Menu**, click **Customize the Start menu**.

3. Display the **Taskbar** tab and clear the **Lock the taskbar** check box, if necessary. This enables you to move the taskbar.

4. If necessary, select **Auto-hide the taskbar**. This option will hide the taskbar when it is not being used.

5. If you made any changes, click **Apply**; otherwise, click **OK**. The taskbar slides off the screen. **Close** all windows. Move the pointer to the bottom of the screen where the taskbar is usually located. The taskbar reappears.

6. Move the pointer to the top edge of the taskbar where it turns into a double-headed resizing arrow. Drag the top edge of the taskbar upward until it doubles in width, and then release the mouse button. If this does not work, right-click an open area of the taskbar, and the click Lock the taskbar.

7. Use the skills you practiced previously to start the **Snipping Tool** and create a **Full-screen snip** of the desktop. Save a copy of this dialog box to the folder where you store your files. Name the file U1Ch06TaskbarStudentName substituting your name as indicated. Close the Snipping Tool.

8. Drag the taskbar to the sides of the screen to see if you like the taskbar in a different location. Drag the taskbar back to the bottom of the screen.

9. Change the settings back to the original settings on your computer, and then submit your snip as directed.

2. Searching for Files that Contain a Particular Word

Windows 7 has the capability to find documents by locating words in the documents, not just by title or date. To search the documents on your computer for files that contain a particular word, follow these steps:

1. Display the **Computer** window. Select your flash drive or other storage location that contains the files for this chapter.

2. In the **Search** box, type coop and notice the files that are displayed.

3. Under the search results, click the **File Contents** button. This will enable the program to search the contents of the file, not just the file name. There should be at least two files displayed: Letterhead and Cooperative.

4. Use the skills you practiced previously to start the **Snipping Tool** and create a **Full-screen snip** of the desktop. Save a copy of this dialog box to the folder where you store your files. Name the file U1Ch06CoopStudentName substituting your name as indicated. Close the Snipping Tool.

5. Close the **Computer** window, and then submit your snip as directed.

3. Locating and Adding Gadgets from Online Sources

There are fewer than a dozen gadgets installed with your Windows 7 operating system. There are, however, many more available online.

To add gadgets from online sources, follow these steps:

1. In an open area of the desktop, right-click, and then from the shortcut menu click **Gadgets**.

2. At the bottom of the **Gadget** window, click the **Get more gadgets online** link.

3. Locate two gadgets that are not available on your computer and follow the directions to add them to the desktop.

4. Use the skills you practiced previously to start the **Snipping Tool** and create a **Full-screen snip** of the desktop. Save a copy of this dialog box to the folder where you store your files. Name the file U1Ch06OtherGadgetsStudentName substituting your name as indicated.

5. Right-click one of the gadgets you just added, and then from the shortcut menu, click **Attach to Sidebar**.

6. Right-click each of the new gadgets and delete them.

7. Close the open window, and then submit the snip as directed.

Discover

Discover exercises give you general directions for exploring and discovering more advanced skills and information. Each exercise is independent of the others, so you can complete the exercises in any order.

1. Personalizing the Desktop Background

In this chapter you added shortcuts to the desktop, added icons to the taskbar, and added gadgets to the desktop. There are other things you can do to customize the look and operation of your desktop.

When you first get your computer or install a new version of Windows, the desktop background will display a background created either by the computer manufacturer or by Microsoft. You can change the background image to a picture supplied by Microsoft, or to a picture you have taken with a digital camera. To replace the current desktop image, do the following:

1. In an open area of the desktop, right-click, and then from the shortcut menu click **Personalize**. The Control Panel Personalize window displays.

2. At the bottom of the **Personalization** window, click the **Desktop Background** link.

3. Scroll through the gallery of desktop backgrounds supplied by Microsoft. If you see one that you like, click the image, and then **Minimize** the window to see if you like the new background. If you do, close the window; otherwise, go through the list again and try a different image. When you have selected the background image you want, **Close** the Personalization window.

4. If you have a favorite picture that you would like to use for your desktop, follow the procedure you just practiced, but in the **Desktop Background** window, click the **Browse** button, navigate to the location of the picture, and then select that picture for your new background.

Write a summary of what you learned. Then, reopen the Personalization window and describe other modifications you can make to the desktop. If you use a word processor to write the summary, print a copy if your instructor requires it.

2. Comparing USB Flash Memory Drives

Flash memory drives are also known by their brand names such as Key Drive, Pen Drive, USB Drive, and ThumbDrive. These drives are very easy to use and extremely portable. USB ports and drives are currently available in two speeds, USB 2 and USB 3. The faster USB flash memory devices that work with USB 3 will also work with older USB 2 drives.

To learn more about USB drives, use your Web browser to visit the following sites and read about this topic.

- Wikipedia, The Free Encyclopedia: **en.wikipedia.org/wiki/Keydrive**
- HowStuffWorks.com: **www.howstuffworks.com/flash-memory.htm**
- Amazon.com: **www.amazon.com** (search for *USB 3.0 flash drive*)

Write a summary of what you learn. Include an essay on how USB drives are used and a table that shows at least five different brands, memory size, and cost. If you use a word processor to write the summary, print a copy if your instructor requires it.

3. Uninstalling a Program

When you buy a new computer, you will find that it comes with a number of programs installed by the manufacturer that are advertising samples for programs—for example, limited versions of antivirus programs. Also, after you have owned your computer for a while, you will find that there are programs that you never use.

You might be tempted to find the program files on your hard drive and delete them. This almost never works, however, because nearly all installed programs have hidden system files that are not removed when you delete the program folder. Windows 7 contains a Control Panel utility program that enables you to remove unwanted programs and clean out the hidden system files.

To uninstall a program, do the following:

1. Click the **Start** button, and then from the Start menu, click **Control Panel**.

2. In the **Control Panel** window, under **Programs**, click **Uninstall a program**.

3. Locate and select the program you want to remove, and then in the toolbar, click **Uninstall**.

Follow the previous steps to the point just before making the final decision to uninstall. Write a summary of what you learned. If you use a word processor to write the summary, print a copy if your instructor requires it. If you do not want to uninstall the program, choose Cancel.

4. Adding Files and Folders to the Favorites List

You will find that you have a few files and folders that you use all the time. You can add these files and folders to the Favorites list at the top of the Computer window Navigation pane, which make them easy to find and access.

To learn how to add items to the Favorites list, open Windows Help and Support and use the search box to search for Navigation pane favorites. When you are done reading the information on this procedure, add a file or folder to your own Favorites list.

Write a summary of what you learned. If you use a word processor to write the summary, print a copy if your instructor requires it.

Glossary

8.3 convention An early DOS file-naming convention that used up to eight letters or numbers to the left of a period and up to three characters to the right of a period

A

AAC (.aac) Popular audio compression method

adaptive computer device Input device designed for the special needs of people with different types of disabilities

Aero The advanced graphical user interface introduced in Windows Vista

algorithm A set of instructions that a computer can follow to accomplish a task

All Programs Option on the Start menu that displays all installed programs

alpha version The first version of a software program; it comes before beta testing

Alternate (Alt) key Key on the keyboard intended for use with other keys to provide new functions

American Standard Code for Information Interchange (ASCII) A standard in which 8-bit numbers represent letters, decimal numbers, and special function characters

analog An electronic signal or system that varies in time in a way that is similar to the property it represents

analog-to-digital (A to D) converter A device that takes an analog input, such as a voice recorded by a microphone, and converts it to a digital signal

Android A smartphone operating system from Google

animation The process of making objects on the screen move; in PowerPoint, controls how text and other objects come onto the screen during a slide show

app Short for application program, but generally used to describe very specific programs sold for use on smartphones and tablets

appliance A computer that is dedicated to a particular task or function

application program Program with which you can accomplish tasks such as word processing, photo editing, or sending e-mail

application service provider (ASP) Software provided online for special purposes on a license or per-use basis

asynchronous digital subscriber line (ADSL) Technology used to provide broadband Internet access over telephone wires

B

Back button Navigation button that moves the view to the previous display

backlight Provides illumination from behind for an LCD screen

backward compatibility The ability of a newer version of a program to open and display files that were created using an earlier version of the program

bar code reader Device that translates the flickering reflection of a beam of light from a series of black and white bars into computer code

BD-R Blu-ray disc that can be written to once and read many times

BD-RE Blu-ray disc that can be erased and recorded many times

BD-ROM Blu-ray disc that can be recorded once and read many times

beta tester Person who evaluates a prerelease version of software

beta version Early version of the software released to a limited audience for testing

binary System that has two states (on and off) that can be represented using zeros and ones

biometric device A security device that can match a user's biological information—comparing fingerprints, retinal scans, or voice prints—with patterns stored in a database to confirm the identity of authorized users

bit (b) A single digit—either a zero or a one—in a binary number

bitmap (.bmp) Rectangular array of picture elements where each has a number to indicate color

blog Online personal journal, contraction of the words *Web log*

Bluetooth A wireless standard used for short distances; used to connect cell phones and headsets, MP3 players and headphones, and wireless keyboards and mice

Blu-ray Optical disc technology that enables you to save 25 GB on a single-layer disc and 50 GB on a dual-layer disc that is the standard for recording HDTV

boot To start the computer

Boot Camp A program that provides a choice of operating system when the computer is first turned on

broadband Using multiple signals of different frequency on the same medium to provide fast Internet connections that are always active

bug Error found in programs that causes the program to fail to complete its operation successfully

burn To write data to an optical disc

byte (B) A group of 8 bits used to represent characters, decimal numbers, and other special characters

C

cathode ray tube (CRT) Analog imaging device that uses an electron beam of charged particles in a glass vacuum tube to create pictures on the end of the tube that is covered with light-emitting phosphors

CD-R Optical disc to which data may be written and then read

CD-ROM Optical disc from which data may be read

CD-RW Optical disc from which data may be read and to which data may be recorded and rewritten

cell reference In Excel, the identification of a specific cell by its intersecting column letter and row number

central processing unit (CPU) The "brains" of the computer; performs calculations and controls communication in the computer

chip Another term for microchip

circuit breaker Safety device to disconnect electric power

click Movement of the mouse pointer followed by depressing the left mouse button

click pad Touch pad that can also be depressed to function as a button

clock A device that sends out pulses used to coordinate computer component activity

clock speed The rate at which the clock circuit emits pulses

clone Duplicate of a file or device or the process of making a duplicate

cloud The network of servers and communications systems that comprise the Internet

command Directive to perform a process

Command key Button on an Apple keyboard

command-line interface A way of interacting with the operating system using the keyboard

compact disc (CD) Portable, round optical storage medium

CompactFlash card Removable electronic memory that does not need power to retain data; typically used in digital SLR cameras

computer-based training (CBT) Training that is delivered and assessed using a computer

Computer icon On the taskbar, an image that represents the Computer window in the Windows Explorer program

contrast ratio The range between the darkest black on the screen and the brightest white

Control (Ctrl) key Key on the keyboard intended for use with other keys to provide new functions

Control Panel A set of options that sets default values for the operating system

course management system Software that provides components of a class, either online or in combination with face-to-face instruction; usually provides a syllabus, calendar, lectures, chatrooms, a grade book, and other features

crop To remove an unwanted portion of an image

D

data Raw, unprocessed facts and figures

database Lists of data organized in tables where each column is a type of information and each row is one person, event, or interaction

database management system (DBMS) A relational database that controls large amounts of data, provides data security and

multi-user access, and can be customized to fit the user's needs

debugging The process of removing bugs or errors from a software program

defragment Rearranging data on a hard disk so that files are written on adjacent sectors

desktop The basic screen from which Windows and applications are run; consists of program icons, a taskbar, a Start button, an optional Windows Sidebar, and a mouse pointer

desktop computer A personal computer that fits well in an individual workspace but is not mobile

desktop publishing Creating professional-quality newsletters, flyers, brochures, and booklets on a PC; also a type of software

Details pane Section of the window used to display common properties associated with a file

device driver A small program that is written to provide communication instructions between a peripheral device and the computer's operating system; also called a *driver*

Device Manager Windows dialog box that provides information about devices connected to the computer

dialog box A box where you select settings and choose what actions you want the computer to take

digital light processing (DLP) Projection technology that uses thousands of mirrors that are controlled by the computer

digital single lens reflex (DSLR) Semi-professional and professional still cameras that use interchangeable lenses and give the photographer complete control over the photography process

digital-to-analog (D-to-A) converter A device that takes a digital file, such as an image from a digital camera, and converts it to an analog signal

digital versatile disc (DVD) See *digital video disc*

digital video disc (DVD) Optical storage that can be recorded in layers; also called *digital versatile disc*

digital video interface (DVI) A display standard used to connect video sources to digital monitors or display devices

digitizing tablet Flat surface with an array of crossed wires built into the surface that can sense the vertical and horizontal position of a pointing device

disc Optical media such as CDs and DVDs

disk Magnetic media such as hard disks and floppy disks

Disk Operating System (DOS) An early operating system with a character-based interface

distributed database Related records stored on more than one computer

distributed processing Dividing a task into component parts that can be distributed to other computers

docking station Device into which a camera or other device is attached to transfer data to a computer

document A word-processing file; the main workspace in the Microsoft Word window

dongle A device that attaches to a computer and functions as an adapter or provides additional functions such as security or Bluetooth connectivity

dot matrix printer Type of impact printer

dots per inch (dpi) Measure of printed image quality; usually the higher the number of dots per inch, the better the image quality

double-click Pressing the left mouse button twice in rapid succession

double-data-rate 2 (DDR2) A type of SDRAM typically used in personal computers

drag See *drag-and-drop*

drag-and-drop A technique for moving text, an image, or other object from one location to another by selecting an item and dragging it with the mouse to a new location

driver See *device driver*

dumb terminal A communication device with a keyboard and monitor that depends on another computer for processing and storage

DVD-ROM Optical disc that is read-only; uses the digital versatile disc method of encoding data

E

e-book An electronic book that can be read on a computer or a special e-book reader

edit To revise

electronic learning (eLearning) Computer-supported education

electronic paper Black-and-white display that uses reflective light

electrostatic plotter A plotter that can print large graphics, similar to a laser printer

embedded operating system Compact, efficient, and often single-purpose operating system used in computer appliances and special-purpose applications, such as an automobile, an ATM machine, or a portable media player

end-user license agreement (EULA) Software license that you agree to when you purchase and install commercial software

Ethernet Standard for connecting a network; usually refers to a twisted pair cable

Extensible Markup Language (XML) Framework for writing a language as simple text along with information on how the application software should interpret that text

external hard drive A hard drive that plugs into a computer, usually using a USB connection

F

Favorites list List of commonly used folders

field In a template, e-mail message, or database, a pre-defined area where a specific type of data is entered, such as a file name, page number, or date; in Access, the smallest useable fact collected for each record; a category of data

file compression program Program that reduces the size of files

file extension The letters following a period after a file name that identifies the type of file and often the software that was used to create it

file list Names of documents or other file types arranged in a sequence

file server A networked computer that stores and finds files or data, delivers the information to the user, and manages updates to the files

filter To display only data, Web pages, or incoming messages that meet certain criteria

finite element analysis Dividing a model into small elements and calculating how they interact to simulate behavior of a real system

FireWire High-speed connection developed by Apple and used for data transfer

firmware Programming that controls a device from within the device

flash drive See *USB drive*

flash hard drive Hard drive that uses flash memory and has no moving parts; it uses less energy, breaks down less frequently, and generates less heat than a magnetic hard drive

flash memory Memory with no moving parts; retains its information after the power is removed; used for such things as USB drives and camera digital picture storage

flatbed scanner Device to transfer documents or pictures one sheet at a time

font A set of numbers and letters that have the same design and shape

form Access object that is used to input, edit, or view data, typically one record at a time

format The appearance or layout of a document

formula Symbolic representation of a mathematical process

Forward button Navigation button that moves the view to the next display in a sequence

fragmented Files stored on the hard disk as separate parts in nonadjacent tracks

frames per second Rate at which video images are displayed

freeware Software that is copyrighted by the programmer but for which there is no charge

function A prewritten formula that is used to solve mathematical problems or manipulate text fields

Function (Fn) key Key on notebook keyboards intended for use with function keys to provide additional functions

G

gadget Small program—such as a currency converter, a calendar, or a clock—that displays in the Windows Sidebar

gamepad A game controller held in both hands with buttons and control sticks that is used to play computer games

ghost image Compressed file that contains a copy of the installed software

gigabyte Approximately a billion bytes

gigahertz Approximately a billion repetitions or cycles per second

gold version The final copy of software at the end of the beta process

graphical user interface (GUI) A program interface that includes screen elements such as dialog boxes, windows, toolbars, icons, and menus that is manipulated with a mouse and keyboard to interact with the software

Graphic Interchange Format (GIF) Image storage format that uses only 8 bits of data for each picture element

graphics tablet See *digitizing tablet*

H

handout A printable output in PowerPoint that displays one to nine slides to a page for the purpose of providing an audience with a copy of a presentation

hard disk Magnetic media made of metal; part of a hard drive

hard drive Device to read and write hard disks; usually the main storage device in a computer

head Device in a hard drive that reads and writes data in magnetic form on a stack of thin metal disks

heat sink The radiator fins attached to a processor that help cool the processor when a fan is running

hertz Measure of frequency equal to one repetition per second

hibernate Record the status of open programs and files to the hard drive and shut down the CPU and RAM

high-definition multimedia interface (HDMI) Connector used to transfer digital signals

Hi-Speed USB USB 2.0, which is a faster version than USB 1.0

hot-swappable Can change connected devices without shutting down the computer

Hypertext Markup Language (HTML) A language that is used to create Web pages that can be viewed in a Web browser

I

IBM compatible Platform that used Intel processors and DOS or Windows operating systems

icon A picture that represents a file, program, or other object

impact printer Transfers ink to the paper by striking an ink-impregnated cloth ribbon

information Data that has been processed so it is organized, meaningful, and useful

infrared (IR) light Form of invisible light used to send signals or data

ink-jet printer Creates an image on paper by spraying ink on a page

input The action of adding instructions and data to a computer

insertion point Position where input will go; a blinking vertical line on your workspace that indicates where text or graphics will be inserted

installation The process of copying a program to the computer's hard drive and then making it operational

integrated circuit (IC) Array of transistors and other electronic devices that performs a function

internal hard drive The main storage device in a computer

International Business Machines (IBM) Manufacturer of computer systems and software

iOS Smartphone operating system from Apple

J

Joint Photographic Experts Group (JPEG) Very popular image format that allows variable compression

joystick Pointing device that is a rod connected to a trackball

jumpers Connectors that fit over pairs of pins

jump list Shortened start menu

K

keyboard shortcut Combination of keys that perform a function as an alternative to clicking menu choices or icons on the ribbon

L

land An unmarked spot on a CD that represents the number 1

laptop computer A mobile computer that can be used anywhere and can run on batteries when a power outlet is not available; also called a notebook or portable computer

laser printer Uses a light beam to transfer images or text to paper where powdered ink is attracted and melted onto the paper

legacy Older model or version

Library Collection of items in the navigation pane in Windows

Linux An operating system for personal computers based on the UNIX operating system

liquid crystal display (LCD) Type of digital display that uses electric fields to change the transparency of liquid cells to pass red, green, or blue light to create an image;

typically much thinner than CRT monitors

Lock mode Command from the Shut Down menu that enables a person who wants to leave the computer for a little while without logging off to come back to his or her own personal settings without having to log on again

Log Off Command from the Shut Down menu that closes personal settings and requires you to supply your user name and password to log on again before using the computer

lumen Measure of the brightness of light sources

M

Macintosh (Mac) Model of personal computer by Apple Corporation

mainframe computer Large computer systems, usually very reliable and secure, used to process large amounts of information

malware Programs that are intended to do harm

maximize The process or button that increases the size of a window to fill the screen

media player Program that plays audio or video files

megabyte Approximately a million bytes

megahertz (MHz) One million hertz

megapixel Measurement of the number of pixels (in millions) in a digital camera image

memory Integrated circuits designed to store data before and after it is processed by the CPU

microchip Integrated circuit for computers

microcomputer Another term for a personal computer

microprocessor In personal computers and workstations, the central processing unit (CPU)

that consists of millions of transistors

microSD card Removable flash memory that does not need power to retain data; typically used in point-and-shoot cameras, smartphones, and PDAs

micro USB Very small USB connector that is smaller than a mini USB

minimize The process or button that hides a window and represents the window with a button on the taskbar

mini USB Small USB connector that is smaller than a Type A or Type B connector

modeling Using formulas to simulate the behavior of real systems

monitor Display device used with computers

motherboard Primary circuit board of a computer where the central processing unit and RAM are located

mouse Pointing device that moves on the desktop and controls a screen pointer

MP3 (.mp3) Popular audio compression method

multi-core processor Multiple processors on a single chip

N

nanoseconds Billionths of a second

natural user interface (NUI) Method of interaction between the user and the computer that utilizes finger movements and spoken commands

Navigation pane The area on the left side of a folder window that enables you to view the folder structure in a vertical list; in the Computer window, displays the Favorites list and the Folders list

network license A software license that allows anyone on the network to use a piece of software

nondisclosure agreement An agreement not to share the product's new features with anyone else during beta testing

nonvolatile memory Memory that does not need constant power to function

notification area An area on the right side of the taskbar that keeps you informed about processes that are running in the background, such as antivirus software, network connections, and other utility programs; it also typically displays the time

Num Lock key Key on the keyboard that toggles the function of the numeric keyboard keys from navigation to numeric functions

O

offsite Storage at another location

OpenOffice Suite of productivity applications available for free download that works with Linux, Windows, and Mac platforms

open source The source code for software that is free to distribute and use that meets the criteria of the open-source initiative

operating system (OS) A type of software program that determines how the processor interacts with the user and with other system components

optical character recognition (OCR) Software that converts images of text on paper into editable electronic text

optical mouse Mouse that detects motion using the reflection of a beam of light

Option key Mac computer key that is similar to the Control key on other computers

OS X Macintosh operating system

output The process of displaying, sharing, or otherwise communicating information that has been processed by the computer

P

patch A software program that modifies an existing program to repair minor problems

peer-to-peer network Direct communication between computers

pen plotter A plotter that uses individual pens and different colored inks to create large line drawings

peripheral Device attached to the system unit or case

personal computer Typically operated and customized for use by one person

personal information manager (PIM) Software that tracks calendars, tasks, and contact information, and may be expanded to include other functions such as e-mail

petabyte Approximately a quadrillion bytes

pin To attach a program to the Start menu or the taskbar

pit An indentation burned into a CD that represents the number 0

pixel A single picture element or subdivision of a picture

platform The combination of a particular operating system and the processor that it controls

plotter Computer output device that draws or prints images, often on larger than normal paper sizes

plug-and-play Windows feature that recognizes new hardware and automatically searches for the correct software driver to install the new hardware

plug strip Device with several power outlets

point-and-shoot camera Small, inexpensive digital still camera with mostly automatic functions

pointing stick A pointing device that senses directional pressure

point-of-sale (POS) terminal A type of dumb terminal used

for managing and recording transactions

port Connection device on the computer

Portable Network Graphics (PNG) Graphics format designed for the Web

power strip An extension cord with a box of additional electrical receptacles

primary key field Unique identifier field in a database table

primary storage The type of storage that is used while the computer is processing data and instructions; also known as memory

probe Sensor used to explore places that are unsafe or not easily accessible

processing Manipulating data according to a set of instructions to create information that can be stored

programmable Computers that can change programs

programmer A person who writes computer programs

programming The process of writing software

projector Projects a monitor image for group viewing

Q

query A set of criteria intended to extract the records and fields that would answer a particular question

QuickTime (.mov) Video compression method from Apple Computer

R

radio frequency identification (RFID) A device that enables remote retrieving of information using radio waves

random access memory (RAM) Integrated circuits that work with the CPU

raw Uncompressed video files

readme File with notes from programmers on changes made since the manual went to press

read-only A file that can be opened and read but not edited

read-only memory (ROM) Type of memory that is usually not changed

record Database information about one person, item, place, object, or event divided into fields and displayed in a single row of a data source

Recycle bin Storage location for files that have been deleted from the hard drive, from which they can be restored

reinstall Make a program or device operational again after removal

relational database A type of database that divides data into several tables that can be related to each other by a common field; Access is a relational database

release to manufacturing (RTM) A software version following beta testing that is sent to the companies that process the product for distribution

remote control Wireless control unit typically used with an appliance such as a music player, a television, or a media center on a computer

report The Access object that is used to summarize information for printing and presentation of the data

resolution The level of detail on a computer monitor, measured in dots per inch for images and pixels for monitors

response time Amount of time it takes to change the color of a pixel

restore down Process or button that reduces the size of a maximized window

restore point A representation of the state of your computer's system files at a particular point in time

revolutions per minute (rpm) Rate of spin of a disc

ribbon Area of the screen that contains groups of commands and command buttons

right-click Movement of the mouse pointer followed by depressing the right mouse button

robot A mechanical device programmed to perform special functions

S

Safe Mode A method of rebooting a computer that runs only the essential parts of the operating system, and does not load many of the utilities that typically run in the background

scanner Device to transfer documents and pictures into a digital format; also, a device that checks several different frequencies to detect and receive those that are in use

scanning Act of transferring a document or picture to a digital format one line at a time

scroll bar Horizontal or vertical bars that enable you to navigate in a window, menu, or gallery by manipulating the display of content within the window

scroll box A box in scroll bars that can be used to drag a workspace up and down or left and right; it also provides a visual indication of your location in the workspace

seat One user of a program that is designed for use by many people

secondary storage Type of storage that is used to record information for later retrieval, and does not require constant power to retain the information that is stored

Secure Digital (SD) card Removable flash memory that does not need power to retain data; typically used in cameras, smartphones, and PDAs

sensor Device that reacts to changes in the environment and produces an electrical signal that corresponds to the change

server A powerful computer that provides a service, such as running a network or hosting an Internet site

service pack Major software updates that are just short of an upgrade

shareware Software that can be used for a trial period but must be paid for if used regularly

Shift key Key on the keyboard used to produce capital letters or to be used in combination with other keys to provide new functions

site license A software license that allows anyone in an organization or group to use a piece of software

Sleep mode Command from the Shut Down menu that shuts down nearly all of the power to the computer but keeps power to the CPU and to RAM, while greatly reducing energy consumption

slide Screen intended for projection (see *slide show*); the main workspace in PowerPoint

slide master Slide layout images that contain all of the placeholder formats for each slide layout within a theme, which are used to change theme formats for all slides

slide show Series of screens used to present ideas to an audience

Small Computer System Interface (SCSI) A peripheral connection method used for high-speed data transfer

smartphone A cellular telephone that has a small keypad or touch screen that can run software applications, store and play music, display pictures, and send and receive e-mail

software Written instructions that direct a computer's processor on how to complete tasks; also called *programs*

solid state drive (SSD) Long-term storage device without moving parts

speaker notes A printable output in PowerPoint that provides a copy of the slide image and related notes for the speaker during a presentation

spreadsheet Generic term for financial data arranged in rows and columns with formulas that can recalculate automatically if values in cells change

spyware Program that records and reports user activity to an unauthorized party

Status bar Rectangular area at the bottom of a window that provides additional information about the window

stylus A pen-like input device that is used to tap or write on a touch screen

subwoofer Audio speaker designed for low range sounds and music

suite Collection of software that is designed to work together

supercomputer Extremely fast computers used for research, modeling, and large-scale data analysis

SuperSpeed USB USB 3.0, which is faster than USB 2.0

S-video port Older type of video port that provides better images than a single conductor

Switch user mode Command from the Shut Down menu that closes personal settings and allows another user to log on

synchronous dynamic random access memory (SDRAM) Type of memory typically used in personal computers (see *double-data-rate 2 [DDR2]*)

system clock Circuits that keep time in the computer

system restore Process of reinstating a previous set of values used by the operating system

system unit The part of the personal computer that contains the central processing unit

T

table The Access object that stores the data that makes up the database; each table stores a set of related data; in Word, a list of information set up in a column-and-row format; in Excel, data that is organized into adjacent columns and rows and defined as a table

tablet computer A portable computer designed to enable the user to write on the screen or use a touch screen as a mode of input

taskbar Displays the Start button and the names of any open files and applications. The taskbar may also display shortcut buttons for other programs

task pane Rectangular area at the side of the window that displays commonly used tools or navigation commands

terabyte Approximately a trillion bytes

terminator Required device at the end of some types of buses such as SCSI connections

thermal printing Display of text using temperature-sensitive paper

thumb drive Removable flash memory device

thumb mouse A portable mouse that uses a trackball operated by the thumb

thumbnails Icons that display a small representation of a file or a slide

title bar The bar at the top of a window; often displays the program icon, the name of the file, and the name of the program; the Minimize, Maximize/Restore Down, and Close buttons are grouped on the right side of the title bar

toner Dry ink used with copiers or laser printers

toolbar Rectangular area usually located below the menu bar with command options

touch pad A small, rectangular, flat area below the space bar on many notebook computers that performs the functions of a mouse

touch screen Input device that senses touch on a monitor

track ball A pointing device with a moving ball in a cradle

transformer Converts electrical voltage from high to low or low to high

transistor An electronic device that can switch on or off in response to an external signal

trial version Software that is intended for temporary use to evaluate a product

triple-click Pressing the left mouse button three times in rapid succession

type A USB Connector on the upstream or computer side of the cable

type B USB Connector on the downstream or device end of the cable

U

Unicode A code that uses up to 32-bit numbers to represent characters from numerous languages, including the older ASCII codes

uninstall Remove a program and its associated files

uninterruptible power supply (UPS) A device that uses batteries to keep a computer running when the power fails

Universal Serial Bus (USB) Connection method that replaces many other types of peripheral connectors

UNIX Popular operating system on mainframe computers; the basis for the Linux operating system on personal computers

update Changes to a version of software to fix problems or add minor feature improvements

upgrade Replaces current version with a newer one that has significant changes

USB 2.0 Second version of USB (see *Universal Serial Bus*)

USB 3.0 Third version of USB (see *Universal Serial Bus*)

USB drive Flash memory that plugs into a USB port on a computer

USB hub Provides multiple USB ports and may provide additional power

utility program Small program that does one task

V

version A variation of the original program or file

video graphics array (VGA) port A personal computer display standard

video RAM (VRAM) Dedicated video memory

virtual memory Space on a hard disk used to supplement physical memory

virus Program that makes copies of itself without permission and distributes them as attachments to files or e-mail

virus protection software Program that detects, blocks, and removes virus programs

voice recognition Ability to convert speech into digital files or commands

voice synthesizer Software that translates electronic words into spoken words

volatile memory Memory that needs constant power to function

W

WAV (.wav) Popular uncompressed audio file format

Web cam Video camera intended for use over the Internet

Weblog (blog) A personal online journal

Web server Computer that runs software that provides Web pages and runs scripts

what-if analysis Process of substituting values to see the effect on dependent calculations

window Rectangular area of the screen with a title bar, Close and Minimize buttons, and a Maximize/Restore Down button

Windows Name of Microsoft's operating system that uses a GUI

Windows Explorer The program within Windows that displays the files and folders on your computer

Windows Phone Smartphone operating system from Microsoft

Windows Sidebar Area at the right side of the desktop where gadgets may be placed

wireless fidelity (WiFi) Wireless standard used to connect computers and peripherals; commonly used for home networks

WMA (.wma) Popular audio compression method

WMV (.wmv) Video compression method from Microsoft

word The unit of data with which a processor can work

word processing The process of using a computer to write, store, retrieve, and edit documents

word size The amount of data that is processed in one operation

workbook A collection of worksheets in a spreadsheet program

worksheet The main workspace in Excel, which is a grid of rows and columns, generically referred to as a spreadsheet

workstation A high-powered personal computer designed for specific tasks, such as graphics, medicine, and engineering; the term is also sometimes used to describe a networked personal computer

Index

E

Ease of Access Center, 172

E-books, 11

Edited document, 131

Editing files, 21

Electrical damage, protecting computers from, 95–97

Electronic learning (eLearning), 141

Electronic paper, 11

Electronic waste, 110

Electrostatic plotters, 57

Embedded operating system, 157

End User License Agreement (EULA), 127, 174

Ending tasks, 178

Ethernet, 89

Expansion cards, replacing or adding, 101

Extensible Markup Language (XML), 159

External hard drives, 49

F

FamilySearch.org, 135

Fan noise level, 91–92

Fans, adequate, 94

Favorites list, 201, 213

Fields, 134

File compression programs, 140

File extensions, 158, 223

File formats, identifying, 139–140

File list, 213

File management across platforms, 80–81

File servers, 8

Files
    backing up, 180, 227
    blockage of downloading, 177
    clearing stored, 100
    copying, 220–222
    corrupted, 159
    deleting, 220–222
    editing, 21
    identifying types, 217, 222
    managing, 226
    managing with Windows Explorer, 216–222
    moving, 220–222
    naming, 225–226
    opening, 21
    opening problem, 227
    printing, 21
    saving, closing, 22
    searching for, 222–224
    selecting, 220–222
    sorting, 217–218

Filter, 133

Finite element analysis, 8

FireWire, 62

Firmware, 180

Flash drives, 48

Flash hard drives, 48

Flash memory, 14, 48

Flatbed scanners, 53

Flow of information, 17–18

Fly by wire, 142

Folders
    copying, renaming, 219–220
    creating, 213–220
    creating, moving, nesting desktop, 213–215
    deleting, 219–220
    described, 212–213
    managing, 226
    moving, 219–220
    naming, 219–220, 225–226
    searching for, 223–224
    using on desktop, 213–215

Font, 131

Format, 131

Forms, 134

Formulas, 132

Forward button, 213

Fragmented, 99

Frames per second, 52

Freeware, 91

Function (Fn) key, 45

Functions, 132

G

Gadgets
    adding to desktop, 198–199
    described, 198

Game controllers, 51

Gamepads, 51

Gaming software, 139

Ghost image, 180

Gigabytes, 13, 16

Gigahertz, 13

Gold version, 126

Google Docs, 128, 176

NOTES

NOTES

NOTES

NOTES

NOTES

NOTES

NOTES

NOTES

NOTES

NOTES

NOTES